THE EFFICACY OF ARCHITECTURE

A significant ideological transition has taken place in the discipline of architecture in the last few years. Originating in a displeasure with the 'starchitecture' system and the focus on aesthetic innovation, a growing number of architects, emboldened by the 2007–8 economic crisis, have staged a rebellion against the dominant mode of architectural production. Against a 'disinterested' position emulating high art, they have advocated political engagement, citizen participation and the right to the city. Against the fascination with the rarefied architectural object, they have promoted an interest in everyday life, play, self-build and personalization.

At the centre of this rebellion is the call for architecture to (re-)assume its social and political role in society. *The Efficacy of Architecture* supports the return of architecture to politics by interrogating theories, practices and instances that claim or evidence architectural agency. It studies the political theories animating the architects, revisits the emergence of reformist architecture in the late nineteenth century, and brings to the fore the relation of spatial organization to social forms. In the process, a clearer picture emerges of the agency of architecture, of the threats to as well as potentials for meaningful societal transformation through architectural design.

Tahl Kaminer is Senior Lecturer in Architectural Design and Theory at the University of Edinburgh, UK. He co-founded and edited the journal *Footprint*. His publications include the monograph *Architecture, Crisis and Resuscitation* (Routledge, 2011) and the co-edited anthologies *Houses in Transformation* (2008), *Urban Asymmetries* (2011) and *Critical Tools* (2012).

"*The Efficacy of Architecture* is a book like no other I have come across. Offering insight into how socially motivated architects, urbanists, and theorists have been misrepresented and marginalized, it highlights the co-optation of publicly-minded work, yet its analysis is ultimately not depressing; it offers precise direction for those so-minded to maneuver dexterously through our complex 21st-century politico-economic system."

Peggy Deamer, Professor of Architecture at Yale University, USA,
Principal of Deamer Architects

"Is there a place for a more politicized and emancipatory architecture in our depoliticized times? This is the central question that *The Efficacy of Architecture* takes up. For those engaged in urban and architectural thought and practice, this book is desperately required reading."

Erik Swyngedouw, Professor of Geography, University of Manchester, UK

THE EFFICACY OF ARCHITECTURE

Political Contestation and Agency

Tahl Kaminer

LONDON AND NEW YORK

First published 2017
by Routledge
2 Park Square, Milton Park, Abingdon, Oxon OX14 4RN

and by Routledge
711 Third Avenue, New York, NY 10017

Routledge is an imprint of the Taylor & Francis Group, an informa business

© 2017 Tahl Kaminer

The right of Tahl Kaminer to be identified as author of this work has been asserted by him in accordance with sections 77 and 78 of the Copyright, Designs and Patents Act 1988.

All rights reserved. No part of this book may be reprinted or reproduced or utilized in any form or by any electronic, mechanical, or other means, now known or hereafter invented, including photocopying and recording, or in any information storage or retrieval system, without permission in writing from the publishers.

Trademark notice: Product or corporate names may be trademarks or registered trademarks, and are used only for identification and explanation without intent to infringe.

British Library Cataloguing-in-Publication Data
A catalogue record for this book is available from the British Library

Library of Congress Cataloging-in-Publication Data
Names: Kaminer, Tahl, 1970- author.
Title: The efficacy of architecture : political contestation and agency / Tahl Kaminer.
Description: New York : Routledge, 2017. | Includes bibliographical references and index.
Identifiers: LCCN 2016027792 | ISBN 9781138909854 (hb : alk. paper) | ISBN 9781138909861 (pb : alk. paper) | ISBN 9781315693750 (ebook : alk. paper)
Subjects: LCSH: Architecture and society. | Architecture--Political aspects.
Classification: LCC NA2543.S6 K245 2017 | DDC 720.1/03--dc23
LC record available at https://lccn.loc.gov/2016027792

ISBN: 978-1-138-90985-4 (hbk)
ISBN: 978-1-138-90986-1 (pbk)
ISBN: 978-1-315-69375-0 (ebk)

Typeset in Bembo
by Saxon Graphics Ltd, Derby

CONTENTS

List of Illustrations   *viii*
Acknowledgements   *x*

Introduction: The Return to Politics   1
Architecture and Agency 1
Architectural Discourse in the 1970s 2
Politics and Agency 10
Contents and Structure 13

PART ONE
Critique, Reformism and Co-optation   **17**

Critique and Change   19
Social Architecture 19
The Role of Critique 20
Evolutionary Socialism 23
Korsch's Hypothesis 26

The Ascent of Reformism   28
Social Stratification 28
The Sanitary Movement 31
Model Housing 33
The Strengthening of Government 37
Averting Class War 41
The Ascent of Town Planning 43
Testing Korsch's Hypothesis 46

The Integration of Critique 53
Societal Integration 53
Towards a Theory of Récupération 57
Récupération in Architecture 59

PART TWO
The Architecture of Radical Democracy 65

The Post-Fordist City 67
Park Hill 67
The New City 70
The Return of Participatory Architecture 74

Theories of Participation 79
Participation and Agency 79
Citizens' Will 83
Consensus and Discontent 86

Theories of Contestation 91
The Global 91
Conflict 96
Aesthetics' Dissensus 100
Mediating Theories 103

Praxis 108
Community Gardening 108
Expanding the Role of the Architect 113
Anti-statism 120
Personalization 123

PART THREE
Languages of Architecture 133

The Political as the Symbolic 135
Architecture and Symbolism 135
The Symbolic Constitution of Society 136
Architecture's Political Symbolism 139
Collège de Sociologie 144
Aesthetics and Politics 147
Architectural Opposition 148

Urban Form 152
After '68 152
Spatial and Societal Organization 157
Urban Form and Economic Organization 162
Reformist Architecture 165

'Vulgar' Architecture, 'Vulgar' Politics 175
The Semiotics of Architecture 175
Empty Signifiers 177

Notes *182*
Bibliography *189*
Index *205*

ILLUSTRATIONS

Cover

Collage by M. Ben-Yitzchak, license CC BY 2.0. The collage is a derivative of 'My own world' by A. Pagliaricci, used under a Creative Commons Attribution 2.0 Generic (CC BY 2.0) with attributions to 'Urban Dandscape' by Sascha Kohlmann under CC BY-SA 2.0, 'Stars Complex Urban Garden' by Gabriel Kamener, sown together and used under CC BY 2.0, 'Anonymous Protest – 15 March 2008 – Queen Victoria Street, London' by Paul Williams used under CC BY 2.0, 'Street Composing' by Kevin D. used under CC BY 2.0, 'Volkswagen' by grassrootsgroundswell used under CC BY 2.0, 'Fukuoka Tower' by Pedro Serapio used under CC BY 2.0.

1.1	Henry Roberts, model housing near Bagnigge Wells, between Pentonville and Gray's Inn Road, London, 1840s	34
1.2	Boundary Street Estate, London	38
1.3	A student strike in Paris, France, 3 May 1968	60
2.1	Park Hill, Sheffield, 2015. Remodelled section on the left, non-refurbished section on the right	69
2.2	A poster of the layout of the London Docklands being shown to Prime Minister Margaret Thatcher during a visit to the area, 1987	71
2.3	A hop farm by the artisan brewery Meantime at the Greenwich Peninsula development in south-east London	73
2.4	Occupy Wall Street demonstration on 15 September 2012	85
2.5	Passage 56, an 'ecological interstice' by atelier d'architecture autogérée (aaa) in St. Blaise area, Paris, 2006	110
2.6	A visualization of communal rooftop gardens in the Elephant Park development in south London	112
2.7	Assemble, Folly on the Flyover, London, 2012	115
2.8 and 2.9	Lacaton and Vassal, FRAC, Dunkerque, 2013	118
2.10	Truck supervisor Bernard Levey with his family in front of his new Levitt-built home, New York, 1950	127

2.11	Quartiers Modernes Frugès, Pessac, 2010	129
2.12	Lacaton and Vassal, Mulhouse, 2005. Interior view of personalized apartment	130
3.1	Ground Zero/World Trade Center winning competition entry, the Freedom Tower on the left, Studio Daniel Libeskind (SDL), 2003	141
3.2	One World Trade Center, Skidmore, Owings & Merrill (SOM)	143
3.3	The shanty town of Nanterre in 1961. Quiet streets and police presence as All Saints' Day coincided with the seventh anniversary of the FLN's rebellion	155
3.4	Plan of Karl Marx Hof, Vienna, showing the permeability of the perimeter blocks	159
3.5	Battery Park City, Manhattan, buildings by Cesar Pelli in the foreground, in front of the World Trade Center, 1996	163
3.6	Model of Canary Wharf master plan by SOM	164
3.7	Plan of Weissenhofsiedlung, Stuttgart, master planned by Mies van der Rohe, 1927	167
3.8	Plan of the 'zigzag' complex at Bruchfeldsstrasse, Frankfurt, master planned by Ernst May, 1926/7	168
3.9	View of courtyard of the 'zigzag' complex, 1927	169
3.10	Excerpt from the 1811 Commissioners' Plan for Manhattan (1807) showing the iron grid layout for urban expansion to the north (right)	170
3.11	Perspective view of North–South Street, Highrise City (Hochhausstadt), 1924	172
3.12	Dogma, A Simple Heart, Amsterdam, 2002–10	178

ACKNOWLEDGEMENTS

This book would have not been possible without the support of my family, friends, colleagues and students. Whether by critiquing the work or by unwitting comments, by taking part in discussions or challenging assumptions, these diverse contributions aided in developing the book's arguments. The editors and referees of books and journals who allowed me to 'test' some of the material present in this book contributed considerably to the development of *The Efficacy of Architecture*: Ana Jeinic and Anselm Wagner, *ARQ*, Hilde Heynen and Jean-Louis Genard, Tom Avermaete and Dirk van den Heuvel. In particular, I would like to thank Isabelle Doucet, Maros Krivy, Heidi Sohn, Erik Swyngedouw, Peggy Deamer, Adam Kelly and Miritte for their diverse support.

INTRODUCTION

The Return to Politics

Architecture and Agency

The role of architecture vis-à-vis society has been intensely contested since the emergence of 'the social' as a specific category in the nineteenth century. That architecture represents society in diverse manners; that architecture is created, to a certain degree, by forces external to it such as technology, economics, or politics, is rarely questioned. Yet the extent to which these external forces leave their mark on the completed building has often been debated, and the idea that architecture, architectural design or the building are not merely passive, formed by society, but rather a participatory force in creating or shaping society has been fiercely contested, and, more often than not, rejected.

For some, the political dimension of architecture is self-evident. The Spatial Agency Group in Sheffield contends that '[t]o say that architecture is political is to state a truism' (Awan, Schneider, Till 2011: 38). Others vehemently disagree. 'Architecture is not political,' Léon Krier unequivocally stated, 'it is only an instrument of politics' (Krier 1998: 411). 'Architecture cannot be an emancipatory project; it never was and never will be', argued geographer Erik Swyngedouw (2016: 48). In her 1929 essay 'A Room of One's Own', Virginia Woolf supplied an example of the relation of architecture to society by arguing that the absence of privacy – of a room of one's own – is one of the causes for the limited number of great women authors. Concisely outlining a history of feminine literature, she asserted that '[i]f a woman wrote, she would have to write in the common sitting-room', and concluded that a 'woman must have money and a room of her own if she is to write fiction' (Woolf 2015). Woolf's emphasis was on material concerns: the man owns property, owns resources, whereas the woman has no access to money, to a counterpart to the male's study or other abode. Indirectly, the essay indicted the programme and the layout of the home in which the woman could find no space of real privacy for contemplation and writing. Woolf inferred that the absence of 'a room of her own' was not only the expression of the suppression of women, but was also, indirectly, one of the causes of suppression, or, in other words, attributing affirming or determining powers to the programme and layout. Historically, however, it is the client rather than the architect who, by a brief, controls the architect's programme.

The lack of clarity regarding architecture's relation to society is complicated by the question of the structure and constitution of society. The question posits, at its polar extremes, Max Weber's argument in *The Protestant Ethic and the Spirit of Capitalism* against orthodox Marxism. The former portrays a society that is primarily constructed by ethics, morals, and ideals, whereas the latter argues that society is determined by the structural base, that is, by the forces and means of production. Weber describes how Protestant theology was central in shaping puritan communities through the work ethic, transposed from ethics to societal organization and much more, and leading to the emergence of a modern, capitalist society (Weber 2012). In contrast, Karl Kautsky and other leading members of the Second International led a narrow reading of Marx that dismissed the superstructure – beliefs, ideals, politics, culture – as merely a product of the economic base. 'The economic conditions are […] not the only things which determine "human affairs" the "processes of human life,"' stated Kautsky in 1902, 'but they are, among the determining factors, the only variable element. The others are constant, do not alter at all, or only under the influence of the changes of the variable element' (Kautsky 1902).

Architectural design is placed in such models within the superstructure, associated with art and culture. A model that claims the superstructure has agency ostensibly supports the idea that architecture takes an active part in shaping society; a model that denies agency to the superstructure suggests architecture is fully determined by economic forces. These questions can only be partially circumvented by focusing on the building itself: the building, as an object in reality that participates in daily life, is created by both superstructure and base; it reflects society's structure but is also part of lived experience; its presence and its materiality mean that it is necessarily more than merely a representation of society.

Significantly, positions suggesting that only superstructure *or* base constitute society have been rejected as too deterministic. Already in the interwar period, 'Western Marxists' such as the scholars of the Frankfurt School and Georg Lukács rejected the views of Kautsky as 'vulgar' (Jay 1973; 1984). In the 1960s in particular, figures such as the sociologist Henri Lefebvre or the literature critic Raymond Williams searched beyond the superstructure–base dichotomy (Lefebvre 1991; Williams 2005). The philosopher Louis Althusser convincingly argued by the late 1960s that the structural base does not mono-directionally determine society, but that superstructure takes an active part in steering society through its ideological state apparatuses (Althusser 1969; 2001). He identified the locus and role of ideology as a mediation between an individual and reality, with ideology responsible for the manner in which individuals experience and comprehend the reality that engulfs them. In other words, ideology mediates between lived experience and structure. Michel Foucault portrayed modern societies in which adherence to societal worldviews and codes is no longer driven by the threat of punishment but by the internalization of the societal demands by individuals (Foucault 1980; 1991; 2008; Hindess 2001: 96–136). In all these endeavours and many others, a mono-directional, 'one-way' deterministic understanding of society was rejected in favour of more nuanced and complex positions.

Architectural Discourse in the 1970s

Interest in the political dimensions of architecture waxes in certain eras and wanes in others. During economic restructuring or political upheavals, architects seek relevance by politicizing their work and by engaging with political issues that are otherwise ignored or overlooked, superseded by a professionalism that masks the ideological content of the work. The most recent era of intense interest in the political predating the current upheavals was the 1970s, following the events of May '68, and was provoked by political agitation, the 1970s economic meltdown, and cultural renewal. In many senses, this earlier interest in architectural agency and efficacy set the stage for contemporary debates and practices. The discussion of architectural efficacy in that era was never concluded, was never 'resolved' – rather, it dissipated, petered out, once architects lost interest and moved on. But the ideals, ideologies and practices, and many of the positions, theories and interests, animate the parallel contemporary movement: anti-statism, citizen participation, everyday life, temporality and ephemerality, play and much more.

During a brief period, approximately 1966–76, numerous young and small architectural groups and offices experimented with spatial frames, pneumatic balloons and other forms of what Felicity D. Scott described as 'techno-utopia' (Scott 2007). Developed from the interest in the early 1960s in flexibility, in technology and cybernetics, in superstructures and megastructures, these groups associated their work with emancipation – from labour, from bureaucracy, from capitalism, and from architecture. Many of these projects, by groups such as Utopie, UFO, 9999, Coop Himmelb(l)au, Haus-Rucker-Co. or Walter Pichler proposed inclusive forms of architecture: 'plugging in' a self-build unit into a spatial matrix, for example, or creating new collective space with membranes. The interest in emancipating citizens by empowering non-professionals to take control of their environment was the ideological kernel of the parallel – though disparate – nascent participatory movement of the same era. It promoted democratization by empowering citizens, primarily within urban renewal and mass-housing projects. Other interests that surfaced in the same years included emergency housing, early forms of environmentalism, 'ideal' alternative communities, low-cost housing, and self-build. Already in 1966, the British sociologist Maurice Broady wrote that 'most of the designers I meet now, especially at the A.A. [Architectural Association], are better described as "social consciences". They are idealists – even radicals' (Broady 1966: 149). The fervent mood of May '68 took further hold in architectural circles following the events in Paris and elsewhere, castigating 'architecture' for its subjugation to state capitalism and to a technocratic society. An article published in the journal of the French group Utopie and penned by Henri Lefebvre's collaborators Hubert Tonka, Jean-Paul Jungmann and Jean Aubert, stated that:

> It took May 1968, [...] for a majority of conscious architects to define themselves no longer in grudging silence but in active criticism; that is, no longer in union demands stuck in the perspective of bourgeois liberalism, but in a socialist perspective. The search for the fragments of democracy in capitalist society and the residence of 'latent socialism' (Marx) are part of theoretical practice. The advocates of structure and, more exactly in architecture, the advocates of redeeming technology, delude themselves when they place their 'positive' solutions on the crumbling ground of a capitalist society unable to listen to them.
>
> *(Tonka, Jungmann, Aubert 2011: 124–25)*

'When the university protest exploded,' Giancarlo de Carlo commented in 1969, 'the most important event since the end of the Second World War – the architecture faculties found themselves immediately in the vanguard. In many universities in Europe and in the wider world, students of architecture were the first to demand a radical renewal of organisational structures and teaching methods' (de Carlo 2005: 3).

In Britain, *The Architectural Review* magazine was slow in responding to the politicization of the architectural discussion, to sit-ins by students in academies of art and other forms of protest. In contrast, its younger competitor, *Architectural Design* (*AD*), which had become a platform for disseminating cutting edge architecture ranging from pneumatic balloons to temporary structures, was the ideal locus for the development of a politicized discourse. Yet *AD* struggled to free itself from the depoliticized professional language of architectural discussion. Initially, the manifestoes and designs of the young architects were distributed and disseminated primarily through pamphlets and self-published magazines. Gradually, *AD* began paying more attention. It reported in February 1968 on an international symposium on architectural theory, held in TU Berlin on 11–15 December 1967, an event which would become pivotal for German architecture. The symposium, organized by architect and professor Oswald Matthias Ungers, captured the radicalizing mood of the young architects of the time and the fiery tone of the discussion, overshadowed by Berlin's history. During the symposium, the magazine reported, in response to a talk by Reyner Banham:

> Ungers was prompted to point out that Scheerbart's ideas led directly to the mysticism and social ideals set out by Bruno Taut in *Alpine Architektür* (1919). Non-conformists in this ideal society were to be branded on the forehead and to be branded again until they conformed. For Ungers the dictatorial attitudes and even the architectural forms of this millennial world were no different from those associated with Hitler's mountain retreat in Berchesgarten.
>
> (AD *1968/2: 51*)

'Banham,' the article continued, 'felt it was somewhat unsporting to introduce politics into an academic architectural discussion' (*AD* 1968/2: 51). On the final day of the symposium, students hung two banners inside the hall, 'all houses are beautiful' read one in German, 'stop building' read the other, a sign of the turn against the systematic destruction of the supposedly 'dull' nineteenth century *Mietskaserne* in Berlin, a process in which Ungers was implicated.

The magazine reported, rather laconically, on the student occupation of the Milan Triennale in May 1968:

> Fired by German and French student protests Italian youth had effectively closed down most universities and institutions during the month of May; the occupation of the Triennale was simply another protest aimed against the archaic disciplines of art and architectural training and the organization of arts in Italy. […] 'No more power from the top', an aging lady painter cried. For ten days they held the building, organizing meetings, preparing press handouts. […] Aldo van Eyck, one of the contributors, has called them a host of failed bourgeois artists.
>
> (AD *1968/7: 298*)

Later that year, at the International Design Conference in Aspen, the programme chairman – the indefatigable Banham – calibrated his words to address 'politics' while steering the discussion to a depoliticized territory of professional practice:

> If politics is the art of the possible, so is design, perhaps to an even greater degree. Designers, architects and planners are, in a phrase current in England at the moment, among the world's proud doers; their pride is in getting things to happen, their pleasure in seeing business done. To me as an academic and journalist, their professional discussions were always fascinating – but also baffling, because designers themselves seemed to be vaguely ashamed of them. Rather that they ought to be talking about something else. The subjects, the topics which design conferences are officially called together to discuss are never 'how to get it done' or 'how to make it happen', but 'why aren't we worrying more about the state of the world' or 'the impending doom of Western civilization'.
>
> (Hollein 1968: 397)

AD's main feature in the August issue was titled 'Architecture of Democracy'. The contributors were Rolf Gortze, Robert Goodman, Peter Grenell, Carl Linn, Lisa Peattie, Donald Terner, and John Turner. The issue included articles about squatter settlements in Latin America, emergency housing, and mobile homes. The squatter settlements were commended repeatedly for their 'freedoms'. The articles called for 'self-determination', the 'creative shaping of one's own environment', citizen participation and self-build. The contributors argued that:

> In contrast [to squatter environments in developing countries], the world which we saw around us in the United States, with all its relative economic lavishness and technical virtuosity, often seemed outside the control of its inhabitants, even alien to men. […] the means of making and controlling are tied together in experience with their physical product, and aesthetic judgements must be penetrated by human meanings and relevance. […] This requires us to look at the city, its neighbourhoods and its dwellings, as not simply artifacts and/or as the format of human activity, but as the vehicle and expression of our human life which, being human, is also communal, in the Greek sense, political.
>
> (Rolf Gortze et al. 1968: 354)

In the same issue, James Redfield argued that '[a] city is the environment and the property of a community; it should express that community's sense of the commodious and the beautiful. Since the basis of community life is not love but justice, or rather justice made vital by occasional love, so the final product will not be reached by pure agreement, but by the rough-and-ready consensus of politics' (Redfield 1968: 389).

The December issue of *AD* was dedicated to 'Cities and Insurrections' and included an article by the Marxist historian Eric Hobsbawm. A few months later, in 1969, Nick Jeffrey wrote:

> Can the architect contribute much? – Little perhaps, while working for the establishment culture, but more perhaps outside it; one could work on schemes which would demonstrate how things could be in a society without artificial constraints on resources ([Herbert] Marcuse's second dimension). One could participate in peoples' day-to-day struggles for a dry house, a safe play area; and one could participate in counter-action: for instance against the encroachment of high-rental flats (Mies in Detroit) into the low rent housing stock.
>
> (Jeffrey 1969a: 237)

6 Introduction: The Return to Politics

The anthropologist Edmund Leach delivered a lecture at the Architectural Association, later published in *AD*, which studied the idea of 'community' in contemporary society. The argument of the talk developed from a general sociological–anthropological survey to a normative, political argument:

> If we want to revive a 'sense of community', we would need to forego many of the freedoms of movement which are intrinsic to the capitalist system. If on the other hand we concede that, […] the idea of a kin-based community is just a lot of old hat, we need to recognize that we have no idea how to handle the psychological strains of non-communal living. […] Social theorists of the last 200 years have never understood that if you want Liberty and Equality, you can't have Fraternity as well.
> *(Leach 1969: 354)*

In the same issue, Martin Pawley reviewed the widely published Dronten Agora community centre in the Netherlands (1966). The Agora's experimental design by van Klingeren emphasized flexibility and adaptability in order to rethink the relation of individual to community. Pawley characterized the design as 'democratic' (Pawley 1969: 358–62). The August issue was devoted to Venezuela, edited by Walter Bor and with articles on urban and periphery issues, informal development and more. The September issue focused on a scientific–reformist agenda of amelioration – architecture and planning as a scientific endeavour aimed at bettering living conditions and quality of life. Informatics, computer science, cybernetics, and linguistics mix here, with the political as a subtext rather than at the fore. In the November issue, Nick Jeffrey published an article titled 'Techniques for Democratic Planning', positing a rather technical–managerial systems approach to democratizing planning processes (Jeffrey 1969b). The architectural critic Kenneth Frampton, agitating by the early 1970s on both sides of the Atlantic, was pursuing a Hannah Arendt-inspired humanist approach to architecture, posited against the excessive critiques of modernism and against the techno-utopian tendencies of the younger generation. In addition to cybernetics-inspired articles about scientific–technocratic design and planning, ensuing issues included numerous articles about the work of Cedric Price and Archigram,[1] 'paper', pneumatic and 'dome' architecture,[2] citizens' participation,[3] low-cost and emergency housing,[4] play,[5] environmentalism and the *Whole Earth Catalog*,[6] the 'Joint Struggle Committee to Crush the 1970 World Exposition',[7] and rock festivals.[8]

Having ignored much of the dissent in architecture schools in Paris, Rome, Turin and elsewhere, the mutiny at the Architectural Association received the magazine's attention:

> The 'guerrilla' group on the council, elected the previous June by the newly restored student vote, demands that all non-members leave the chamber, Principal Lloyd, administrator Bernstein (popularly believed to be in the pay of the CIA), staff representative Jencks, and student representative Hammill leave in a wild surmise. In the bar they speculate on their fate. Hanging may be too good for them, perhaps the birch? Downstairs the guerrillas in trembling voices demand the immediate standing down of the President, the Principal and the Treasurer. Uproar results.
> *(Pawley 1971b: 190)*

This interest peaked with the publication of an extensive special section in the September 1971 issue devoted to May '68 in Paris via the lens of architecture students. 'The Beaux-Arts

Since '68', written by Pawley and Bernard Tschumi, introduced the *AD* readers to the militant and radicalized discussions of the students, to the events themselves, to some of the theory animating the demonstrations, and to the aesthetics of the *événements*: the cut-up posters and fliers, the caricatures and 'zines (*AD* 1971/9: 533–66). The authors announced that the issue of *AD*:

> is devoted to an account of militancy among architectural students in Paris. […] turning the very basis of their studies towards the exposure and uprooting of the social evils which our present system of environmental design and construction seems unable to ameliorate. Inadequate housing, the destruction of communities by redevelopment, the harsh treatment of building workers and immigrants, the ecological absurdities of our technological society; above all the idiocy and criminal irresponsibility of professionals who refuse to acknowledge their role in the whole process of economic growth and industrial development.
>
> *(Pawley, Tschumi 1971: 533)*

Most of the articles mentioned above and the ensuing discussions in later issues of *AD* tended to address the political obliquely, through issues such as public space, community, planning, technology, needs, or cities. Increasingly, though, the political became a focus.

As the political agitation of the architectural groups consolidated, a critique of the self-perception of architects' agency and the discipline's efficacy emerged as well, directed first and foremost at the social ambitions associated with modernism, but with repercussions for all forms of architecture. Already in 1968, the Heideggerian architectural critic Christian Norberg-Schulz argued that 'Architects' publications are at present dominated by studies on topics taken from sociology and psychology, economy and ecology, mathematics and communication theory. The only subject that, paradoxically, is missing, is *architecture*' (Norberg-Schulz 1968: 257). In a similar vein, Robert Venturi wrote that '[t]he architect's ever diminishing power and his growing ineffectualness in shaping the whole environment can perhaps be revised, ironically, by narrowing his concerns and concentrating on his own job' (Venturi 1977: 14).

In his 1973 book *Modern Movements in Architecture*, architectural critic Charles Jencks admitted to some degree of political content in architecture, but restricted any conception of architectural agency to a minimal level. Jencks identified three areas in which ideology and politics intertwine with architecture. First, by working for a specific client – public or private, government or corporate – and on specific projects – housing or munitions, shopping or offices – the architect necessarily accommodates a political position, conceded Jencks. Second, architecture affects those who inhabit it – though 'in a very *loose* way' (Jencks 1973: 30). And third, the shaping of public space by architecture has political resonance.

Jencks accurately described the potpourri of conflicting political positions in Congrès Internationaux d'Architecture Moderne (CIAM), highlighting the conflicts and contradictions. He outlined the pragmatic, opportunistic streak in Le Corbusier and the apolitical stance of Mies and of the technocratically-inclined Buckminster Fuller and 'systems' architecture. The post-war 'triumph' of modernism, according to Jencks, meant that such architecture was to be found everywhere, in all countries, commissioned by very different regimes. '[T]he architect,' wrote Jencks, 'is particularly prone to the influence of such factors because he has to depend more directly than any other kind of artist on social patronage' (Jencks 1973: 50-51). Jencks demonstrated how Stalin's Soviet Union propagated Social Realism and legitimized it as 'socialist architecture', while only a few years earlier the Constructivist architects had used the same argument to support their own work. In this example and others, architects' rationalizations appear detached from the actual design, merely a means of gaining legitimacy or, more opportunistically, gaining commissions. At the end of the day, while Jencks afforded architecture some efficacy, his argument was aimed to counter perceptions of architectural agency.

Jencks claimed architecture was necessarily apolitical and allied to the reigning government. His evidence, then, included the realization of similar buildings in capitalist democracies and in communist states, as well as the apolitical or politically ambiguous stance of CIAM and of many of its leading architects, and a lack of relationship between the architects' argument and their design. The debate Jencks was involved in was problematic in a number of senses, and primarily in the type of 'politics' he was attempting to ascribe to or deny architecture. Contrasting the Western bloc to the Eastern bloc of the Cold War, Jencks was indeed contrasting two very different political systems and ideologies, but ignoring the fact they had a very similar political economy, based on Keynesian theories of governmental intervention, and, to different degrees, planned economies and planned societies. Working within a similar political economy, the architecture realized in these different political contexts was often similar. The differences that Jencks conveniently ignored emerge not so much in social housing in Western Europe versus housing in Eastern Europe, but in corporate skyscrapers in the United States and in the symbolism and monumentality of the 'people's palaces' realized in several capitals of the Eastern bloc. The corporate skyscrapers, commissioned by private corporations in conditions of a real estate market, are restricted to capitalist cities, and the people's palaces demonstrate the huge centralized power of the states of the Eastern bloc, far exceeding that of Western governments in the same era. Modernism did not play a significant part in either of these typologies, but instead contributed significantly to the design of mass housing – precisely the type of architecture found in West and East. Yet the similarities in mass housing did not derive only from architecture, but from similar conditions (government commissions rather than private market; technocratic oversight; questions of quantity at the fore), needs (a response to similar demands posed to architecture), techniques, and worldviews (a focus on 'modernization', efficiency, and development).

The rejection of architecture's political dimensions would lead architect Léon Krier, a few years later, to argue that 'there is neither authoritarian nor democratic architecture, no more than there are authoritarian or democratic Wienerschnizel' (Krier 1998: 411). The onslaught on ideas of architectural efficacy was mostly led by architects and critics associated with conservative or centrist positions. But some figures heavily invested in the question of efficacy, including Marxists such as the architectural historian Manfredo Tafuri, launched their own attack. Tafuri famously wrote that 'just as it is not possible to found a Political Economy based on class, so one cannot "anticipate" a class architecture (an architecture for "a liberated society"); what is possible is the introduction of class criticism into architecture. Nothing beyond this, from a strict – but sectarian and partial – Marxist point of view' (Tafuri 1980: xv).

Tafuri was greatly influenced by the work of his peers, particularly the philosopher Massimo Cacciari and the political scientist Mario Tronti. Some, if not most, of the social and political theory that pervades Tafuri's writings and informs his assessment of architecture, was developed from Cacciari's and Tronti's work. In his *Architecture and Utopia* (1976), a specific model of organization of production, the assembly line, is reproduced in diverse forms on all levels of society, including the infrastructural base and the superstructure, the city and architecture. In such a worldview, the negative forces, such as irrationalism or nihilism, appear as necessary counter-reactions that are part of the system and prevent real change. In other words, a very different theory of society than a Hegelian idea of progress, which identifies the determining role of the negative in societal transformation. The reproduction of the assembly line form on diverse levels of society is similar to the social theory developed and deployed by Cacciari and Tronti, a theory of 'levels' or 'instances'. Such theories were common among 1960s Marxists in Italy and France and allowed a limited autonomy of the different 'horizontal' levels, while in the specific theory in question the levels are tied together 'vertically' by the reproduction of a model or form, by its realization within the organization of labour, social relations, culture, politics and so on. Tafuri's pessimistic comment – 'one cannot "anticipate" a class architecture' – has to be read as the statement of a radical or revolutionary rather than a reformer.[9] It rejects the possibilities of a revolutionary architecture preceding a social revolution. It is a narrow argument; it does not necessarily preclude all forms of architectural agency.

In 1966, the sociologist Maurice Broady published in the Architectural Association journal *Arena*, an article critiquing determinism in architecture. A well-disseminated critique of the use of social theory in architecture delivered by a sociologist, it intervened in the discussion of architecture, agency and politics in Britain, and its fingerprints can be found in Jencks's argument in *Modern Movements*. Broady wrote that architectural determinism:

> asserts that architectural design has a direct and determinate effect on the way people behave. It implies a one-way process in which the physical environment is the independent, and human behaviour the dependent variable. It suggests that those human beings for whom architects and planners create their designs are simply moulded by the environment which is provided for them.
>
> *(Broady 1966: 150)*

Broady's argument was about the degree to which the environment shapes society. He admitted that an environment can 'induce' certain social practices and much more; his objections were to a one-way determinism. The intervention by a sociologist was significant. The architects who had recruited sociologists for support in teaching and practice expected endorsement, but instead were rebuked for their simplistic social theory. While the main target in Broady's article was the kind of quasi-scientific architecture that was influenced by crude behaviourism, his critique had wider implications. The article provided ammunition for confronting all societal pretensions in architectural and urban design, for rejecting any idea of agency. '[A]rchitectural design […],' Broady summarized, 'is complementary to human activity, it does not shape it. Architecture, therefore, has no kind of magic by which men can be redeemed or society transformed. Its prime social function is to facilitate people's doing what they wish, or are obliged to do' (Broady 1966: 153). Rather than introducing nuance, the article ended up supporting a very different form of 'one-way determinism': the argument that architecture is fully determined by society.

Broady's critique was reflected in another article, published in 1969 in *The British Journal of Sociology* by Alan Lipman. Lipman, a trained architect, criticized architects' propensity to argue for the societal efficacy of their work, to claim that their designs determine human behaviour. He explained this propensity by changes in the profession itself – the rise of mass-housing commissions, of a mass clientele from diverse and unfamiliar backgrounds. Architects, in reaction, turned to science as a means of addressing new unknowns (Lipman 1969).

Curiously, the perception of architecture as completely determined by society took hold precisely in a period in which scholars in other fields renounced mono-directional ideas about the shaping of society. Raymond Williams called for abandoning the base–superstructure model; the work of Althusser, Foucault and others described intricate and complex societal structures; many neo-Marxists focused on issues of consciousness and culture as co-determining factors which supplemented society's infrastructure. The need to supersede 'one-way' determinism was precisely the point Broady was trying to make. Nevertheless, while the understanding of the diverse factors and forces that shape society was widening, in architectural circles it was narrowing.

The retreat of architecture from societal ambitions marked a turn to experimentations in the field of communication – postmodernist architecture – and the focus on the formal linguistics of architecture – the so-called neo-avant-garde. The former opted for a representational architecture that accepts its pre-determination by society, and the latter preferred an aesthetic architecture centred on its supposed disengagement with society. Architectural autonomy was deployed as an argument in favour of architecture's focus on its own features, such as type, form, composition or materiality (Kaminer 2011a: 71–113). While the Italian neorationalists, led by Rossi, understood architectural autonomy in terms similar to Tronti as a limited freedom of a specific 'level' within society's structure, for Eisenman and American East Coast architects' autonomy meant a refusal of consumer culture and freedom from subjugation to a compromised society.

Following four decades in which these positions dominated architecture – a longer period, in fact, since the 1966 publication of Venturi's *Complexity and Contradiction* and Rossi's *The Architecture of the City* – and following the attempt by Rem Koolhaas to break open architecture's closed system only in order to subjugate it to economic forces, a new generation of architects and theorists have been busy reclaiming a political role for the discipline.[10] Many of the contemporary architectural returns to politics have resurrected radical 1960s critiques, strategies and tactics, though often with little recognition of the changes that have taken place in the decades that have elapsed: the collapse of the Keynesian order, the passage to a post-Fordist, neoliberal, post-industrial society; the weakening of the state by deregulation, by freeing economy from the edicts of politics and society, by globalization, by new forms of capitalism that, in fact, addressed much of the 1960s critique by infusing spontaneity, creativity and difference into their products and organization. *The Efficacy of Architecture* attempts to add rigour, clarity and coherence to the return of architecture to politics by providing a critique of previous attempts to engage the political and their assumed 'failures', by studying the contemporary loose participatory movement, and by interrogating the linguistics of architecture. The point of departure of *The Efficacy of Architecture* is a rejection of 'one-way' determinism or causality. Architecture, architectural designs and buildings are not only expressions of society, politics, technology or economics, outcomes moulded by external forces. They necessarily partake in shaping society as well, even if in a limited sense. And consequently, even if restricted, the architect has some degree of agency. The moments and forms in which such agency becomes discernible stand at the centre of this book.

Politics and Agency

The prescription of austerity by governments and international institutions once the stimulus packages of 2008 succeeded in preventing a depression, ostensibly placed economy at the fore: fiscal debt-reduction as the major goal of societies and nation states. But austerity policies defied accepted economic rationale. Rather than based on economic urgencies, austerity was politically driven. In 1929, following the Wall Street Crash, governments in Europe reacted by imposing austerity, and these actions were complicit in generating the Great Depression (Hansen 1981). Austerity – the curtailing of governmental programmes and investment – is considered high risk during downturn, when the private sector is weak, and can cause high unemployment, under-consumption and deflation. The stimulus packages of 2008, in contrast, were a textbook Keynesian solution to economic crisis. Initially a means of preventing restructuring in a Keynesian direction and of maintaining the status quo, austerity quickly developed into a grab, an attempt to restructure societies in an opposite direction. Most visibly, austerity enhanced not only inequalities, but also increased the democratic deficit: debt was used to undermine democratically elected city councils and national governments, replacing them where possible with technocratic, 'apolitical' administrations.[11] The process inferred that societies in debt no longer had the right to democracy, and, essentially, were placed under receivership, like failed corporations. As a result, the discussion of the democratic deficit and the discussion of social inequalities, which have in the past taken place in parallel,[12] appear evermore intertwined, placing politics at the fore of debate.

Change and transformation take place in diverse forms, often at a distance from 'politics', sometimes unwittingly and unintentionally rather than driven by clear plan, demands or ambitions. But the interest of this book is in agency, and particularly in human agency: how can architects who are committed to societal transformation contribute to the steering and determining of society? What degree and what forms of agency do architects possess? The political terrain is the main locus of contestation in the struggle over society's future, and consequently, politics stands also at the centre of *The Efficacy of Architecture*.

The recent surge of interest in politics by architects is driven by discontent with the contemporary role of architecture in society, by a desire to take part in the shaping of society, by positing to architecture a demand to do more than merely fulfil its given tasks. The use in recent decades of landmark buildings and stunning designs to 'sell' cities as global and relevant to the market, to sell housing to international speculators, to add the veneer of gravitas or spectacle to crude commercial endeavours, has left a bad taste. In reaction, a growing number of architects have turned to voluntarism of diverse modes, to the enhancement of citizens' participation, to an 'everyday' architecture, self-build and forms of architecture that have not been discredited by an overt relation to or dependence on neoliberalism.

But what is 'politics'? The term is deployed very differently by diverse scholars, activists, and practitioners. It is used in a multiplicity of disparate 'lay' and colloquial forms. *The Efficacy of Architecture* will introduce and study diverse notions of politics, derived from political theory, unfolding a wide array of conflicting ideas. The understanding of the political will change and develop throughout the book. Yet a definition of sorts is required as a point of departure. 'Politics' will be understood here simply as the area in which power is organized and contested in modern society.[13] But even in modern society, with its specific locus of politics – parliaments, trade unions, political parties, etc. – 'politics' can be observed and identified in territories outside this defined field. Not just as the 'politics' of specific non-political institutions, but also in families, in consumer decisions and much more. Politics, evidently, are not restricted to the territory dedicated to them, and pervade disparate areas of life.[14]

The dictum 'everything is political' was, at a certain moment, very useful as a means of enhancing awareness of the existence of political issues in everyday life, yet it has also had the effect of expanding the idea of politics to the extent that it meant little, blurring the differences between actions with relatively minor political efficacy and those that have wide-ranging consequences. 'If everything is political,' commented the political scientist Mark Lilla, 'then strictly speaking nothing is' (Lilla 1998). Terry Eagleton has argued that:

> Those radicals who hold that [...] 'everything is political' seem not to realize that they are in danger of cutting the ground from beneath their own feet. Such slogans may valuably challenge an excessively narrow definition of politics and ideology, one convenient for ruling power intent on depoliticizing whole sectors of social life. But to stretch these terms to the point where they become coextensive with everything is simply to empty them of force.
> *(Eagleton 1991: 8)*

In this book, following the work of the political theorist Chantal Mouffe (1999; 2005), the term 'politics' will be used for the specific terrain of power contestation, whereas 'the political' will be used to describe the type of contestations that are animated by moral and ethical passions and concerns.[15] The latter can be found both within and without the official territory of politics. Mouffe writes that:

> By 'the political', I refer to the dimension of antagonism that is inherent in all human society, antagonism that can take many different forms and can emerge in diverse social relations. 'Politics', on the other hand, refers to the ensemble of practices, discourses and institutions that seek to establish a certain order and to organize human coexistence in conditions that are always potentially conflictual because they are affected by the dimension of 'the political'.
> *(Mouffe 1999: 754)*

Here is also where ideology enters the equation. Ideology and politics are intertwined, each deploying the other as its extension: ideology realizing its goals via politics, and politics achieving hegemony by the penetrations of its ideology into areas of everyday life to which politics have no access. It is thus impossible to speak of the political outside the official realm of politics without speaking also of ideology, which is the major form in which the political affects and is affected in these areas (Eagleton 1991). 'Ideology' is a term restricted neither to the powers-that-be (dominant ideologies), nor to oppositional forces (oppositional ideologies). It is the 'filter' through which individuals read their reality (Althusser 1969; 2001). In its coherent, structured form, ideology is the vehicle of organized political movements, and in its more murky, veiled, and abstract sense it becomes a motivation for individuals to accept reality and their social conditions by naturalizing or legitimizing the reality – a worldview or 'spirit' that motivates individuals and explains to them their place in the world (Boltanski and Chiapello 2005: 10–11).

The process by which an ideology is 'naturalized' is one that engenders depoliticization. An issue that is ideological and political, and thus ought to be contested within politics, is removed from this arena, integrated, instead, into society's worldview, into everyday life, and into social relations to the extent that the ideology driving it becomes invisible to citizens. 'Naturalization' is a typical feature of dominant ideology, constructing a consensus and a supposed 'common sense' shared by a significant section of society, preventing the formation of meaningful critique. The reverse process involves the de-naturalization of issues and their politicization, dragging them back into the territory of politics.[16]

Significant for any discussion of agency and the political is the current post-political condition. While diverse explanations for this condition and its causes are provided by disparate scholars, there is a loose agreement that it describes a condition in which politics are too weak to address the great societal challenges of our times, whether the environmental threats, economic instability, forms of radicalization, inequality or other. For Mouffe, the post-political condition stems from the political order established after the Second World War, in which the 'irrational' passions were excluded from politics as a reaction to the instability of democracies in the interwar years; namely, the threat of fascism or communism. For others, the post-political is the condition of the post-Cold War era, once ideological strife was supposedly superseded. Politics have become evermore a locus of depoliticized, technocratic–managerial forms of governance. Japhy Wilson and Erik Swyngedouw have characterized Mouffe's argument as 'the post-political as the repression of antagonism'; Jacque Rancière's perspective as one in which the post-political is the denial of equality; and Slavoj Žižek's as the 'foreclosure of class struggle' (Wilson and Swyngedouw 2014b). 'In post-politics,' write Wilson and Swyngedouw, 'political contradictions are reduced to policy problems to be managed by experts and be legitimated through participatory processes in which the scope of possible outcomes is narrowly defined in advance' (Wilson and Swyngedouw 2014b: 6).

In *The Efficacy of Architecture*, the post-political condition is understood primarily as a recent phenomenon, related to the process of neoliberalization and the freeing of economy from the dictates of society. This took place deliberately by weakening governments and limiting their control and steering of the economy. Power has increasingly been transferred from elected governments to unelected international or transnational bodies (such as the World Trade Organization, the International Monetary Fund, the World Bank Group), arbitrators (through agreements such as the Transatlantic Trade and Investment Partnership, the TTIP), and corporations. As a result, governments today, compared to the significant powers of governments in the post-war era, can affect life only in a restricted area. The economy, which shapes life in numerous manners, ranging from social mobility to equality, from housing to employment, operates largely outside the control of citizens and their representatives.

Contents and Structure

The Efficacy of Architecture studies, first and foremost, the agency of the architect and architectural efficacy. 'The concept that design matters,' wrote architect and consultant Alexi Marmot, 'that it can make a real difference to people's lives, is a fundamental tenet for most design activity' (Marmot 2002: 252). 'Architecture' is here understood as a discipline and as a practice, but also as a project and a building. Each of these four senses in which the term 'architecture' operates delineates a somewhat different territory, overlapping and differentiated from the three other. The unrealized project, 'paper architecture', emphasizes the architects' decisions, but its efficacy is restricted to the architectural discipline, or, in other words, it is allowed 'to speak' in the broadest sense, while constrained in what it can 'do'. The building, in contrast, is necessarily a compromise between diverse forces and conditions, but its presence and materiality allow it a more direct efficacy – constrained in what it can 'say', but less so in what it 'does'. While not at the centre of this study, these differences nevertheless inform the book.

The book offers neither a comprehensive history nor an all-encompassing overview of architectural efficacy and agency. Rather, it provides analyses and understandings of diverse modes in which architectural design attempts and in some cases succeeds in (co-)producing meaningful change. Considering the breadth of the topic, and the significant history of architecture's attempts to engage with the political and the numerous analyses and assessments of such engagements, there are expectedly many absences in the book. Arguably the most glaring absence is Constructivist architecture and the discussions and theories of Osip Brik, Alexei Gan, Moisei Ginzburg and others. In contrast, the parallel architecture of Weimar, while not at the fore of the book, is nonetheless represented. Weimar is present here in Part Three, in the discussion of Tafuri's conception of urban form. Due to the limitation of scale, to the book's particular interests, and to the numerous studies of Constructivism available,[17] the preference for Weimar architecture was based on its clearer affinity to social democracy and reformism, which are the key protagonists of Part One.

The mixing of canonic work – the Weissenhofsiedlung, for example – and less familiar work – such as Assemble's Folly for a Flyover – may be disconcerting. The work analysed here that is outside the canonic history was selected not in order to introduce a history 'against the grain' but simply because it offers understandings of the efficacy of architecture that more familiar work does not. The canonic architecture is valuable here for its familiarity, which enables the book to draw out the issues that matter while providing contextualization and general introduction to the projects only when relevant to the issues discussed. Together, the diverse work critiqued in this book elucidates a wide array of strategies, techniques and understandings which claim political or societal efficacy, allowing a proper and informed discussion of the means of employing architecture as an agent of change.

But how to assess societal transformation, or, alternatively, how to evaluate the benefits and disadvantages of contemporary projects – of specific architectural designs, buildings, or urban interventions? How to identify a causal relationship between a community garden and stronger community cohesion or dislocation and gentrification? Researchers in social sciences apply diverse methodologies to parse and evaluate case studies such as these. The methodologies range from ethnographic interviews to the study of statistical data regarding relocations, employment, crime, health and other. As Marmot points out, however, there is:

> genuine difficulty of understanding what conclusions to draw from results that may be established. After moving to a newly designed office, people may confess themselves to feel more productive. But what factors were responsible for this? It may be the new building, or the new furniture, or the new location, the new telephone and computer systems, the feeling of involvement in the process or simply the fact that the new location is less cluttered, cleaner, fresher and more up to date than the former setting. Or, it may simply be the fact that a change has been made, that management has valued them enough to invest in alterations.
>
> *(Marmot 2002: 252)*

Diverse measurements provide disparate knowledge, and each contributes to some understanding of the societal impact of a project, yet they are unable to 'isolate' the case study as a means of narrowing down the complexity of reality, reducing the amalgam of forces and conditions shaping the project and its outcome. They cannot account in aggregate for a project as a totality – they fall short of providing a comprehensive account, offering, instead, a set of diverse narrow accounts. Consequently, assumptions regarding the significance of specific criteria must precede the studies, and in order to produce a comprehensive account there is need for some level of speculation regarding the interpretation of the results. While both the assumptions and the speculations are necessary, they demonstrate a limited capacity to proceed from collecting 'objective' empirical data to evaluations that are wholesome and comprehensive, and also fully validated in the empirical sense. The research on which this book is based has employed, to a limited degree, such methodologies – primarily observations and semi-structured interviews, as in the case of an Amsterdam community garden, or the study of data regarding housing prices in Britain. Such information is not at the fore; it feeds into the assessments and evaluations, but is secondary. More attention is given to key questions such as the level of involvement or lack of involvement of government, the empowerment of citizens or business, or the ideological alignments of diverse ideals.

The Efficacy of Architecture consists of three sections. Part One, 'Critique, Reformism and Co-optation', is historic in its outlook. The material it unfolds is familiar: the emergence of the ideas, theories, practices and positions, later embodied in the welfare state and its architecture, from the nineteenth century to the Second World War. Rather inexplicably, despite the numerous studies of this era, social history and architectural history have been mostly studied separately, bar a small number of publications.[18] This history is typically narrated by planning or housing literature rather than architectural literature. The purpose of this section is threefold: to establish the role of critique in societal transformation, to elucidate the process of co-optation, and, most importantly, to demonstrate that architecture can reproduce oppositional ideologies in its own ideas, practices and built forms. The rise and triumph of reformism serves as an example of the potential of architecture to engage with and support societal transformation, to ally itself with alternative or oppositional movements rather than be subjugated to hegemonic ideologies and worldviews.

Part Two, 'The Architecture of Radical Democracy', is focused on current movements and contestations. It interrogates the contemporary loose participatory movement in architecture – the amalgam of small vanguard practices which have coalesced around banners such as 'the right to the city', and which emphasize issues such as citizens' participation, everyday life, environmental concerns, and much more. The section looks at the post-Fordist condition against which the rebellion of young architects is posited, examines the political theory which feeds, directly and indirectly, into the designs, and studies the work of architects who have contributed to architecture's return to the political. Leading this critique is the question whether the practices exalted by the architects, including 'urban acupuncture', temporary structures, and participatory tactics, are prone to co-optation by capitalism, or, even more unsettlingly, are the flip side of the same coin as neoliberalism. The purpose of problematizing aspects of current practice is to generate a critical self-assessment by the relevant architects of the processes, procedures and practices they espouse, particularly at a moment in which these are still unsettled, have not yet been 'sublimated' or enshrined in the type of myth that limits critical judgement.

Part Three, 'Languages of Architecture', disengages from the current discussion of participation and efficacy in order to examine avenues that the contemporary architects committed to radicalizing architecture have mostly ignored. It studies three issues related to the linguistics of architecture: symbolism, form, and the poverty of architectural language. The section's first chapter enters the discussion of symbolism from a different perspective than that of the 1970s. Instead of 'communication' or the relation of signified to signifier, the chapter asserts that the symbolic is at the heart of the political. Sidelining the symbolic, it contends, entails a transition from the political to the technocratic–managerial. The chapter interrogating urban and architectural form delineates an argument that societal organization is reflected in spatial organization, an argument that shifts the focus from the political to questions of political economy and social forms. The last chapter suggests that the poverty of architecture as language, its inability to produce 'refined' and 'precise' statements, enables rather than limits political efficacy. The 'vulgarity' of its deployment of social theory and of erroneous 'one-way' determinism can be, it is argued, productive in the most positive sense, whether architecturally, socially or politically.

The two contrasting perceptions of the architect as, on the one hand, powerless, a 'head bricklayer' in Giancarlo de Carlo's terms (2005: 5), subjugated to society, and, on the other, an all-powerful demiurge, are untenable. '[B]oth go too far', wrote Umberto Eco (1986: 82). But the intention of *The Efficacy of Architecture* is to do more than simply confirm a limited level of efficacy or a narrow scope of architectural agency. It wishes to promote a tight relationship between political movements and architecture, to argue that architecture can, in effect, precede political economy in identifying new trajectories for society, and that it can provide valuable support not only to dominant ideologies and hegemonic politics, but also to alternative and oppositional movements.

PART ONE
Critique, Reformism and Co-optation

CRITIQUE AND CHANGE

Social Architecture

Many of the architects currently struggling to identify a politically and socially affective architecture have been drawn to May '68 and the theories and practices developed in that radical era. Yet it was precisely the society against which the students in Paris demonstrated that had developed an effective architecture. Such architecture accounted for one of the two main trajectories of modernism: while one sought innovative architectural composition and form, the other foregrounded the social responsibilities of design, and produced, primarily, mass social housing and planned cities.

Marinated for decades in formal and phenomenological explorations, the discipline has preferred to adore the modernist formal experiments, while the social and political project of the modernist avant-garde receded from view. Architecture, as a discipline, merely echoed society and the desire to erode and repress all memory of the era of an interventionist state. Systematic demolition has been applied to *Betonbau* in Leipzig, to housing estates in London and to slabs in Amsterdam, threatening even Robin Hood Gardens. George Ferguson, while president of the Royal Institute of British Architects, prepared an 'X-list' in 2004 of buildings worthy of demolition, populated primarily by post-war 'social' architecture.

The architecture of the *betonbau* and of Robin Hood Gardens was neither subversive nor transgressive. It reacted to and fulfilled demands posited to it by the society of its era, which demanded equality, better conditions of living, and stability. In this sense it was dominant, and was part of the hegemonic order of a specific period that will be here characterized as the nadir of reformism. The lack of desire on the part of architects to return to familiar forms of politically and socially effective architecture is worth interrogating, but the purpose of this first section is to identify the manner in which such architecture ascended to become dominant – the changes of circumstances, conditions, worldviews and ideologies that enabled the success of a hegemonic process driven by oppositional movements and their architecture.

This section does not pretend to provide a complete picture of these transformations – much of the material is, in any case, familiar. Rather, it brings to the fore certain moments and details that illuminate the transformation and the process involved. The argument itself is completed only in Part Three of the book, which returns, concisely, to the early moment of the Weimar Republic and the experiments in social-democratic architecture by Ernst May and Hilberseimer, as seen through the eyes of the architectural historian Manfredo Tafuri. 'Critique, Reformism and Co-optation' will tie together critique and reformism, and unfold the importance of the revolutionary movement for the success of the reformists. It will describe the manner in which reformism recruited architecture to aid in achieving its goals, and will demonstrate how the reformist movement and its architecture facilitated integrating the working class into bourgeois, capitalist society. It will delineate the gradual transformation and agitation that led to the broad implementation of economic, social and spatial planning – 'the Plan' – in the post-war years.

The relationship of critique to political movements, and particularly to the nineteenth-century reformist movement, is at the centre of this section of *The Efficacy of Architecture*. The first chapter, 'Critique and Change', sets the stage for later discussions. It concisely studies the emergence of critique and its role. The chapter introduces reformism and outlines Karl Korsch's hypothesis regarding critique and revolutionary praxis, which will enable characterizing different eras as inherently reformist or revolutionary. The second chapter, 'The Ascent of Reformism', follows the rise and triumph of reformism, with particular attention to the manner in which reformism leveraged critique and architecture for societal transformation. The last chapter of the section discusses the hijacking of critique, *récuperation* – namely, the process by which the state or capitalism respond to critique not by satisfying its demands, but by co-opting it. Part One, 'Critique, Reformism, and Co-optation', is thus a means of introducing issues such as reformism and revolution, critique and co-optation, which are significant for later discussions. But it also demonstrates, by looking back to a familiar history, that architecture can, in effect, be instrumental to producing positive change led by oppositional movements and ideologies.

The Role of Critique

In the eighteenth century, publications such as Addison's *Spectator* and Steele's *Tatler* in Britain and the work of Diderot, Voltaire, and Rousseau in France, presented a new voice, characterized by moral indignation, 'a struggle against the absolutist state' (Eagleton 1996: 9), and an intertwining of political, ideological, cultural, and social concerns. These critical eighteenth-century endeavours owed their existence to the emergence of egalitarianism and journalism, and were developed, according to the historian Reinhart Koselleck, from late Renaissance practices of re-reading ecclesiastical texts (Koselleck 1988; Eagleton 1996). By the seventeenth century, figures such as Richard Simon and Pierre Bayle had developed criticism as a specific methodology of rational judgement. Critique thus played a key role in the advent of reason, in delineating a public sphere for civil society, and, unintentionally, in the creation of a schism between reason and religion.[1]

Koselleck traces the contribution of the eighteenth-century Illuminati and Freemasons in demarcating a specific territory for critique, formulated as a moral critique of the state, of social stratification, and of religion. It was a critique that was necessarily political, tailored to advance the interests of the bourgeoisie against the entrenched powers of the nobility and absolutism, yet appeared ostensibly apolitical, produced in the non-political and protective context of the lodge (Koselleck 1988: 75–97). 'On the plane both of the *Règne de la Critique* and of the lodges,' wrote Koselleck, 'the bourgeoisie used indirect methods to bring about a new order' (Koselleck 1988: 96). Terry Eagleton highlighted the relation of critique not just to the ascent of the bourgeoisie, but also to the logic of capitalism: 'What could better correspond to the bourgeoisie's dream of freedom than a society of petty producers whose endlessly available, utterly inexhaustible commodity is discourse itself, equitably exchanged in a mode which reconfirms the autonomy of each producer?' (Eagleton 1996: 17).

The modern process of compartmentalization of life into specific and separate spheres of which Max Weber would later write, was already evident in the eighteenth century, yet in this transitory period a pre-modern 'absolutist' separation of moral and political spheres was still dominant. In the absolutist state, morality was deemed a private concern, whereas politics focused on power and policy. The bourgeois critics argued that morality is 'above' politics, calling for the subjugation of absolutist power to a universal, humanist morality. This allowed Schiller to conceive of art – and particularly theatre – as an autonomous domain from which a moral critique of the shortcomings of politics and of society could be produced.

A key aspect of critique was its ability to claim an apolitical position, indirectly assaulting the state or the church – and it is precisely this apolitical claim that, on the one hand, protected critique from its adversaries, and, on the other, provided it with legitimacy. The distance of the lodge and Schiller's 'moral' stage from politics and state, a critical distance, therefore enabled the formation of rigorous critique by providing a totalizing overview, the (relative) disassociation of the critic from the object of criticism, and moral protection from the powerful subjects of criticism.

At the close of the eighteenth century, Immanuel Kant perfected critique as a methodology, a means of drawing distinctions and discriminations. Kant wrote:

> Our age is, in especial degree, the age of criticism, and to criticism everything must submit. Religion through its sanctity and law-giving through its majesty may seek to exempt themselves from it. But they then awaken just suspicion, and cannot claim the sincere respect which reason accords only to that which has been able to sustain the test of free and open examination.
>
> *(Kant 1966: xxiv)*

The philosopher and physiocrat Anne-Robert-Jacques Turgot attempted to reform the absolutist state as finance minister in France (1774–76). This was a reformist endeavour to transform and rectify the state from within, by a figure who embodied the rationale and spirit of Enlightenment. Many of Turgot's influential supporters belonged to the Enlightenment secret societies, which were also the power base of the radical Jacobins who agitated for revolution only a few years later. Eighteenth-century critique was thus both reformist and radical by nineteenth-century standards. Reformist, because of its apolitical claim and its indirectness; radical, because of its unequivocal opposition to the absolutist state, an opposition at the level of complete disavowal. Terry Eagleton has written of Enlightenment criticism that:

> while its appeal to standards of universal reason signifies a resistance to absolutism, the critical gesture itself is typically conservative and corrective, revising and adjusting particular phenomena to its implacable model of discourse. Criticism is a reformative apparatus, scourging deviation and repressing the transgressive; yet this juridical technology is deployed in the name of a certain historical emancipation.
>
> *(Eagleton 1996: 12)*

In the following century, this field of intellectual work was increasingly split as a result of growing specialization and the division of labour into two different operations: the application of critique as method, following the work of Kant, and criticism as a sub-literary genre limited to the discussion of the arts and disseminated primarily via journalism. The broad and sweeping 'amateurish' critiques of the eighteenth century were now replaced by more narrow and specialized exercises in moral judgement and (socially irrelevant) evaluation of aesthetic quality (Eagleton 1996: 69–71), yet, as will later be discussed, critique's political role became also more lucid in this era, with the apolitical veil gradually, though only partially, lifted.

The sociologist Luc Boltanski argues that critique necessarily finds itself caught between contradictory demands.[2] On the one hand, critical theory is expected to appear objective, non-biased or partisan, and on the other, it depends on a relation to 'ordinary critiques', the '[m]oral judgements formulated by actors in the course of their everyday activities' (Boltanski 2011: 3). It is the relation of critique to such 'ordinary critiques' that gives critique force and offers it a political dimension. Appearing too tightly related to 'ordinary critiques', too impartial, and insufficiently objective undermines not only scientific rigour and its positivist impetus, but also the political efficacy of critique. Boltanski differentiates between critique as formulated via forms of systematic critical theory and the more evidently morally driven partial critiques that are overtly embedded in 'ordinary critiques'. He writes:

> Unlike 'traditional theory', 'critical theory' possesses the objective of *reflexivity*. It can or *must* (according to Raymond Geuss) grasp the discontents of actors, explicitly consider them in the very labour of theorization, in such a way as to alter their relationship to social reality and, thereby, that social reality itself, in the direction of *emancipation*.
>
> (Boltanski 2011: 5)[3]

A critical theory 'that is not backed by the experience of a collective' results in a pointless critique for critique's sake and lacks efficacy (Boltanski 2011: 5). Boltanski's argument rephrases that of Koselleck: the tension within, and internal contradiction of a critique that is political yet postures as apolitical, is here cast as the tension between moral judgement empowered by 'ordinary critiques' and the maintaining of a quasi-objective stance.

Critique requires a critical distance: a position of exteriority to the object being studied. Such a distance enables the development of metacritiques of society; it allows the formation of an objective (or quasi-objective) description of society's structures that, from 'within', seem to coincide with reality – that is, appear naturalized rather than constructed. The description of the structures, which de-naturalizes them, makes visible what was previously veiled, and is supported by a judgement of the structures in question. It is in this dual operation of distanciation and judgement that critical theory attempts to satisfy the conflicting demands for objectivity and for a relation to ordinary critiques.

Critique is also a necessary vehicle for questioning what Boltanski and Eve Chiapello identify as 'tests' – 'an event during which beings, in pitting themselves against one another [...], reveal what they are capable of and, more profoundly, what they are made of' (Boltanski and Chiapello 2005: 31). A critique of a test can be reformist ('corrective') and demand making the test stricter and more just, or be, alternatively, 'radical', demanding to replace one test with another. Reformist critique proved to be a means of survival for capitalist, bourgeois society: the ability to respond to critique, to address demands raised by elements within society, and to allow its own transformation in order to rectify inadequacies – all this meant the longevity and subsistence of the capitalist order, defying the predictions and hopes of revolutionaries.

Evolutionary Socialism

The term 'reformism', as a political category, owes its meaning primarily to the work of the socialist Eduard Bernstein. In a series of publications at the end of the nineteenth century on 'evolutionary socialism', Bernstein critically interrogated Marx and Engel's work. He questioned the deterministic understandings of the orthodox Marxists of the Second International, according to which only the structural base steers and determines society's development, understandings that rendered the political merely a reflection of the base. '[T]he point of economic development attained to-day', countered Bernstein,

> leaves the ideological, and especially the ethical, factors greater space for independent activity than was formally the case. In consequence of this the interdependency of cause and effect between technical, economic evolution, and the evolution of other social tendencies is becoming always indirect, and from that the necessities of the first are losing much of their power of dictating the form of the latter.
>
> (Bernstein 1978: 15–16)[4]

The 'necessity' doubted here by Bernstein is the idea of 'historical necessity': the idea of a predetermined direction of progress from feudalism via capitalism to socialism, driven by the inevitable progress of society's means of production.

Bernstein outlined in his book *Evolutionary Socialism* several recent developments, which seemed to contradict Marx's predictions – primarily, doubting the existence of processes of centralization and concentration of capital, according to which the capitalists become a relatively smaller group within society whereas their overall wealth, both in absolute terms and proportionally, grows. Bernstein initially pointed out that contrary to expectations, the best-paid workers were to be found in the sectors in which the rate of surplus value – supposedly an indicator of exploitation – is highest (Bernstein 1978: 39). Next, he presented diverse data for Britain, France, and Germany to demonstrate that the relative and absolute size of the capitalist group was growing rather than shrinking; that small and medium size businesses have not necessarily suffered from the expansion of large-scale manufacturers, but, rather, remain a significant element in the market; likewise, the increase in large-scale farming had not eliminated small- and medium-scale farming. 'It is thus quite wrong to assume that the present development of society shows a relative or indeed absolute diminution of the number of the members of the possessing classes', he concluded (Bernstein 1978: 48).

The emergence of trusts and growth in shareholding, Bernstein argued, served to expand the capitalist class, to expand the lower strata of the middle class, and hence, instead of the social strata becoming more polarized between capitalists and workers, they became increasingly diversified. 'If the working class waits till "Capital" has put the middle classes out of the world,' wrote Bernstein, 'it might really have a long nap' (Bernstein 1978: 50–51).

Bernstein highlighted two important stages en route to socialism: the development of the capitalist mode of production beyond a certain level, and, subsequently, the workers, organized as a 'class party', would need to 'take possession of the political government' (Bernstein 1978: 97). He pointed out that such political empowerment can happen either via parliamentary struggle, or via revolution (Bernstein 1978: 101). He proceeded to argue that the working class is far from homogeneous; that, once power is assumed, government cannot, in any immediate sense, take over businesses and factories and successfully run them without a transition period or alternative measures, such as employing the previous proprietors, or leasing factories to their employees.

Democracy, for Bernstein, has to be considered 'as an absence of class government' (Bernstein 1978: 142). He argued that social democracy had no choice except for 'taking its stand unreservedly on the theory of democracy – on the grounds of universal suffrage with all the consequences resulting therefrom to its tactics' (Bernstein 1978: 145). 'The right to vote in a democracy,' wrote Bernstein, 'makes [the working class] members virtually partners in the community, and this virtual partnership must in the end lead to real partnership' (Bernstein 1978: 144). And while he acknowledged the shortcomings of contemporary democracy, he envisioned a process in which workers' suffrage would 'transform the representatives of the people from masters into real servants of the people' (Bernstein 1978: 144).

Moreover: Bernstein pointed out that socialists are already invested in 'bourgeois' democracy and in democratic expansion, in forwarding universal suffrage, and in achieving gradual betterment, and therefore his proposition was merely to acknowledge this reality as desirable, and to address this in socialist theory, shedding, en route, the revolutionary rhetoric. He emphasized the emancipatory character of socialism, tying progressive social legislation to 'liberalism', understood not as the political face of capitalism, but as a doctrine which is aimed at maximizing freedoms. Further, he wrote:

> If democracy is not to excel centralised absolutism in the breeding of bureaucracies, it must be built up on an elaborately organised self-government with a corresponding economic, personal responsibility of all the units of administration as well as of the adult citizens of the state. Nothing is more injurious to its healthy development than enforced uniformity and a too abundant amount of protectionism or subventionism.
>
> *(Bernstein 1978: 155)*

Bernstein's propagation of gradual, piecemeal change rather than an abrupt total transformation, and hence 'evolutionary socialism' rather than revolutionary change, was heresy to orthodox Marxists such as Karl Kautsky or George Plekhanov. Bernstein's self-description as a 'revisionist' was subsequently used by his adversaries as a derogatory term to delegitimize his work. But Bernstein had an audience among socialists, and his work sowed the seeds that would lead to the break between the social democratic and the communist movements, the former adopting Bernstein's reformist 'evolutionary' route to socialism.

The improvements in the conditions of the working class that Bernstein observed, however, were largely achieved by the work of another reformist movement, significantly less radical than Bernstein's social-democratic milieu. The agenda of this earlier movement would increasingly coincide with that of the social democrats in the twentieth century until the two would completely converge, yet up until the adoption of a gradualist approach by the social democrats, this second, 'bourgeois' reformist movement remained largely distinctive. This earlier reformist movement stands at the centre of the following chapters. Already when Bernstein wrote *Evolutionary Socialism*, some of the distinctions between the two were dissipating: the 1875 Gotha Programme of the German Social Democratic Party (SPD), which Lassalle's socialists helped found, was reformist in character; though the 1891

Erfurt Programme, to which both Bernstein and Kautsky contributed, was more solidly Marxist and revolutionary, it nevertheless focused on legislative betterments via bourgeois politics and state; and while originally the new trade unions and co-operatives were viewed negatively by revolutionaries, they were, by the late nineteenth century, more of an organ of radical socialism than of more moderate and 'bourgeois' social reformers.

Expectedly, radical and revolutionary movements scorned all forms of reformism, perceiving it as an organ of bourgeois society intent on protecting the hegemony of the bourgeoisie. Lenin, writing disparagingly on the British 'bourgeois democratic system' some years later, asserted that:

> I would call this system Lloyd-Georgism after the English minister Lloyd George, one of the foremost and most dexterous representatives of this system in the classic land of the 'bourgeois labour party'. A first class bourgeois manipulator, an astute politician, a popular orator who will deliver any speeches you like, even revolutionary ones, to a labour audience, and a man who is capable of obtaining sizable sops for docile workers in the shape of social reforms (insurance, etc.), Lloyd George serves the bourgeoisie splendidly, and serves it precisely *among* the workers, brings its influence *precisely* to the proletariat, to where the bourgeoisie needs it most and where it finds it most difficult to subject the masses morally.
>
> *(Lenin 1964: 118)*

Elsewhere, he announced that:

> Nothing in our time can be done without elections; nothing can be done without the masses. And in this era of printing and parliamentarianism it is *impossible* to gain the following of the masses without a widely ramified, systematically managed, well-equipped system of flattery, lies, fraud, juggling with fashionable and popular catchwords, and promising all manner of reforms and blessings to the workers right and left – as long as they renounce the revolutionary struggle for the overthrow of the bourgeoisie.
>
> *(Lenin 1964: 117)*

Zinoviev, in 1924, was even more explicit:

> Bolshevization means a firm will to struggle for the hegemony of the proletariat, it means a passionate hatred of the bourgeoisie, for the counter-revolutionary leaders of social democracy, for centrism and the centrists, for the semi-centrists and the pacifists, for all the miscarriages of bourgeois ideology.
>
> *(Laclau and Mouffe 2001: 61)*

The threat of powerful revolutionary movements aided reformers in advancing their causes, posited as a middle ground between revolt and the status quo. The reflexivity of middle-class society and the centrality of critique, reason, and the public sphere for debate and opinion formation enabled the dominant forces – capitalism as the mode of production, the state as the dominant institution, and the bourgeoisie as the dominant class – to react with some precision to changing circumstances and contingent conditions, whether by satisfying the demands raised by 'respectable' citizens, by repressing them, or by co-opting them.

Korsch's Hypothesis

The renegade Marxist Karl Korsch argued in the 1920s that in specific eras in which revolutionary ferment wanes – primarily due to a lack of opportunities, conditions and hope for an imminent revolution – it is substituted by a reformist agenda (Korsch 2008: 55–65). It is precisely in these eras that oppositional intellectuals turn to critique. The logic is simple: critique, as an instrument that relies on a critical distance, can support action only indirectly, via a necessary praxis-oriented mediating theory. In a condition that lacks a revolutionary horizon, critique becomes the only viable instrument available to oppositional movements, deployed as a means of delegitimizing the existing order. In his analysis of the development of Marxist thought and the workers' movement, Korsch described the period of 1843–48 as one of revolutionary ferment; he defined the period spanning from the repression of the events of 1848 until the end of the nineteenth century as a 'quite unrevolutionary' period of regenerating the movement (Korsch 2008: 57); the period from the early twentieth century until 1923 – his own era – was characterized as one of growing revolutionary conditions. In the second, reformist period, critique became one of the two dominant schools of Marxist thought that 'treated Marx's materialist principle as merely a "subjective basis for reflective judgement" in Kant's sense' (Korsch 2008: 62–63). Korsch explained the rise of this school as follows:

> a unified general theory of social revolution was changed into criticisms of the bourgeois economic order, of the bourgeois State, of the bourgeois system of education, of bourgeois religion, art, science and culture. These criticisms no longer necessarily developed by their very nature into revolutionary practice; they can equally well develop, into all kinds of attempts at *reform*, which fundamentally remain within the limits of bourgeois society and bourgeois State, and in actual practice usually did so.
> (Korsch 2008: 63–64)

Whereas Korsch's understanding of 'reformism' is indebted to Bernstein, the era he defines as 'reformist' preceded the conception of 'evolutionary socialism'. The reformism Korsch refers to in the second half of the nineteenth century is primarily focused on radical circles within the nascent socialist movement, yet his depiction of the era itself as reformist acknowledges a broader movement that advanced social betterment in a non-revolutionary piecemeal manner: the 'bourgeois' reformism mentioned above. And indeed, this movement systematically deployed critique for its own ends.

Critique served the struggle of the bourgeoisie in the eighteenth century against the absolutist state, and in the nineteenth century, following the repression of radical Jacobinism and later of the Chartists, political reform – first and foremost the demand for universal suffrage – remained high on the agenda of oppositional movements. But now the need to better the lives of the many, which increasingly included the new urban migrants and the emerging working class, became an urgent issue.

Until the formation of grass roots labour movements in the late nineteenth century, reformers in Britain were primarily members of the middle class, including lay preachers of puritan, non-conformist sects, conscientious traders and factory owners, as well as radical politicians. The reformist movement included organizations such as the Fabian Society, the various reformist charities and associations of the era, such as The Metropolitan Sanitary

Association or The Society for Improving the Condition of the Labouring Classes, and figures such as Octavia Hill and Lord Shaftesbury. Consequently, reformism often prescribed the 'embourgeoisment' of the workers: betterment via integration, and integration by the emulation of the middle class.

The arguments of the reformists leveraged critique to their advantage, providing a rigorous assessment and judgement of existing conditions supported by pragmatic proposals. Consequently, critique played an important ideological role. It became the basis for the creation of a popular force that shaped society. A critique that tightly related to 'ordinary critiques' and was buttressed by concrete proposals of change could, in effect, bring about the transformation of society. The ability to address demands raised by 'respectable' elements within society, and to allow society's own transformation in order to rectify inadequacies – all this meant the longevity and prowess of the capitalist order, defying the predictions and hopes of revolutionaries.

The radicals' position towards critique was more ambivalent than towards reformism. On the one hand, they associated critique with Kantian philosophy, which was perceived as the 'high philosophy' of the bourgeoisie (Jay 1973: 57; H. Marcuse 2007: 210). They were familiar with the role of critique in the bourgeois reformist movement, and the manner in which it prevented revolution and helped capitalism persevere. On the other hand, despite these doubts, radicals developed their own means of critique. Yet, in many senses, critique remained suspect, not least because critique required critical distance and eschewed a theory–praxis relation necessary for revolutionary action. In the following description of the emergent bourgeois reformist movement, and later in this section in the discussion of the twentieth century, Korsch's hypothesis will be used as a means of assessing the radical or reformist agendas dominating specific periods as well as the role of critique in social transformation.

THE ASCENT OF REFORMISM

Social Stratification

> [T]he awakening of the labouring classes, after the first shock of the French Revolution, made the upper classes tremble.
>
> *(The Diary of Frances Lady Shelley: 8)*[5]

The modern reformist movement is unprecedented in its longevity and efficacy. Its roots, as discussed earlier, are in the Enlightenment era and its project: the spreading of reason, liberty, equality, and justice. It developed in the early nineteenth century into a middle-class reaction to the hardship of labourers, and increasingly, as the century unfolded, intertwined and converged with grass roots working-class organizations agitating for change. Initial concerns of reformism in the nineteenth century were the police reform, the prison reform, and the reform of the Poor Law. The latter would bring about a convergence of issues regarding poverty, sanitation and housing (Hall 1998: 658–83). The hardship at the centre of concern was caused by industrialization and mass urbanization. It was exacerbated by the laissez-faire capitalism of the era: the speculation and profit involved in the construction of shoddy tenements for the poor, the exploitative and inhuman conditions of work, the limited access of the poor to health services, education and other resources. The health hazards found in working-class neighbourhoods, as well as the presumed 'moral depravity' of the poor – their involvement in crime and prostitution, their absence from church, the lack of basic privacy in their living quarters – only added to the concerns. A segment of the middle class developed in the early nineteenth century compassion towards the poor, and developed a consciousness of the unacceptable conditions of a large segment of society.

Beyond such compassion, another motivation was the fear of the disorderly, uncultivated, 'criminal' lower classes, a fear of the faceless 'masses'. This anxiety would grow once the working class consolidated, once rebellious social and political movements such as anarchism and communism would attempt to overthrow the existing order, beginning with the massacre of Peterloo in 1819, the Canut revolt of 1831 in Lyon, the events of 1848 in Europe, and followed by the Paris Commune of 1871. 'At no time did the Victorians feel completely safe from the possibility of social unrest,' wrote the historian Anthony Wohl, 'and it was against the backdrop of fear and uncertainty that the housing reformers proffered better housing as a bulwark against revolution' (1977: 64).

Class war could be averted only by significant changes in society, by integrating the working class into bourgeois society. The philosopher and activist Antonio Negri has written that '[w]orking-class political revolution could only be avoided by recognizing and accepting the new relation of class forces, while making the working class function within an overall mechanism that would "sublimate" its continuous struggle for power into a dynamic element within the system' (Negri 2003: 27). Thus, the reformist movement was driven by a mixture of genuine concern and anxiety. Rather than a unified movement, it included several movements dedicated to specific causes, and in the United States took the form of the Progressive Movement.

Whereas in France violent revolution was necessary for the bourgeoisie to seize political power, in Britain the parallel transition required a lower key and gradualist struggle. The 'foot soldiers' of these struggles, however, were not the rich traders. They included the poor, in the form of the destabilizing 'mob', and the various artisans and journeymen concentrated in the large cities. In London, the latter social group frequented many of the coffee shops of Oxford Street in the eighteenth century,[6] and formed the base for many of the secret societies mentioned earlier. Its members were literate, engaged, and had some – though very limited – economic means and free time, to an extent that they formed a very different social group than the poor masses. Their importance to reformist and revolutionary agitation was central, for they were excluded from the new, bourgeois order, but were very aware of the universality of the demands for liberty and equality that legitimized the ascent of the bourgeoisie, and consequently demanded their share. While the bourgeoisie used these ideals to delegitimize the old order of hereditary power and privilege, the same ideals were soon deployed against the bourgeoisie themselves by those who were excluded from the new structures of power and privilege. A trajectory leads from the development of a bourgeois ideology, via that of the middle-class reformers and revolutionaries of the early nineteenth century, to the ideology of the late nineteenth-century reformist labour movements.

By the 1880s, the journeymen and artisans of the beginning of the century would form the core of the 'labour aristocracy', as Victorians called this social group (Hobsbawm 1964; 1984a; 1984b; 1984c: 182–83). The aristocracy of labour included, increasingly, skilled and unionized labour. It lived above the poverty line, and was 'respectable' to an extent that it was sometimes referred to by members of the middle class as a lower middle class. This social group, in effect, mediated between the working class and the middle class. Its members were often involved in the organization of labour movements such as trade unions and co-operatives, and in this sense the 'aristocracy of labour' was the representative of the working class as a whole towards its social superiors; though, as this social group was placed in proximity to the middle class, it was susceptible to 'embourgeoisement' in conditions that encouraged social mobility. Yet such conditions hardly existed before 1914, to the extent that the historian Robert Roberts commented that 'skilled workers generally did not strive to join a higher rank' (Roberts 1971: 13).[7] Lenin identified the existence of an 'aristocracy of labour' as the source of the reformist character of the British labour movement; the historian Eric Hobsbawm qualified such perceptions, yet admitted that 'there is really no denying that the labour aristocrats, so long as their privileged position lasted, were not aiming at the overthrow of capitalism, and were indeed both subjectively and objectively furthering the subaltern integration of workers into the system' (Hobsbawm 1984a: 222-23). It was precisely this social group that often benefited from early council housing, and it was its members who moved into early council housing together with the clerks and shopmen of an emergent lower middle class.

'Respectability', as an important social value that contributed to the standing of a family and individuals in society, reflected a further breakdown of the working class into social subdivisions, and played a role in the politics and policies of housing. Those who could maintain a 'respectable' household – assessed by cleanliness, neatness, and by the existence of normative household 'necessities' – were positioned socially above those who could not. As housing and urbanism historian Alison Ravetz argues, '[f]inding and maintaining a home and using it to establish a particular social position were all, by definition, individual and therefore divisive actions' (Ravetz 2001: 28).

At the end of the nineteenth century, another, newer social group consolidated, a lower middle class of white collar workers, placed socially between the 'labour aristocracy' and the more affluent middle class. The members of this group were often conservative and eager to emulate the bourgeoisie as a means of differentiating themselves from the working class. The existence of this social group and its politics initially created a counter-reaction by radicalizing the 'labour aristocracy' (Hobsbawm 1984c: 184), but in the long run would facilitate a smoother route to social mobility by 'completing' the social strata of British society, bridging the gap that had separated the working class from the affluent classes.

One of the major sources of reformism, particularly in Britain, was religion.[8] Many of the leaders of the reformist movement were dissenters or non-conformists who rejected the institutional Anglican Church. The Jacobinism imported from France in the eighteenth century blended with the worldview of diverse groups of dissenters, whether Calvinist, Quakers, Baptist, Unitarians, or other Puritans. A special place, in this sense, is reserved in England for John Wesley's Methodist Church, which played a double role: producing, on the one hand, some of the most influential reformers, and, on the other hand, aiding in subjugating the working class. As E.P. Thompson pointed out (1966: 350–400), Methodism, which spread in the early nineteenth century among the English working class, despite its roots in radical Jacobinism, renounced radicalism. Methodism explained to members of the working class their place in the world and preached submission, and consequently served to pacify the workers and affirm the existing conditions. It was a means of producing the ideal factory workers – submissive, disciplined, and lifeless to the extent that they could cope with the long hours of repetitive labour activating machinery. An 1835 text by the scholar Andrew Ure, *The Philosophy of Manufactures*, preached to factory owners to get their 'moral machinery' in shape in order to guarantee workers' cooperation and higher productivity (Ure 1835: 417; Thomspon 1966: 361–62).

Yet Methodism also gave birth to its own dissidents, many of whom were lay preachers, who contributed to the consolidation of the working class and to reformist agitation, initiating movements such as the Chartists. The Methodists demonstrated the advantages of well-organized and centralized administration to the reformers and to the nascent labour movements of the first half of the nineteenth century. Organizational rigour and centralized administration would later become one of the demands addressed to government by many of the reformers, as an alternative to the loosely administrated liberalism of the era, and would be implemented also in the self-organization of labour. Thus, like reformism itself, Methodism had a double role, both pacifying the workers and radicalizing them.

The Sanitary Movement

Of particular interest within nineteenth-century reformism is the sanitary movement. It identified housing as one of the causes as well as solutions to the malign of the working class, and gave birth to the housing reform movement. The sanitary movement, which coalesced in the first decades of the nineteenth century, was informed by advances in science, and railed against the poor hygiene conditions that allowed epidemics to rampage through vast areas of cities such as London and Manchester, against high death rates of infants and adults, and against diseases that reduced many urban inhabitants to pauperism once they lost their ability to work. The cholera epidemic of 1832, and, around 1848–49, outbreaks of smallpox, measles, and scarlet fever further galvanized the sanitary movement. Most epidemics spread from the areas inhabited by the working class to other districts, and the majority of the victims were among the urban poor. The living conditions in areas such as London's East End, with their tenements, shacks, filth, open sewage, cesspools, and squalor, were targeted by the sanitary movement and its call for governmental or philanthropic intervention. The sanitary movement thus identified the spatiality of epidemics and disease, and tied it to social class. It proceeded by claiming that the living conditions of the urban poor were the cause of the epidemics, as the overcrowding and lack of sanitary systems led to decrepit conditions and brought about the fast spread of disease.

An exemplary figure in the British movement was Edwin Chadwick. His work demonstrates the manner in which social reform became intertwined with sanitary issues and housing.[9] The 1842 report by Chadwick to the Poor Law Commissioners (Chadwick 1842) was a watershed for the sanitary movement in Britain. In the report, Chadwick extensively cited local medical officers. He highlighted the relation of health to living conditions. '[T]he deaths from the chief diseases,' he wrote, 'which the medical officers consider to be the most powerfully influenced by the physical circumstances under which the population is placed – as the external and internal condition of their dwellings, drainage, and ventilation' (Chadwick 1842). He described a scene he had encountered in Glasgow:

> We entered a dirty low passage like a house door, which led from the street through the first house to a square court immediately behind, which court, with the exception of a narrow path around it leading to another long passage through a second house, was occupied entirely as a dung receptacle of the most disgusting kind. Beyond this court the second passage led to a second square court, occupied in the same way by its dunghill; and from this court there was yet a third passage leading to a third court, and third dungheap. There were no privies or drains there, and the dungheaps received all filth which the swarm of wretched inhabitants could give; and we learned that a considerable part of the rent of the houses was paid by the produce of the dungheaps. Thus, worse off than wild animals, many of which withdraw to a distance and conceal their ordure, the dwellers in these courts had converted their shame into a kind of money by which their lodging was to be paid. The interiors of these houses and their inmates corresponded with the exteriors.
>
> *(Chadwick 1842)*

Much of the report was aimed at arguing that employers should improve their employees' work and living conditions by applying a typical reformist ploy: identifying both a financial and moral imperative in such improvements. The report also called for the creation of boards of health, and was particularly focused on agitating for sewers and water supply (Hall 1998: 685). Critique was thus instrumental for the reformists' demands for improvements. Chadwick argued for greater governmental powers and authority to intervene, a demand that created powerful enemies among politicians and free-market interest groups, which depicted him as authoritarian and tyrannical (Porter 2000: 315–17).[10] Despite such opposition, mounting death tolls from epidemics exerted a pressure that brought about the gradual strengthening of government at the expense of laissez-faire.

One of the main agitators for better sanitary conditions was Hector Gavin, a lecturer and the author of *Sanitary Ramblings*, an influential study of London's Bethnal Green. Gavin claimed that the limited number and bad condition of privies were a cause of disease; like Chadwick, he identified the overcrowding of working class neighbourhoods as a health hazard. Gavin argued that mortality and sickness rates directly relate to the number of inhabitants per area in households. He scrutinized ventilation, heating, structure, drainage, paving, and sewage. By calling for help for the working class to be able to live in 'the modest comforts of an English home' (Spriggs 1984: 286), Gavin was suggesting that by emulating the middle class mode of living, the concerns regarding both the physical and moral health of the working class would be resolved.

In 1848, a General Board of Health was created, and John Simon was appointed Medical Officer of Health for the City of London, while a new independent organization, Metropolitan Sanitary Association, took the helm of agitation in London, with Hector Gavin as one of its three honourable secretaries. The Association and the General Board demanded that the government be given more power to intervene in health issues, adding to the pressures to limit laissez-faire by regulation and governmental authority.

From early on, the issue of hygiene was linked to morality. Beyond the association of filth and squalor with immorality, overcrowding was a major concern, for it led to unmarried women and men sharing rooms, whether in lodging houses or in workers' homes (Evans 1997). Gavin quoted in a report evidence by a Mr Paine regarding lodging houses:

> In one house I visited in Stanley-street, I found an adult man and woman, brother and sister, occupying the same bed, labouring under fever. In another house in the same street, I found a similar case. In another house, where I had occasion to attend an inmate, I found a lad of 17 or 18 years of age sleeping in the same bed with his father and mother. It is a consistent custom for four or five families to sleep in one bedroom.
> *(Gavin 1851: 54)*

While Chadwick and Gavin must be credited for bringing the issue of overcrowding, and hence also housing, into discussion, neither gave it much weight, preferring to focus on sewages, water and drainage (Wohl 1977). Gradually, though, overcrowding and housing moved to the fore of concerns. The Health of Towns Association was formed in 1844 in order to exert political pressure for sanitary reform, and showed more interest than other organizations in housing issues. *The Builder*, an illustrated weekly trade journal, was founded in 1842, and soon became the mouthpiece for housing reform. Aiming at an inclusive readership – architects, constructors, art connoisseurs, engineers and more – *The Builder* provided a platform for discussing housing reform and its architecture in an era in which more narrowly architectural publications took little notice. On its pages, model housing was dissected, and building know-how was disseminated. A third element in nudging the discussion towards housing was the 1844 Royal Commission on the Sanitary State of Large Towns, which focused on overcrowding and its causes more than any of its predecessors (Wohl 1977: 7–8).

The initial concerns with health thus led the sanitary movement to increasingly focus on bettering the living conditions of the poor. Consequently, the Metropolitan Board of Works, formed in 1855 to provide London with adequate infrastructure, became involved in slum clearances, but was empowered only to demolish decrepit buildings rather than build new homes. Instead, it was involved in constructing new roads and widening existing ones, which often meant demolishing existing dwellings of the poor and causing more overcrowding.[11]

At this stage, as reformism itself developed from eighteenth-century resistance to despotism, its own gravitation towards stronger government was slow. As late as 1885, the radical liberal Joseph Chamberlain lamented the inadequacy of legislation regarding housing, claiming that previous housing acts were 'tainted and paralysed by the incurable timidity with which Parliament is accustomed to deal with the sacred rights of property' (Porter 2000: 327).

These conditions led many reformers to channel their ideas through charity and philanthropy. Octavia Hill famously re-fitted cottages for the working class and employed female rent collectors. The Society for Improving the Condition of the Labouring Classes, founded by Lord Shaftesbury, constructed a series of model housing developments. The first was the 1844 model housing near Bagnigge Wells in London. This was followed by the Metropolitan Dwelling in the same area in 1847, and the 1848 Model Houses for Families near New Oxford Street.

Model Housing

> All the secret forces which set on fire the volcano called the social question which glows under our feet, the proletarian bitterness, the hatred ... the dangerous confusion of ideas ... must disappear like mist before the morning sun when ... the workers themselves enter in this fashion into the ranks of the property owners.
>
> *(Dr Sax, quoted in Engels 1872)*

The architect commissioned by The Society for Improving the Condition of the Labouring Classes was Henry Roberts. In 1851, Roberts published an illustrated pamphlet titled *The Dwellings of the Labouring Classes, Their Arrangement and Constructions* (H. Roberts 1853). This document was one of the first professional publications to address the role of architecture in improving the living conditions of the working class.[12] Roberts himself notes this in the opening of the book: 'The subject now submitted to the consideration of the INSTITUTE OF BRITISH ARCHITECTS is one to which their special attention has not been previously invited' (H. Roberts 2007: 1). He also acknowledges the limited appeal the topic may have to architects who understand architecture as an art, or as a scientific–technological pursuit, admitting that it is 'a field of labour, which apparently offers little scope for scientific skill, and but few attractive points to an artist's eye' (H. Roberts 2007: 1). Among the arguments Roberts unfolds in order to convince architects of the need for such architectural endeavours, is that architects have an obligation and responsibility towards the well-being of working-class labourers involved in construction.

The change that took place over the following century – for transition was gradual rather than immediate – was nothing less than profound, and meant an unprecedented expansion of the field of architecture. The gradual transformation in architectural interests that Roberts foresaw meant that public buildings, once considered the locus of architecture, retreated from the fore of the profession, and housing took over as the major architectural concern. With this change, architecture could shape the manner in which people lived, address social experience, and was no longer limited to symbolic representations and communications. If, circa 1850, the large majority of urban dwellings were created without the involvement of architects, by the 1950s the reverse was true. But in 1851 these changes were still distant, and Roberts's publication was merely an early step in the direction architecture would take.

The model housing near Bagnigge Wells by Roberts consisted of two rows of double-storey buildings facing each other (Figure 1.1). With very minimal ornamentation and a repetition, they resembled, to some degree, barracks. The central section of one of the two buildings was a home for widows, organized by rooms flanking a central corridor. The rest of the development consisted of two apartment types, one of which was duplex housing. The staircases were not shared, each apartment had its own. The emphasis on privacy is evident also in the provision of different rooms within the small apartments, allowing the parents to enjoy separation from children, and a separation of sexes in the case of adult children. Thus, three bedrooms became the preferred solution, as it allowed the minimum separation: one room for parents, one room for girls, one for boys. Privacy was therefore one of the distinctive marks of the model housing. The George Street Model Lodging-House, for example, also by Roberts, included dormitories, but they were 'subdivided with movable wood partitions 6ft. 9in. high; each compartment, enclosed by its own door, is fitted up with a bed, chair, and clothes-box' (H. Roberts 2007: 9).

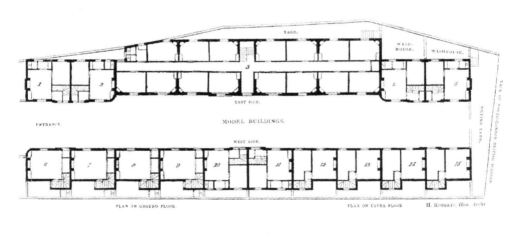

FIGURE 1.1 Henry Roberts, model housing near Bagnigge Wells, between Pentonville and Gray's Inn Road, London, 1840s. From Roberts, H. (1853) *The Dwellings of the Labouring Classes, Their Arrangements and Constructions*, 3rd ed., London: The Society for Improving the Condition of the Labouring Classes.

A telling passage from Roberts's publication outlines in the most lucid manner the decisions with which the providers of the model housing wrestled and the intentions driving the layout of the housing:

> The question of lodging a large number of families in one lofty pile of building has been the subject of much discussion, and in reference to it the most contradictory opinions were stated before the Health-of-Towns Commission. Some thought it the best adapted and most economical plan to provide in one house, with a common staircase and internal passages, sufficient rooms for lodging a considerable number of families, giving them the use of a kitchen, wash-house, and other necessary conveniences, in common; others objected that such an arrangement would lead to endless contentions, and be attended with much evil in cases of contagious disease.
>
> It must be obvious that in many localities where labourers' dwellings are indispensible, it is impossible to provide them with isolated and altogether independent tenements; and therefore, though modified by local and other circumstances it will be found the general practice in Great Britain, as well as in large towns on the Continent, for several families of the working classes to reside in one house. […]
>
> In providing for the accommodation of a large number of families in one pile of building, a leading feature of the plan should be the preservation of *the domestic privacy* and *independence* of each distinct family, and the *disconnexion of their apartments* […]
>
> (H. Roberts 2007: 10, my italics)

The desire to supply the working class with the type of detached houses favoured by the middle class was not feasible, of course. The debate was therefore between an economistic, quantitative approach, which meant a stress on collective dwellings in order to reduce costs and provide more homes, and the attempt to preserve as much privacy as possible in the model housing in order to offer the inhabitants conditions similar to those enjoyed by the middle class.

The Thanksgiving model buildings in Portpool Lane and the model houses for families on Streatham Street seem to owe their solid, robust appearance to the Albergo de Poveri in Naples (1751), which had left an impression on Roberts in 1829. A superblock even in contemporary terms, the Albergo, according to Roberts, housed 2,600 impoverished Neapolitans, but was kept in a remarkably good order. The Streatham Street model houses are of particular interest, because they demonstrate some of Roberts's conclusions: shared staircases and galleries in order to reduce costs, yet an organization of the layout of the apartments that maximizes privacy. The specific solutions outlined here to balance the need to economize with privacy will become ubiquitous in the mass social housing of the twentieth century as well as in for-profit mass housing intended for the lower middle class, offering to the financially limited masses a way of living that had been the privilege of affluent middle class citizens, and consequently bringing the masses a step closer to the middle class by sharing a way of habitation. 'If the working man has his own house,' Lord Shaftesbury stated in the 1860s, 'I have no fear of revolution' (Porter 2000: 329).

The reception of model housing by the working class was hardly favourable. The inhabitants often altered the layout of the homes, slept in a single room, vandalized the fixtures, and many of the homes remained empty. Many of the problems were not new. Chadwick's 1842 report already contained examples of the explosive situation and rebelliousness in some slums:

> In the course of the Constabulary Inquiry I was informed by the superintendent of the old police of that town that one of the most dangerous services for a small force was attending to enforce ejectments. This they had often to do, cutlass in hand, and were frequently driven off by showers of bricks from the mobs.
>
> *(Chadwick 1842)*

However, the new dwellings were supposed to solve such issues. An 1857 editorial in *The Builder* noted, regarding a refurbishment project by the Metropolitan Association, that '[a]lthough the collector had formerly felt very little difficulty in collecting the rents when the place was a scene of dilapidation and ruin, it has become, strange to say, not easy now to collect the rent; and many doors are fastened with a padlock, the tenants having left' (Evans 1997: 111).[13]

Roberts, studying a failed 1845 housing project in Birkenhead, built by a local dock company for its workers, offered his own interpretation:

> These building have been completed upwards of three years, and it was with much regret, when visiting Birkenhead in October last year, that I found them tenantless, owing doubtless, in a considerable measure, to the suspension of the Dock-works in contemplation when they were erected; yet being within accessible distance to a numerous and increasing working population, I apprehend another cause may be, that the gloomy appearance of the narrow alleys, on the pavement to most of which the sun can never shine, has had a repulsive tendency.
>
> *(H. Roberts 2007: 14)*

In the absence of sociological or anthropological surveys or interviews with the inhabitants of the slums of the period, it is only possible to speculate on the reasons for this rejection. One reason may be the dislike for charity among London's poor, and the 'top-down' aspects of the model housing, which may have offended their pride and dignity. To the 'free-born Englishman', being told where and how to live may have seemed unacceptable, and the elaborate codes of conduct enforced by the philanthropist could not have added enthusiasm. The restriction or prevention of subletting parts of the homes,[14] which was a common practice in the slums, meant a significant loss of income. But it is also important to stress that in this era the working class shared relatively little with the middle class in terms of aspiration, culture, or worldview. The middle-class ideal home, the *pavillion*, the terraced, detached or semi-detached house, was not the ideal home that the working class desired, let alone conceived of as a possible abode.

Some years later, Engels, countering the reformist proposals of a Dr Sax, claimed that Sax 'seems to assume that man is essentially a peasant, otherwise he would not ascribe to the workers of our big cities a longing for property in land, a longing which no one else has discovered. For our workers in the big cities freedom of movement is the first condition of their existence, and landownership could only be a hindrance to them' (Engels 1872). Wohl wrote that '[i]t took a very long time before the idea of an imposed communal landscape began to yield to the wish for the kind of individualized suburban domain invented by the English middle class' (1977: caption to illustration 31). As Robin Evans speculated (1997), it may be precisely the aspect of privacy in the model housing that the working class resented. It contrasted, after all, with their own experience of domesticity and habitation, and undermined the immediacy of the types of social networks that had sustained their lives in harsh conditions.

The limited effect of charity work encouraged other ideas, such as for-profit philanthropic ventures, intent on increasing the amount of decent housing on offer for the poor by allowing a limited, non-exploitive profit. The Society for Improving the Condition of the Labouring Classes had already presented its claim that modest profit could be made from philanthropic housing. The Metropolitan Association for Improving the Dwellings of the Industrious Classes, Alderman Sydney Waterlow, and Angela Burdett-Coutts were among those who pursued this mode of urban development, but it was particularly associated with the Peabody Estates, noted for their strict control and management as a means of preventing moral and physical deterioration. Peabody Estates opted for the 'economistic' solution, offering shared toilets and sinks, and therefore falling short of the desired improvements.

The Strengthening of Government

The prevalence of liberalism, of laissez-faire and its ideology, the importance given to freedom and liberty meant an uphill struggle for those reformers who demanded governmental intervention. The entire reformist movement, driven by middle-class and bourgeois concerns, embodied an idea of superiority to its subject, and was often animated by a belief that while there may be 'deserving' poor, many had only themselves to blame for their circumstances. The solution offered, initially via the model housing, expressed the desire to 'rectify' the working class by bringing it closer to the middle class. As mentioned above, until quite late in the nineteenth century most reformers, including figures such as Lord Shaftesbury, were themselves reluctant to move beyond the idea of charity. 'In hostility to the increase in the powers of any centralised authority,' wrote E.P. Thompson (1966: 82), 'we have a curious blend of parochial defensiveness, Whig theory, and popular resistance.'

In the 1880s, London's newspapers, pamphlets, and books were paying increasing attention to the overcrowding and inhumanity of the working class dwellings, reflecting the manner in which such concerns spread from a minority of reformers to a wider segment of the public, and consequently increasing the pressure on politicians to act (Porter 2000: 334). Andrew Mearns' 1883 pamphlet *The Bitter Cry of Outcast London* (Mearns 1970), a sharp critique of the immorality and destitution caused by poverty, was discussed in the *Pall Mall Gazette*, *The Times*, and *Punch* (Hall 2014: 14–15). It argued that '[t]he State must make short work of this iniquitous traffic, and secure for the poorest the rights of citizenship; the right to live in something better than fever dens; the right to live as something better than the uncleanest of brute beasts' (Mearns 1970).

Despite an explosion in charitable and for-profit organizations, trusts, and associations building for the poor, it was becoming clear to reformers that charity could not provide a complete solution to the problem of housing the poor. The Charity Organization Society (COS), formed by different philanthropic organizations, created the Dwellings Committee in 1873, and came to the conclusion that a problem of such magnitude is beyond the scope of charity. It recommended to enable the London authorities to build for the needy (Ravetz 2001: 25). An important acknowledgement of the problem and a new focus on the issue of housing rather than sanitation must be credited to the British Royal Commission on the Housing of the Working Classes of 1885. Among its (limited) recommendations, implemented in the Housing for the Working Classes Act of the same year, were the transfer of local powers in London to the Metropolitan Board of Trade and the enablement of local authorities to borrow money from the Treasury at minimum interest rates.

38 Critique, Reformism and Co-optation

The London Trades Council, giving evidence to the Royal Commission examining the condition of the urban poor in 1887, argued that 'it is totally impossible that private enterprise, philanthropy and charity can ever keep pace with the present demands [...] But what the individual cannot do the State municipality must seek to accomplish' (Pawley 1971a: 14). Increasingly, the British press and public perceived its emerging competitor, Germany, as more modern and successful, not just in economic terms, but in terms of welfare, governance and administration as well. The Imperial Decree of 1881 and Bismarck's programmes for sickness (1883), accident (1884), old age and invalidity (1889) insurances, which for the German Chancellor formed part of his plan to undermine the ascending socialists, provided an example of government-led progressive social reform. Edward Bellamy's 1889 utopian story *Looking Backward* was widely read. *Looking Backward* advocated a strong state, run by benevolent technocrats, offering its citizens complete security in a planned economy. While the book was seen by some as a call for despotism and an attack on freedom, others found the argument compelling, and groups and societies advocating the nationalization of industries were formed in reaction.[15]

All this meant a gradual shift in worldview and a growing demand to accept governmental intervention and limit the free market. *The Times* commented that '[i]t can hardly be doubted by any one who watches the tendencies of the time that *laissez-faire* is practically abandoned and that every piece of state interference will pave the way for another' (Hall 2014: 19). Important legislation for the reformist housing agenda came in the 1885 Housing Act and the 1890 Housing of the Working Class Act, which included in its Part III the empowerment of local councils to build for the needy. London's Boundary Estate (1900), on the site of the former Old Nichol rookery near Shoreditch, the locus of Morrison's *A Child of the Jago* (1896), was the first completed council housing in Britain and a direct result of the legislation.

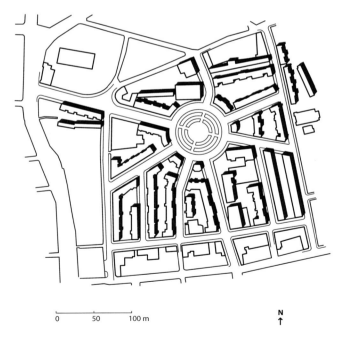

FIGURE 1.2 Boundary Street Estate, London. Drawing by Adam Kelly (2015) based on LCC area plan from around 1900. By permission of the London Metropolitan Museum.

The estate, created by the Housing of the Working Classes Branch of the London County Council (LCC, replacing in 1888 the Metropolitan Board) and designed by Owen Fleming, was organized radially, with Arnold Circus and an elevated garden in its centre as the focal point (Figure 1.2). It housed 5,000 people. The five-storey brick buildings reflected the ideas of the Arts and Crafts movement. The residential area was supported by some shops and two schools. It was an exemplary project, which served the LCC as a showpiece of its housing policies and models. However, the cost of building the estate required rents that excluded the very poor, and the first residents included members of the fast-growing tier of lower middle class, such as teachers and clerks. The next project, completed by 1903 at Millbank, was likewise too expensive for a majority of the working class. Many of the tenants of the estates, being relatively upwardly socially mobile, moved on within a short period, which inevitably meant new residents with limited finances moving in, a growing bad reputation, and many evictions due to unpaid rents.

The formation of an organized grass roots labour movement and its increasing involvement in the issue of housing hardly altered the conclusions the bourgeois reformers had reached by the 1880s. Rather, the emerging movement accepted the general solutions in the field of housing in the manner that they were already framed and developed. The British Labour Party, as much as its formation was the outcome of a genuine working-class organization, was also the product of middle-class advocacy and associations. The trade unions, by far the most grass roots of the working class organizations, and the Workmen's Housing Council, established in 1898 in London to bring about municipal solutions to housing shortages, entered late into the question of housing. They entered a debate in which the reformist position was already clarified and the boundaries of discussion were delineated. Their agitation was necessarily limited by political compromise with the other groups that were part of their political bloc.

The desire for 'respectability' by the 'aristocracy of labour' meant emulating the lifestyle of the middle class. Respectability, beyond inferring a capitulation to the social pressures involved in enforcing normative behaviour and lifestyle, was also a key to social mobility, as limited as it was until the second half of the twentieth century. In 1917, in a meeting with the Local Government Board, the demands outlined by the Workmen's National Housing Council – the successor of the Workmen's Housing Council – were precisely those of the reformers' 'miniaturized' middle-class dwelling: three bedrooms as a minimum, a separate bathroom, enforcement of minimum space standards. Thus, organized labour adopted the solutions to housing issues outlined 'top-down' by earlier reformers, and a radical rethinking of housing solutions was pre-empted.

Throughout the nineteenth century, architectural discourse was preoccupied with the debates between advocates of neoclassicism and Gothic, ignoring the significant changes to practice under way, and led by the demands for the provision of mass housing. Instead of circumventing time, as neoclassicism attempted to do, Gothic Revival looked back in time, to a pre-modern, pre-industrial era of a supposedly 'high Christianity' and better society. While no less hostile to industrial, modern society than neoclassicism, Gothic Revival and Arts and Crafts, by 'looking back', inevitably recognized the linearity of time and would end up allowing the ideas of progressive time and *zeitgeist* to take hold. Moreover, while neoclassicism futilely attempted to establish rules and codes to prevent transgression, Gothic Revival remained relatively general in principles, and this meant constant change and adaptation of the style. The religious morality preached by Pugin was in Ruskin and Morris coupled with a social consciousness. While the ad-hoc resolution of the nineteenth-century 'battle of styles' meant that Gothic was mostly applied to churches whereas neoclassicism to civic buildings, the social consciousness of the advocates of Arts and Crafts and its 'down to earth' ideology – a medieval simplicity and disposing of the typical clutter of the bourgeois' interior – meant that Arts and Crafts was applied to model and social housing. Subsequently, once mass housing was assimilated into a recognizable and established architectural style, the architectural discourse, long focused on public buildings, would increasingly address issues of housing the many, just as Roberts had wished.

An important figure in the garden city movement, in the introduction of council housing, and in the agitation for planning legislation was Raymond Unwin. Unwin, involved in the New Earswick and Letchworth Garden City experiments, contributed to the development of the typologies for council housing in Britain and to the integration of Arts and Crafts ideas into governmental policy via reports, books and articles, and diverse committees with which he was involved in the early twentieth century, such as the Tudor Walters Committee (commissioned in 1917). While a strong supporter of the low-density housing solutions of the garden city, including the detached or semi-detached house, he nevertheless questioned some of the prevalent ideas regarding the layout of homes. Following ideas of utility and simplicity, he wished to dispose of all 'unnecessary' aspects of housing, including 'indulgent' ornamentation and the underused parlour (Swenarton 1981).

By the close of the First World War, the innovations at the Ford factory were the centre of discussions in Britain and elsewhere. Unwin identified Fordist simplification and standardization as a key to the economy of housing, and already in his First World War scheme for Gretna moved away from Arts and Crafts to simple neo-Georgian, neoclassical homes, stripped of almost all excess (Swenarton 1981: 24–25, 58–62; 2008: 95–124). A solution of sorts to the contradiction between individualism and standardization was offered by the designs of Adshead, Ramsey, and Abercombie for the industrial village of Dormanstown (Powers 1981). Dormanstown was designed for the workers of the nearby steelworks at Redcar. Like Gretna, the First World War concern for the housing of munitions workers played a part in instigating an ambitious new 'industrial village' based on garden city principles. By this time, a level of consultation with workers, and particularly workers' wives, was established. The Women's Labour League and the Women's Co-operative Guild reported on the women's demands for separate bathroom, parlour and other amenities (Buckley 2010: 25). The avoidance of 'barracks' row housing, the front and back gardens and other amenities offered by the design of Dormanstown drew press attention. The unity of the ensemble is accorded a higher value here than the individuality of the singular buildings, with a repetition of simplified houses (Swenarton 1981: 63–64). But individuation is maintained in the preference for semi-detached housing rather than row housing. Here, like Unwin in Gretna, the architects originally associated with the Arts and Crafts movement designed neo-Georgian homes inspired by Enlightenment simplicity and efficiency.

The town's designers were taught in Liverpool by Charles Reilly, an advocate of Fordism and consequently were immersed in the discussion of and concern for efficiency and standardization. Stanley Adshead had already shown interest in the question of standard cottages in a 1916 article (Adshead 1916; Buckley 2010: 22, 31). He wrote that '[t]he standard cottage is an essential appendage of a highly organised social system, and without it we cannot have that which lies at the very root of national efficiency, organisation, and economy' (Adshead 1916: 245). Neo-Georgian architecture allowed standardization in a sense that the romantic Arts and Crafts did not. Its simplified forms seemed to bridge tradition and modernity and to offer a simplicity that was morally suited to a condition of limited resources.

Averting Class War

The transition from free market and private urban development to governmental development was still far from complete. Important political discussions concerning housing took place during the First World War, in the years 1914–18. The government was clearly anxious of instability following several rent protests. The war meant a very different political condition and economic paradigm, in which the government's role was paramount, and speculation and free market curtailed. The 1915 Rent Restriction Act, stabilizing rents, was a necessary means of pacification that corresponded to the commandeering of factories for war purposes (Ravetz 2001: 74–77). Industrial unrest in 1917 raised concerns regarding Britain's ability to pursue the war without a 'contented working class' (Swenarton 1981: 71). As the war drew to a close, anxiety in government regarding the aftermath increased. The 1917 Bolshevik Revolution in Russia was a lucid example of social and political unrest caused by lack of reform, and the situation in which millions of British working-class soldiers would return to poverty and unemployment loomed as an existential threat to the existing order. The threat grew in late 1918 and early 1919, with more industrial unrest, including a major strike in Glasgow. A senior member of the Conservatives stated that 'we were up against a Bolshevist movement in London, Glasgow, and elsewhere' (Swenarton 1981: 77).

It was the threat of revolution, then, that forced the hand of the British government. The 1918 Tudor Walters Report and the 1919 housing acts that ensued were a victory for the reformists, initiating council housing in Britain in a sense the 1890 Act did not. The new commitment was articulated in Lloyd George's 'homes fit for heroes' speech and in the government's ambitious housing plan. However, at this moment, the British government envisioned a period of controlled economy only as a gradual transition to free market economy, not as a long-term solution.

The council housing and its management in the interwar period would form an important step in the integration of the working class, despite the continuing tensions between the economistic and qualitative approaches to housing. Universal suffrage and other reformist legislation, as well as the strength of grass roots labour movements and representatives meant that the working class was increasingly being included in bourgeois society. Trade unions, in particular, negotiated and compromised with the existing system, and thus played an important part in the pacification of the class tensions. The First World War, as a shared national experience, which circumvented class distinctions, meant that the working class increasingly felt it had a stake in bourgeois society.

By the end of the First World War, the aspirations of the members of the 'aristocracy of labour' were becoming increasingly similar to those of the middle class, even if their politics were radicalizing and their identity remained unequivocally 'working class'. Social respectability was dependent on emulation of the socially superior, pressurizing the working class to integrate, to accept the lifestyles and values of the middle class. The importance to the aspiring and better off segments of the working class of a parlour in their housing was one example of the convergence of tastes and demands. The removal of the parlour in some of Unwin's designs met with dismay among the aspiring 'aristocracy of labour': Unwin encountered entrenched social habits, which were not easily circumvented (Swenarton 1981:

20–21; Ravetz 2001: 63). Similarly, at Dormanstown, the homes without parlours 'were harder to let' (Buckley 2010: 37).

Important here is the subdivision of council housing into different strata, according to quality, and allocated to different tenants. This was particularly visible in Glasgow, where three types of housing were defined: 'Ordinary', 'Intermediate', and 'Rehousing' (Ravetz 2001: 93), with a clear differentiation in quality and designated social groups from which tenants would be drawn. The better quality housing was given to the 'aristocracy of labour', and the more economistic and inferior housing to the weaker segments. This meant that members of the working class entered a visibly socially stratified and encoded system that encouraged, on the one hand, envy and feelings of discrimination for being 'marked downwards', but, on the other hand, identified a clear aspiration and trajectory to a better position in the social hierarchy.

This was supported by the private market housing for the new lower middle class. Usually of higher quality and more spacious than the council housing, a typical layout emerged in the interwar years, designed for homes without servants, and boasting new sanitary and cooking modifications. These houses included relatively wide façades, which allowed better light conditions and enabled placing the scullery within the house itself rather than in a projection at the back of the home. This layout was used at Bournville, and later by Unwin, and included in the typical plans suggested by the Tudor Walters Report (Swenarton 1981: 22). The layout was later universalized and standardized by speculative developers, adapted to both working and middle class needs and means, leading to a shared experience of habitation and aspiration.

In this era, the vast majority of private development housing was of either cottage, detached, or semi-detached type. With a back garden, and when financially possible, a front one as well, this would become the ideal home coveted by all classes. Such housing was preferred by the bourgeoisie already in the second half of the eighteenth century; it was a means of emulating the aristocratic country house, a sign of the social status gained by the bourgeoisie.[16] In the second half of the nineteenth century smaller versions of this housing type proliferated, built for the emerging middle class. As mentioned above, the workers of mid-nineteenth century Britain did not idolize such an abode: its reality was extremely distant from their own experience. Yet for housing reformers, it was the ideal model, providing privacy and respectability. And indeed, model cottages were built in the mid-nineteenth century, and in the interwar years city councils across Britain developed such housing for the working class in cottage estates. By the 1920s, however, the poor and working class had come to see the detached house as an ideal form of living no less than the middle class.

Such low-density social housing was, of course, untenable in cities bar some historic exceptions, as Roberts had understood long beforehand. Yet the discussion regarding densities continued into the interwar years (Swenarton 1981: 34). A solution of sorts was found thanks to a housing shortage for the lower middle class, coupled by a reasoning that had been used again and again in the past decades – 'filtering', or 'housing flow': namely, that by expanding the housing stock for the lower middle class and 'aristocracy of labour', better housing became available to others, allowing members of lower social rank to improve their living conditions (Swenarton 1981: 10, 77; Ravetz 2001: 86). This reversed version of the infamous 'trickle-down' argument, applied to housing policy, allowed authorities to build at the lower densities they cherished, applying garden city ideas in houses that were directed to the middle classes, yet believing that the development would also benefit the poor.

The 'homes for heroes' programme was axed only a few years after it commenced, and British governments encouraged a return to pre-war conditions. By 1931, the Labour Party would encounter significant setbacks. While the Liberal Party dissipated, it was the Conservatives who dominated British politics between the wars. Stanley Baldwin, the leader of the Conservatives, was conservative on civil liberties issues and a defender of laissez-faire. Yet the Conservatives, during these years, did expand social security. Programmes that Britain had already initiated before the First World War, such as workers' compensation (1897), old age pensions (1908), health insurance (1911), and compulsory unemployment insurance (1911), were expanded and new programmes were added by the Conservatives to the extent that by the outbreak of the Second World War Britain was the most advanced country in these issues.

The social hierarchy of dwellings thus placed the detached or semi-detached house with garden at the hierarchical top, with flats in large residential buildings at the bottom. This entire range was provided by council housing, and such policies would later correspond to the post-war Minister of Health, Aneurin Bevan, 'universalizing' the idea of council housing beyond the limitations of working class. All this would explain the process of integrating the working class into a bourgeois society.

The Ascent of Town Planning

> Effective planning necessarily controls, limits or even completely destroys the market value of particular pieces of land.
>
> *(Cullingworth and Nadin 2011: 195)*

In a previous era, towns, man-made environments, were the place of refuge for humans from the ravages of nature. But in the nineteenth century, the expanding industrial cities were seen as a threat to civilization: they were the locus of an unprecedented level of 'moral depravity', of crime, of dehumanization, of epidemics, of extreme poverty and filth. To members of the middle class, cities, with their pollution, overcrowding, and violent mobs, were no minor problem. Consequently, providing adequate housing for the poor was merely one of many concerns addressed by the reform movement, with the city itself being one of the most complex problems it attempted to rectify.

An early attempt to regulate the British cities was the issuing of by-laws – limited regulations put in place by local authorities, which were intended to prevent some of the worst effects of the laissez-faire speculative urban development of the period. Early by-laws typically regulated the relation of the breadth of the street to the height of the buildings. The urban environment produced by the by-laws was scorned by reformers. Such streets were often long, with row housing that was compared to barracks for their monotony, dreariness, and lack of imagination. The by-laws were a first step towards control of the urban environment, but they steered urban development, evidently, towards unwarranted results, to the extent that Letchworth Garden City was built, purposely, in an area not governed by by-laws, and the creation of Hampstead Garden Suburb required specific legislation in order to exempt it from them.

The disgust with the existing city can explain the emergence of blueprints for utopian, ideal cities in this era, as in the Versailles-inspired sketches and diagrams of Fourierists in France, or Owen's ideal communities, initially embodied by his New Lanark experiment. The ideal city severed all ties to the compromised industrial city and offered a fresh, 'uncontaminated' start.

Its focus, initially, was on the formation of an ideal political community, a *cité*, rather than on the physical form such a community would take. The key proposition, which nudged utopian schemes from the realm of fantasy into realization, was Ebenezer Howard's garden city. His book *Garden Cities of To-morrow* (1902) was initially named *To-morrow: A Peaceful Path to Real Reform* (1898), articulating Howard's reformist convictions.

The realization of a utopian model, even in the conditions of a new settlement, ended up in compromise. The difficulties of Letchworth in attracting investors and employers, as well as the unexpected high costs of developing infrastructure, were a significant hurdle, and the outcome was, in many senses, far too similar to the model towns and industrial villages already realized in Saltaire (1853), Bournville (1878), Port Sunlight (1887) and, at about the same time, New Earswick (1902). At the centre of Howard's vision was the communal purchasing of land at agricultural values through a limited-dividend company, which would mean that the higher values brought about by development would be to the community's rather than speculators' benefit. But the control of real estate values and land in Letchworth fell short of Howard's plans. Moreover, the garden city never threatened the existing relations of production, as its focus of change were dwellings and land rent, whereas the factory and the conditions of production were ignored (Swenarton 1981: 6).

Raymond Unwin's picturesque layout of Letchworth evoked an ideal rural village with meandering streets and low-density housing, organized radially. In contrast, in Welwyn, which followed Letchworth, the layout was dominated by an iron grid, and in Hampstead Garden Suburb Unwin's design was compromised by Lutyens's neoclassicist interventions. While the meandering streets of Letchworth and Hampstead Garden Suburb suggested informality, the organization of the settlement retained, nevertheless, some aspects of classicist use of formal strategies such as the radial layout in Letchworth and axes in Hampstead. This model perfectly expressed the ideas of middle class reformers: the detached and semi-detached cottages, with back and often front gardens, offering the privacy so valued by this social group, and the nostalgic appeal of a pre-industrial community.

In the meantime, the reformers' ambitions grew as they increasingly realized the inadequacy of the tools at their disposal for tackling complex and entrenched social problems. British reformers watched in envy Continental cities, and particularly the German cities, expand through planned urban development, guiding development by city councils' centralized power and control. The Garden City movement became the major vehicle for agitating for town planning. It appropriately changed its name to Garden City and Town Planning Association, and was soon joined by the Association of Metropolitan Corporations and the National Housing Reform Council. Birmingham became the first city in Britain to embrace municipal purchase of land and town planning.[17]

A significant legislation aimed at establishing planning was the Housing, Town Planning, Etc. Act 1909. It enabled local councils to prepare town planning schemes for new urban development (Cullingworth and Nadin 2006: 16). It followed a series of acts that had some, though limited, influence on producing tools of controlling the built environment and its development, such as the Torrens' Act (1868) and Cross's Act (1875), which introduced some concerns that would later be assimilated into urban planning, primarily regarding the sanitary condition of urban areas. The London Building Act (1894) expanded the territory of local government to encompass issues such as the creation of streets or their widening, open space required around buildings, and the lines of building edges. While the argument for planning continued to be driven by sanitary demands, the major propagandists for planning, such as Unwin, understood it as a means of socially bettering the working class and restricting the excesses of market capitalism and speculation. Unwin outlined his ideas in the 1909 publication *Town Planning in Practice*. Many of the propositions of this early publication would be included in the 1918 Tudor Walters Report.

Town planning was neither expanded nor strengthened in the initial interwar legislation, such as the Housing and Town Planning Act of 1919. But the 1919 Act was a measure of the commitment of government to intervening in the built environment, to steering its development via regulation, programmes, subsidies, and other means. Arthur Greenwood, Minister of Health in the Labour government of 1929–31, planned comprehensive legislation regarding town and country planning, but the Great Depression and fall of the government meant the legislation ended up weaker and watered down. Nevertheless, the 1932 Town and Country Planning Act was not insignificant. Planners were no longer merely advisers, but had a role inscribed in law. Yet this legislation outlined a cumbersome administrative structure and process for planning, and, consequently, was mostly circumvented in practice.

The Great Depression and unemployment in Britain's north and in South Wales encouraged more governmental intervention. Concerns regarding the location of new factories initiated a call for government to spatially control the expansion of industry; while this was dismissed, it nevertheless expressed a convergence of demands for greater governmental intervention in economy and society, and specifically in the built environment. In 1938 the Barlow Report was commissioned to study the economic and social consequences of industrial conurbations. Frederick Osborn, the secretary of the Town and Country Planning Association, the offspring of the Garden City movement, was among the key figures invited to give evidence to the Barlow Commission (Addison 1975: 42–43). The report recommended that the government would become responsible for decisions regarding land use. It proposed decentralization, including the creation of new garden cities and suburbs, as well as light industry areas. The recommendations included a call for establishing strong planning powers on a national level in order to be able to control and manage resources and issues such as distribution of industries and population on a macro scale.

The Second World War provided the final impetus for town planning in Britain. The war encouraged the dispersal of population in order to reduce vulnerability to aerial bombing. It required, in a manner even more extensive than in the First World War, a planned economy, and the need for government intervention extended into all fields, first and foremost the decreeing of the location of relevant industries. Paul Addison characterized the effects of the war as a transitory process in which 'the optimists who believed that capitalism could be made to work more efficiently, and provide greater social welfare, had ousted from power the pessimist who believed that the conditions of the 1930s were decreed by iron laws of circumstance' (Addison 1975: 21). The physical damage suffered by cities required a well-co-ordinated mass reconstruction effort at the end of the war, whereas the working class expected their concerns and well-being to stand at the centre of the post-war reconstruction of Britain, as society and the state were indebted to them for their wartime sacrifices. In all these endeavours, planning was a necessary tool to rectify society's wrongs. The new administrative system was put in place by the 1947 Town and Country Planning Act, and complemented by the Distribution of Industry Acts, the National Parks and Access to the Countryside Act, and the New Towns Act.

British planning was thus animated by the Garden City movement. It was brought into being by the agitation of the reformist movement, following a lengthy campaign. It was dependent on the demand for a strong, interventionist government,[18] and was consequently part of a general change in which politics assumed responsibilities for territories of society and the economy that were previously left in the hands of the free market. For the radical left, reformism and planning were merely means of preventing revolution by creating a palatable capitalism at the moment of capitalism's weakness, saving the contemporary mode of production from demise.

Town planning in general, and particularly in Britain, did not see the contemporary city favourably. Rather, it saw it via the eyes of the reformist movement as a cesspool of health hazards, hardship, overcrowding, and immorality, caused by the dehumanization brought about by the excesses of industrialization and capitalist speculation. And like the Garden City idea to which it was indebted, British planning often framed its call as a response to the town and country, urban and rural divide. Reformism, and with it the critique of current conditions and the desire to curtail excessive laissez-faire, formed the DNA of planning, inscribed into the discipline and practice to a degree that, once opinions against the reformist remedies formed in the 1960s, planning would also be limited and curtailed, reducing its mandate to purely bureaucratic processes of administration.

Testing Korsch's Hypothesis

The previous pages concisely delineated the ascent of the reformist movement up until its apex – the constitution of the welfare state in the post-war era. They highlighted the deployment of critique by reformists and the process of the integration of the working class – namely, the avoidance of class war by satisfying certain demands made by the workers and their representative institutions. This was a process that was not a simple redistribution from rich to poor, as it also involved the determination of the terms of redistribution to ensure that the process would result in a new labourer who internalized the aspirations, ideals and worldview of middle-class society. In the first chapter of this section, Korsch's theory regarding critique and reformism was outlined: the hypothesis that in eras with a limited revolutionary horizon, 'reformist' eras, intellectuals turn to the production of critique at the expense of a robust engagement with praxis. Korsch's description of the oscillation between reform and revolution ends in 1923, the year he published his essay 'Marxism and Philosophy'. His theory will now be deployed to explain the development of the dialectic of reform and revolution in more recent times.

In the post-war years, the reformist era par excellence, Critical Theory emerged as the major instrument of oppositional thought – initially in West Germany, once the Frankfurt School returned from exile, later in the United States and many other countries. While its conception was related to Max Horkheimer's reading of Kant (Jay 1973: 46), thus tying it to the tradition of bourgeois philosophy and critique, its method was dialectical and it was developed from the commitment of the Frankfurt School to 'exploring the possibilities of transforming the social order through human *praxis*' (Jay 1973: 42). Critical Theory was posited against the loss of human agency in the twentieth century, against excessive empiricism or, alternatively, irrationalism, against reductive understandings of materialism, against the fetishization of labour, against the dominance of utilitarianism, against essentialisms and absolutisms, and for reconciling the dualism of subject and object. Its main characteristics included dialectics, totality, and mediation (*Vermittlung*).

One of the features of Critical Theory was a dialectical relationship between praxis and reason. However, in this relationship it was reason that dominated rather than praxis. Herbert

Marcuse wrote that '[t]heory will preserve the truth even if revolutionary practice deviates from its proper path. Practice follows truth, not vice versa' (Marcuse 1999: 322).[19] Furthermore, Marcuse bemoaned the separation of philosophy and practice in contemporary society (Marcuse 1999: 320–21), a product of the division of labour, and implicitly acknowledged the difficulty of Critical Theory to address praxis in such conditions. Indeed, while the Frankfurt School expressed its support of theory as a guide to action, the work produced by its scholars preferred to maintain critical distance from praxis, to the extent that the sociologist Alain Touraine could write that '[t]he Frankfurt School takes as its starting point what it sees as the obvious divorce between praxis and thought, between political action and philosophy' (Touraine 1995: 151).

The revolutionary horizon was eclipsed in the post-war period, and oppositional forces in West Germany found themselves facing the 'authoritarian, conservative and apolitical ambience of German society' at the time (Krüger 2009: 125), only enhanced by an ever more powerful and centralized Keynesian state. Korsch's hypothesis that critique flourishes in eras of reform is thus confirmed by the turn to the work of Adorno, Horkheimer and their colleagues in this period. As the revolutionary ferment strengthened in the late 1960s, the radicals of the German student movement found Critical Theory to be of little use – they required a theory of revolutionary praxis, not critique.[20] Thus, in West Germany, 'Critical Theory was practically non-existent in the mid-seventies' (Krüger 2009: 129), substituted by other, more praxis-oriented Marxist and anarchist theories. Yet a return to the work of the Frankfurt School began in the late 1970s, 'the more rigid and isolated the left became (a few despaired and turned terrorists and others retreated from active politics into the realm of academic Marxism)', or, in other words, once the revolutionary ferment waned (Krüger 2009: 128–29).

The dissipation of revolutionary agitation led not only to the replacement of radical discourse with Critical Theory, but increasingly to the enthralment of leftists with post-structuralism and postmodernist theories. Most post-structuralists attested to a preference for 'doing' to 'saying', and many presented their ideas as practice-oriented radical theories developed as a dialogue with – though also rebuttal of – Marxism. The postmodernist Jean-François Lyotard, a veteran of the ultra-leftist group *Socialisme ou Barbarie*, was greatly influenced by the unity of theory and praxis he perceived in May '68, and wished to re-establish such a condition as part of his 'desire-revolution'. He castigated the 'therapeutic' ideas of the (reformist) Left as well as critique, for critique was necessarily dependent on the system it criticized and therefore part of it. Moreover: Lyotard claimed that critique was 'authoritarian' and demanded to surpass it (C. Bürger 1992).[21]

The work of Derrida, which would become increasingly popular by the early 1990s in the United States, developed modes of thought that departed radically from the diametric oppositional positions of the Left. Deconstruction was introduced as a form of practice rather than an abstract philosophy, an instrument to undermine the validity of dominant ideologies and of exposing mystifications and paradoxes. According to theorist Paul Patton, it 'seeks to intervene in order to change things' (Patton 2008: 126). Derrida specifically wrote that:

> the most radical programs of a deconstruction that would like, in order to be consistent with itself, not to remain enclosed in purely speculative, theoretical, academic discourses but rather [...] to aspire to something more consequential, to *change* things and to intervene in an efficient and responsible, though always, of course, very mediated way, not only in the profession but in what one calls the *cité*, the *polis* and more generally the world.
>
> (Derrida 1992: 8–9)

Derrida's emphasis on a future 'to come' is an open-ended search for agency within relations of power, for transformation and change, but without drawing a picture of the future, avoiding prescribing a future, and thus, supposedly, also circumventing the flaws of earlier 'utopian' conceptions of future society.

The modes of critique outlined by Derrida and other French scholars dissolved binary structures and dichotomies, and avoided dialectics and historical materialism, rendering them reductivist and unhelpful. The list of prohibitions emerging from deconstruction included binaries, essentialisms, totalizations, and determinisms. The irony, the acute 'awareness', the multiple qualifications, the constant raising of doubt and scepticism, the relativism – all these formed an armour of sorts, defending deconstruction from being castigated as authoritarian, as Euro-centric, as ideological. Deconstruction could thus assume the role of destabilizer yet avoid commitment to 'fixed', 'restrictive' or 'utopian' remedies. The project of Derrida can be described as an attempt to construct a novel way of thinking, new descriptions and concepts, which are completely severed from existing models – consequently overturning not only the dominant ideology and the legitimacy of existing institutions, but also those propagated by the Left.

However, despite the emphasis on 'doing', deconstruction remained abstract. It tended to support individual transgressions and avoid collective action, and it increasingly became an instrument of academic, textual practices rather than a praxis taking place in everyday life. Some of this was caused by the centricity of philosophy to deconstruction, a discipline in which 'doing' is necessarily abstract, text-based and harbours a keen interest in ideas. But beyond the limitations of philosophy as practice, the deconstructivists specifically drew the contours of an adversary of infinite scale: society in all its diverse forms, political, economic, social, ideological, organizational, and cultural. The mission of generating transformation on such a scale is far more challenging, even 'utopian', than the typically narrow and specific ambitions of political activism. '[D]econstruction,' Eagleton wrote,

> operated [...] as an ersatz form of textual politics in an era when, socialism being on the run, academic leftists were grateful for a displaced brand of dissent which seemed to offer the twin benefits of at once outflanking Marxism in its audacious avant-gardism, and generating a sceptical sensibility which pulled the rug out from under anything as drearily underconstructed as solidarity, organization or calculated political action.
>
> *(Eagleton 2008: 84)*

Moreover, the avoidance of prescribing the future, while helpful in defending deconstruction from assimilation and from certain critiques, meant an absence of concrete propositions regarding just processes of decision-making or of just institutions of power. The literature critic Fredric Jameson has written that the solution outlined by deconstruction to the 'tired status quo' is 'the avoidance of the affirmative sentence as such, of the philosophical proposition. Deconstruction thus "neither affirmeth nor deneith": it does not emit propositions in that sense at all' (Jameson 1999: 33).

The slippage from radical engagement with theory–praxis to abstract thought can be demonstrated by the development of *Semiotext(e)*, the radical journal and publishing group that was founded in 1970s New York by veterans of the May '68 radical movements, and run by a group of anarchists and ultra-leftists headed by Sylvère Lotringer. In the 1970s, they dedicated a special issue to the Italian autonomist movement, including interviews with the radicals behind the journal *Lotte Continua* and Radio Alice. In another publication, *Semiotext(e)* published an interview with a member of the German urban guerrilla movement the Revolutionary Cells while in hiding (Lotringer 2009; Lotringer and Marazzi 2007). Yet *Semiotext(e)* gradually introduced the work of the French post-structuralists to American intellectuals, replacing the revolutionary theories with textual transgressions, a passage from one form of radicalism to another – more abstract, cultural, and textual.

These developments were related to the omnipotence of 'the cultural' as a category that replaced 'the social' as the focus of contestation.[22] Critique, addressing the lack of cultural analysis in Marxist theory and influenced by the growing importance of culture in society, focused on cultural critique and emphasized its critical distance as a means of preventing its contamination by consumer culture – following, in effect, the trajectory identified by Korsch. Critique, however, was not only attacked by post-structuralists and abandoned by the vanquished praxis-oriented revolutionaries, but was also assaulted from the centre and from the right. The rebirth of pragmatic philosophy in the work of Richard Rorty demonstrated that a demand for a relation between theory and practice was not limited to the left-wing radicals, but belonged also to a pragmatic agenda that was interested in circumventing critique by focusing on 'doing', and consequently also affirming the status quo.

These challenges to critique in the realm of thought were buttressed by the 'roll back' neoliberalism of the 1980s and 'roll out' neoliberalism of the 1990s, which meant the Left was increasingly battling to defend previous achievements. On a micro and individual scale, one example of the changes was the pressures on workers to leave trade unions and curb their critique of work conditions to guarantee their employment or promotion (Boltanski and Chiapello 2005: 274–96). The economic upturn of the 1990s further eroded critique by emphasizing opportunities available to hands-on, uncritical approaches, perfectly represented by the 'third-way' politics of Blair, Schröder and Clinton. The pragmatist, centrist thought, which increasingly challenged post-structuralism and other radical theories,[23] was enthralled with the possibilities of creativity and entrepreneurship offered by post-Fordism and neoliberal economy. Nor did the new consensus hesitate to direct its attacks on the type of benign critique associated with reformism. Critique, in all forms, was rendered quixotic, useless, unnecessary.

Korsch's hypothesis of the rise of critique during periods of reform and its wane during revolutionary periods can thus assist in understanding the attacks on critique in recent decades. From Korsch's perspective, the periodization of the years spanning 1848–1923 fits neatly the categories of reform and revolution. The post-war years of reformist triumph and Critical Theory, as well as the revolutionary period around 1968 and the dominance of revolutionary praxis, confirm Korsch's theory. Yet the last thirty years, 1978–2008 approximately, have been marked by neither reform nor revolution, as delineated above. Rather, they have entailed a total retreat from reform as well as revolt. This period has thus been one in which many of the successes of the reformist movement have been undone, and the revolutionary movement completely suppressed. In this sense it is hardly surprising that critique found itself under direct assault by forces which are hostile not only to revolution, but also to reform, and are prepared to dispose of the instrument which had, in fact, aided the survival of capitalism and the bettering of society for about two centuries. Consequently, critique, instead of being considered an instrument of social betterment which is subservient to the greater good of society, has become the last trench preventing the dismantling of the remaining alternative and oppositional forces, however limited in their ambition.

The development of reform and revolution had a direct impact on the fields of architecture and urbanism. As outlined earlier in this chapter, the reform movement was responsible for the birth of social housing, which by the mid-twentieth century became the bread-and-butter of many practising architects, particularly in Europe.[24] Regional planning would have never been established without the agitation of reformists, and planning would have probably been limited to zoning and streamlining urban development to suit the needs of land speculation and capital accumulation. Le Corbusier's infamous 'architecture or revolution', the title of the last chapter of *Towards a New Architecture* (2008: 267–89), thus perfectly expresses the reformist agenda of mainstream modernist architecture. The book's closing sentences, 'Architecture or Revolution. Revolution can be avoided' (Le Corbusier 2008: 289), leave little doubt regarding the allegiances of modernist architecture.

The attacks on modernism in the late 1960s must therefore be understood as attacks, on the one hand, by radicals who demanded a total revolution rather than reform (Scott 2007), and, on the other, by forces allied with the market that demanded the freeing of urban development from the constraints of planned society and a return to land and property speculation. The main feature of the reformist Keynesian state, the Plan, whether in the form of the planned economy or spatial planning, was criticized by figures on the architectural Left ranging from Andrea Branzi to Manfredo Tafuri as a vehicle of social integration and control, an accessory of capitalist development. Yet the diverse forces that attacked modernism and its reformist agenda did not hesitate to deploy critique for advancing their causes: a critique of the corporate architecture erected in city centres, of the lack of personalization and individuality in mass housing, of the absence of spontaneity and freedom in the new towns, of the standardization of the housing and building industry. Such critique, both within and without architecture, aided in consolidating and voicing strong opposition to modernism, which inevitably led to its demise.

The dissolution of modernist architecture and planning was thus related to the dissipation of reformism. In the aftermath, critique found itself lacking the support of a powerful movement. Moreover, without the threat of revolution, the battered reformist movement could no longer argue its agenda convincingly, could no longer offer a 'middle ground' between revolt and laissez-faire. Critique thus increasingly became limited to the production of knowledge.

Tafuri, positioned on the side of the radicals, declared that a revolutionary architecture was impossible before a social revolution (Tafuri 1980: xv). Instead, he developed the argument that Walter Benjamin had articulated in 'The Author as Producer':

> In the questions posed in 'The Author as Producer', there are no concessions made to proposals for salvation by means of an 'alternative' use of linguistic techniques; there are no longer any ideological distinction between a 'communist art' as opposed to a 'fascist art'. There is only a genuinely structural consideration of the productive role of intellectual activities and, consequently, a series of questions regarding their possible contribution to the development of the relations of production.
>
> *(Tafuri 2000b: 166)*

The Italian architectural historian proceeded from this conclusion to call for increased reflexivity and self-critique in the work of architecture critics: 'The very same questions that criticism puts to architecture it must also put to itself: that is, in what way does criticism enter into the process of production? How does it conceive its own role within that process?' (Tafuri 2000b: 167). Critique was thus requested not to consider what is 'said' – represented, symbolized etc. – but what is 'done' in the sense of production, and, furthermore, to assess its own participation in the capitalist relations of production.

Particularly in the United States, a generation of architecture critics, ranging from K. Michael Hays to Joan Ockman, mostly influenced by Tafuri's writings, turned to such production of knowledge in the academia, utilizing critical distance in their analyses of architectural production. A parallel generation of practising architects with limited commissions, mostly dependent on academic positions for income, could embrace Critical Theory, post-structuralism, and the work of the architectural critics without hesitation. These practitioners, with Peter Eisenman at their helm, could posit their own distance from large-scale commercial commissions, a consequence of external conditions as much as choice, as a critical distance of sorts. Critique was thus preserved primarily as an academic pursuit rather than as a political instrument of social transformation.

Once the economic boom of the mid-1990s set in, critique seemed increasingly unnecessary; the discipline of architecture was no longer confronted with mediocre, commodified corporate architecture that needed challenging. Instead, architecture was offered opportunities of realizing daring designs unthinkable a generation earlier (Kaminer 2011a: 71–113). The conditions seemed so favourable to architecture that critique appeared to be the last refuge of pessimists who refused to acknowledge how good things actually were – scholars trapped in their old habits, unable to adapt to the new post-political situation.

It is in this context that within architecture a specific route of attack opened on critique, launched by Sarah Whiting and Bob Somol and later developed by Michael Speaks and others (Somol and Whiting 2002; Speaks 2003; Baird 2004). The so-called 'post-critics' accepted, in effect, Eisenman's characterization of autonomous architecture as 'critical'. Their onslaught against architectural autonomy thus took the form of an attack on critique, and called for architecture to engage with its outside, with the compromised and 'dirty' world of daily life, economic exploitation, and mass culture. Hence, they demanded the elimination not only of critical distance, but of critique. Instead, they endorsed developing theories that support practice, though the support offered was primarily a legitimation of already existing practices via a pragmatist argument: dissolving the critical distance, but not in order to produce a radical theory–praxis relationship and to challenge current architectural production, but in order to sanction, in effect, the current social and political conditions, while questioning the need for an alternative vision.

To conclude, critique must be seen as a benign but necessary steering instrument that aids in bettering society. Critique, which emerged in tandem with reason, belongs to modern society. It is a reflexive apparatus of a modern, bourgeois society, a society that can conceive of itself. Identified primarily with reformist movements, critique poses limited danger to current conditions. Its abolishment should be understood as a direct threat to the reflexive and reflective qualities of modern society. Boltanski and Chiapello have written that '[a] critique that is exhausted or defeated, or loses its vigour, allows capitalism to relax its mechanisms of justice and alter its production processes with total impunity. A critique that increases in vigour and credibility compels capitalism to strengthen its mechanisms of justice' (Boltanski and Chiapello 2005: 30).

It is necessary to acknowledge that without a radical alternative, posited as a revolutionary threat to existing order, critique has limited efficacy. Its ability to leverage politics to generate change is curtailed. Critique may not be directly involved in practice, but it indirectly generates theory and praxis which attempt to respond to the critique, and via this mechanism transforms reality. The absence of critique, or its reduction to a marginal 'academic' position, means the closure of opportunities of steering society towards self-improvement.

THE INTEGRATION OF CRITIQUE

Societal Integration

> [Power] integrates the force of protest by approving it on the one hand and, on the other, gives the appearance of respecting its message.
>
> *(Hubert Tonka 2011: 169)*

The co-optation or *récupération* of alternative or oppositional ideas and practices by society's mainstream is a familiar phenomenon. Well-documented examples include the manner in which alternative lifestyles, such as the reuse of ex-manufacturing loft spaces, practised by artists since the 1950s, have become ubiquitous. Integrated into contemporary living practices, they have become nowadays merely a lifestyle choice among several, rather than a potential for a very different social practice (Zukin 1989). The use of provocation, mobilized in the 1920s by Dada artists as a weapon against the bourgeoisie, has become a standard tool of public relations and a means of self-promotion, exemplified by the provocative advertisements of Benetton and Calvin Klein in the last decades. Shklovsky and Brecht's 'de-familiarization' and 'estrangement', once avant-garde instruments of formulating a cognition and consciousness of compromised daily life, have been integrated into a Disneyfied, irrationalist method of adding colour, wit and surprise to otherwise vacuous and dour environments, and consequently an instrument of pacification and 'quietism'.

The migration of ideas or practices from the periphery to the centre stage of thought, practice, or discourse has encouraged the creation of popular terms describing such processes, such as 'paradigm shift' and the more recent 'tipping point', coined by Thomas Kuhn (1962) and Malcolm Gladwell (2001), respectively. Clement Greenberg's understanding of the artistic avant-garde expressed a similar idea of diverse cutting edge notions and techniques developed by small vanguard groups of artists and later trivialized by their broad dissemination to a wider public. However, *récupération* is a different type of gravitation from margin to centre:[25] it is a process in which critique and oppositional ideas and practices are absorbed by society and transformed from a threat to the status quo into an integral part of it. This is precisely the process that exposes the resilience of middle-class, capitalist society: its ability to counter threats and critique from its periphery not by exclusion, but by a selective inclusion, which transforms the threat into something more benign and palatable. The potency of co-optation is precisely in its ability to undermine the efficacy of critique. This chapter will open with a review of some of the relevant literature on the topic, leading to the outlining of the process of societal integration and culminating in two examples of *récupération* in architecture.

The expectation for a response to critique by the state and the process of *récupération* have become ubiquitous in recent decades as never before. The liberal model of sovereignty and citizenship, which is prevalent in contemporary understandings of the relationship of the democratic state and its citizens, prerequisites the consent of a civil society for the legitimacy of government, a consent that civil society can, it is presumed, withdraw if necessary (Hindess 1996: 19–22). Civil society, in turn, consists ostensibly of autonomous, rational subjects, and critique, according to such models, is formed by civil society and addressed to the state. An early version of such a model can be found already in the writings of Locke (1988), and this model has since become part and parcel of the self-perception of modern Western societies. As these positions have been widely disseminated, society has increasingly developed refined mechanisms and strategies of addressing critique, *récupération* being one such instance.

This emphasis on response to critique can be attributed, first, to the institutionalization of critique – the broad expectation that the state respond to critique, on the one hand, and the related measures taken by states to enable rather than repress critique on the other; and, second, to the ever more sophisticated apparatuses steering society, which in the political field include a legion of strategists, political and media consultants, work groups, pollsters, think tanks, and similar organizations.

Capitalism and the state have learned to avoid, when required, response to critique by repression and exclusion,[26] and developed their means of reacting to critique, balancing the need to satisfy demands raised by 'respectable' citizens with the desire to avoid change which limits profits or erodes bases of power. *Récupération*, in this context, proved to be a useful instrument of status quo, or, rather, of change without substantial change. Such non-substantial transformation has become a constant, an essential ingredient of the 'fashion machine'. The sociologist Jean Baudrillard described the situation as one in which '[e]verything is in movement, everything shifts before our eyes, everything is continually being transformed – yet nothing really changes' (Baudrillard 2005: 167).

Whereas this chapter discusses critique and *récupération* in a general sense, co-optation carried out by the state and co-optation carried out by capitalism are disparate processes. Critique, whether of state, of capitalism or of any injustice, is often directed to the state – the state being the institution expected to respond directly to citizens' demands. Politics and ideology play a role in critique and its integration, often as the battleground for ideas and ideals supporting or undermining the status quo. The state, in some cases, initiates the process of societal integration, though often enough the changes can be generated or shaped by other agencies in society – bringing about a transformation of capitalism, of ideologies, of bureaucracies, of practices and so on. For the purposes of this chapter, no specific differentiation will be made between the diverse types of critique and *récupération*. Rather, co-optation is understood as generally related to the process that leads subjects to voluntarily adopt or accept the positions and worldview of dominant power – subjugation by inclusion.

An early description of co-optation appears in Marx's *Eighteenth Brumaire*. Marx does not present the suppression of the revolt of 1848 as a failure of a working-class revolution, but as an act of betrayal by the bourgeoisie of their own interests, supporting a relapse into an antiquated political system of absolutism. With palpable sarcasm, he writes:

> The Constitution, the National Assembly, the dynastic parties, the blue and red republicans, the heroes of Africa, the thunder from the platform, the sheet lightening of the daily press, the entire literature, the political names and intellectual reputations, the civil law and penal code, the *liberté, égalite, fraternité* and the second Sunday in May 1852 – all has vanished like a phantasmagoria before the spell of one man whom even his enemies do not make out to be a magician.
>
> *(Marx 2003b: 333)*

The growing support of Louis Napoleon by a significant segment of the bourgeoisie, Marx argues, led to a relapse. The bourgeoisie were motivated by their fear of economic instability – and loss of profits – caused by the instability of the democratic, republican model. 'Society now seems to have fallen back behind its point of departure', declared Marx (Marx 2003b: 332). Hence, autonomy relapsed into heteronomy, a process of integration, as the bourgeoisie betrayed their own elected representatives and accepted, in effect, the conditions dictated by Louis Napoleon.

Marx's description suggests that under certain external – 'empirical' – conditions autonomy can relapse into heteronomy, but for Adorno and Horkheimer autonomy is structurally correlated to heteronomy and mass deception, and therefore its relapse is not primarily dependent on external circumstances (Brunkhorst 2004: 260). Rather, heteronomy is intrinsic to autonomy. The two Frankfurt School scholars, as well as their colleague Herbert Marcuse, identified one of the main characteristics of late capitalism as a system of identity – a process of de-differentiation and consequently integration. They claim, basically, that 'there is no longer a revolutionary opening in the negative totality of history at hand' (Brunkhorst 2004: 257); 'Anyone who resists can survive only by being incorporated' (Horkheimer, Adorno 2002: 104). For Adorno, the 'consciousness of the nonidentical' was the negative thought that undermines the compromised common sense, and which was directly under assault by the system of identity. Whereas the thesis of relapse appears in Marx narrowly focused on specific social groups, Adorno and Horkheimer generalize this thesis and the idea of a process of atomization to entire society.

Hannah Arendt, writing in 1960, described the threat posed by an inclusive society. In the eighteenth and nineteenth centuries, she argued, the term 'society' referred to a small elite within the population, an educated and 'civilized' elite (Arendt 1960). It was against this society and its conservatism, its narrow morality and its domination that the modern individual rebelled. The rebellion was enabled by the existence of a 'nonsociety strata' – an area excluded from society, an area that provided an escape of sorts and a critical distance. In contrast, Arendt wrote about the conditions of mass society in 1960, 'the despair of individuals […] is due to the fact that these avenues of escape [the "nonsociety strata"] are, of course, closed as soon as society has incorporated all the strata of the population' (Arendt 1960: 279). In other words, one of the effects of an ever more egalitarian and inclusive society has been the prevention of rebellion, dissent and critique.

A few years after Arendt's article, Herbert Marcuse's influential *One Dimensional Man* directly addressed the process of co-optation. It outlined the paralysis of critique in contemporary society, and identified the causes, including the manner in which the individual subject internalizes the dominant morals, values, worldview, ideology, and lifestyle of society, an internalization facilitated by changes in the diverse processes of production. 'The efficiency of the system', wrote Marcuse,

> blunts the individuals' recognition that it contains no facts which do not communicate the repressive power of the whole. If the individuals find themselves in the things which shape their life, they do so, not by giving, but by accepting the law of things – not the law of physics but the law of their society.
>
> *(Marcuse 1969: 26)*

As a result of expanding automation in the factories during the post-war years, blue collar labour became more similar to the work of white collar employees, namely, the supervision and maintenance of machines rather than physical labour. Consequently, the working class was more easily assimilated into a middle-class society, as it could now identify with white collar employees, sharing their experience and worldview.

In the realm of culture, Marcuse explained the manner in which mass media intertwines art, religion, politics, philosophy, and commercials, applying the commodity form to these very disparate spheres of cultural production. Specific autonomous fields, such as that of high culture, which previously offered an opportunity to transcend and criticize compromised daily life, are consequently integrated; they continue to exist, but without that specific element that sublimated reality. Marcuse, echoing the claims of the art for art's sake movement, identified in the great art of the nineteenth century a certain freedom and rebellion against technocratic, capitalist society, carving out for itself a territory that confronted and contradicted the order of business. This was represented by characters in the literature of the period such as the rebel-poet, the prostitute, the outcast. Their offspring in contemporary literature, claimed Marcuse, 'are no longer images of another way of life but rather freaks or types of the same life, serving as an affirmation rather than negation of the established order' (Marcuse 1969: 60). In effect, '[t]he absorbent power of society depletes the artistic dimension by assimilating its antagonistic contents' (Marcuse 1969: 61).

Marcuse wrote *One Dimensional Man* before the emergence of counterculture; but he already foresaw its integration by identifying the limitation of the rebellion of the Beatniks, the forefathers of 1960s counterculture. Writing of cultural 'alternatives' such as Zen Buddhism and Beat, he argued that 'such modes of protest and transcendence are no longer contradictory to the status quo and no longer negative. They are rather the ceremonial part of practical behaviourism, its harmless negation, and are quickly digested by the status quo as part of its healthy diet' (Marcuse 1969: 28).

While never quite addressing the process of *récupération* as directly as Marcuse, Foucault's studies of power, governmentality, discipline, and biopolitics all touch upon related issues. In his early work, such as the study of insanity, the emphasis was on 'exclusion', often via domination; in later work, 'inclusion' became a major issue. Techniques of power adapt to circumstance, and resistance may bring about a refinement or adaptation of such techniques. Discipline or governing do not merely infer techniques of control and power directed at subjects from without, but take place also within the subject, affecting the subject's conduct – and hence, 'biopower'. Foucault depicted an unstable structure in which balances of power constantly shift and transform, assuming a basic degree of freedom as requisite for a relations of power – 'domination' being the term reserved, at least in Foucault's late work, for describing conditions of extreme imbalance of power leading to extremely limited freedom for subjects. The term 'subjectivization', for example, deployed by Foucault in *Discipline and Punish* (1991), denotes both the emergence of an autonomous subject and the subjugation to power.[27] When Foucault wrote that in neoliberalism '[e]conomics is [...] no longer the analysis of the historical logic of processes; it is the analysis of the internal rationality, the strategic programming of individuals' activity' (Foucault 2008: 223), he was describing a mode of societal integration distinct from, yet in proximity, to the machinations of co-optation.

The studies of co-optation mentioned above, with the exception of Foucault's biopolitics, focus primarily on the causes of co-optation, and less on the specifics of the process. The following theory of *récupération* attempts to unfold the step-by-step process of integration, in the most general sense, and as a means of producing an understanding of a major threat to critique and its efficacy. Its emphasis is on the ideological process rather than on the psychological aspects involved.

Towards a Theory of *Récupération*

The sociologists Luc Boltanski and Eve Chiapello identified three modes in which critique influences the spirit of capitalism – the 'spirit' that is responsible for societal integration: undermining the efficacy of dominating spirits by de-legitimizing them; forcing a reaction that guarantees improvement in terms of justice; allowing, in some cases, society and capitalism to respond not by bettering conditions, but by changing the means of accumulation and profit – that is, voiding the critique without responding to its demands (Boltanski and Chiapello 2005: 28–29). Yet *récupération* does not precisely fit these categories; it is a 'voiding of critique', but not exactly in the sense of the third mode, because co-optation responds to critique by seemingly addressing it – while dismantling its threat. The process of integration is not necessarily a political one in the conventional sense, but it is nevertheless an ideological operation. Even when practices or techniques rather than ideas are being integrated, the integration takes place via ideology.

The work of the political theorist Ernesto Laclau on politics and particularly his work on populism provides a description of a political process that relates to co-optation (Laclau 2005).[28] In an ideal condition, Laclau argues, demands raised by subjects are adequately addressed by the state, treated as different, secluded and particular demands. As such an ideal condition does not exist in reality, demands that are not addressed by the state accumulate over time. At a certain moment, and under particular conditions, these different and isolated demands tend to develop into an equivalential chain – that is, they tend to be seen as a set of demands, despite being articulated originally as isolated and unrelated demands. While demands that originate in a well-defined ideological and political movement contain the same abstract ideas – which coalesce them into a systematic set – these unaddressed demands remain, to some extent, independent of each other. They are initially held together by their common antagonism to the state that fails to address them, and this antagonism allows the subjects from whom the demands originate to construe themselves as 'the people' while excluding their adversaries – the 'elites', in populist jargon, whether the moneyed elites, the political elites, or the intellectual elites.

In order to develop beyond this basic antagonism and division line between 'the people' and 'the elite', the equivalential chain of demands needs further strengthening by a symbolic representation. Such a function can be carried out by elevating one of the demands to the status of representing all others – despite being originally an isolated demand, despite the fact that it does not share an essence or abstract idea with the other demands. Whereas in a systematic, ideological movement the specific demands tend to develop from the general, abstract idea that permeates all demands, and hence all contain it in some form, here the symbolic idea emerges only at a later stage, and is not contained in the separate populist demands. Rather, it functions as a subsequent unifying element. The symbolic idea or demand needs to be emptied, to a certain extent, of its content: in order to be able to represent such diverse and unrelated demands, the symbolic idea cannot be linked too directly and too obviously to any singular element. As a result, populism often appears as an amalgam of contradictory ideas and demands, held together by representations that refer to all and yet to nothing specific at the same time; the symbolic idea can also be a leader, or the name of a leader. Laclau provides the example of the Marlboro advertisement that represents 'America' even though America stands for many things that the advertisement does not represent in any form.

Laclau's ideas regarding the empty signifier develop from Gramsci's conception of hegemony. 'A class or group is considered to be hegemonic when it is not closed in a narrow corporatist perspective,' Laclau writes, 'but presents itself as realizing the broader aims either of emancipating or ensuring order for wider masses of the population' (Laclau 2007: 43). He identifies the empty signifier as a key aspect of a hegemonic operation, as it is the empty signifier that enables the unification of differences without necessarily undermining them by fully assimilating them into the new totality. The empty signifier is, for Laclau, neither the contradictory signifier, which points to diverse and competing signified, nor the ambiguous signifier, which is abstract and vague. Rather, it is a signifier that points to an absence – the absence, which the relevant political movement wishes to fill with its own content, its own symbolic form. The specifics of Laclau's empty signifier are of less significance here, and, for the operation of societal integration, ambiguous and contradictory signifiers can be as potent as the 'absence' – they are, after all, easily emptied, subverted, and filled with new meanings.

The 'empty signifier', and the fact that the equivalential chain is formed in the first place as a result of a shared antagonism, enable the re-alignment of the populist movement – a relatively small shift in the equivalential chain, in the identity of the adversary, or in the meaning associated with the 'empty signifier' can create significant political shifts, which can be as radical as shifting from a left-wing to a right-wing populism. Laclau highlights the contingent aspect of the hegemonic operation, arguing that even when an empty signifier and equivalential chain are successfully produced, 'the chain of equivalences which are unified around this signifier tend to empty it, and to blur its connection with the actual content with which it was originally associated. Thus, as a result of its very success, the hegemonic operation tends to break its links with the force which was its original promoter and beneficiary' (Laclau 2007: 45).

Populism thus emerges as a contingent structure rather than a fixed or stable set of ideas and ideals, and the political shift described here, namely, the re-alignment of the empty signifiers and equivalential chains, resembles and is related to a process of *récupération*. Co-optation takes place by such re-alignment, by shifting the meanings of the symbolic, by taking advantage of the emptiness or contingency of the signifiers, or of the weakness of the chain which holds the diverse demands together. Moreover, co-optation is a process directly related to hegemonic operations. The process of *récupération* and its similarity to a shift within populism will now be demonstrated via two examples.

Récupération in Architecture

Colin Rowe and Fred Koetter's *Collage City* (1978) can serve as an example of co-optation in the realm of architectural theory. The collage city is the idea of a city to which new material – buildings – can be added without causing harm, and a political community, a *cité*, which are pluralist and can contain contradictions and adversity without imploding. Rowe and Koetter aim at enabling a co-existence of utopia and tradition, but in order to allow the inclusion of utopia in their proposed democratic, pluralistic *cité*, they strip it from the excesses that make it, in the first place, utopian:

> [B]ecause collage is a method deriving its virtue from its irony, because it seems to be a technique for using things and simultaneously disbelieving them, it is also a strategy which can allow utopia to be dealt with as image, to be dealt with in *fragments* without our having to accept it in *toto*, which is further to suggest that collage could even be a strategy which, by supporting the utopian illusion of changelessness and finality, might even fuel a reality of change, motion, action and history.
>
> *(Rowe and Koetter 2000: 109)*

In a similar manner, the architectural critic Roemer van Toorn wrote more recently that '[t]he approach I am after carries the charge of an utopian impulse but struggles against reproducing an idealist utopian vision that universalizes experience and promises progress' (van Toorn 1997: 20). The result, in both the case of *Collage City* and van Toorn, is a utopia devoid of anything which is utopian. The term 'utopia' is emptied of its original meaning, and a new meaning appears.

Rowe and Koetter's proposition is a rhetorical resolution to a specific problem: how to create a democratic, pluralistic society, city, and discipline, without shunning uncompromising, intolerant utopia, and the vibrancy and edge it has produced in twentieth-century culture. It attempts *récupération* by following three steps: first, emptying the term from its original meaning and creating a subverted 'utopia' without its excess; second, freeing 'utopia' from its original equivalential chain, which juxtaposed it with radicalism and progress; third, including the subverted 'utopia' in a new equivalential chain held together by the umbrella term 'collage city' and by its antagonism to progress. Yet, on the level of co-optation, the success is limited; utopia was never an empty signifier to those who followed a doctrine that can be identified as 'utopian', but filled with specific meaning, such as 'Socialism'. In fact, utopias are considered utopian *only by those who do not believe in them*: the detractors of utopia, such as Marx or Karl Popper,[29] ironic agnostics who bask in the excesses of 'utopia', such as Archigram, or disbelievers who nevertheless call for a reinstatement of a utopia and decry its absence, such as David Harvey. The operation carried out in *Collage City* thus aims at *récupération* by its tactics of subversion of meaning and inclusion in a new equivalential chain, but the subject of the operation – 'utopia' in general rather than a specific utopia – is not one which lends itself to the process. In fact, rather than the *Collage City* text and theory, it is the collage city principle that is here proposed as a machine of co-optation: the collage city as a society- and city-making principle that absorbs utopian fragments and removes, in the process, their threat to the status quo, leaving a 'cultural' or 'aesthetic' shell devoid of menace.

An example of a successful *récupération*, which took place on a much grander scale – that of society – than the attempted co-optation by Rowe and Koetter, relates to the critiques of the 1960s. The May '68 protests (Figure 1.3) have been characterized by scholars such as Fredric Jameson and Alain Touraine as a reaction to the emerging post-Fordist, post-industrial society (Jameson 1985: 67; Touraine 1971: 90), but a close inspection of the demands of the May '68 students by Boltanski and Chiapello draws a different picture: while the overt targets of the protests were Gaullism, American Imperialism and capitalism (Ross 2002: 8), the less visible adversaries of the students were state authority, Fordism, and bureaucracy (Boltanski and Chiapello 2005: 39).[30] The students demanded freedom, spontaneity, self-realization, creativity – demands which are associated with the artistic critique of society, as opposed to the social critique and its demands for higher wages and job stability, prevalent since the mid-nineteenth century. The new demands and change in worldview followed structural changes in Western societies, including a fairer distribution of wealth, more opportunities of social mobility, and a limited dissolution of class differences thanks to the successes of the reformist movement and the creation of the welfare state and Keynesian policies, all of which enabled, structurally, greater amplitude for individualization (Honneth 2004).

The artistic critique of society became intertwined with the critique of modernist architecture and the modernist city: the absence of spontaneity and life in the assembly line architecture of mass social housing, the lack of creativity and freedom in the modernist city. Many of the alternatives spelled out in this period, ranging from Constant's New Babylon of 1958–74 to the early work of Peter Eisenman, construed as an opposition to the mainstream

FIGURE 1.3 A student strike in Paris, France, 3 May 1968. By permission of AP/Press Association Images.

'Fordist' architecture of the period, emphasized difference and creativity in their designs. New Babylon foregrounded the ideas of 'play' and indeterminacy, imagining life without labour as an emancipation of the human subject, a stark contrast to the subjugation of human subjects by the all-powerful Keynesian state, to a life of labour as mere cogs in a 'total' machine. The reification and objectification of the human subject is replaced by a subjectification, 'desire' supplants 'basic needs', and imagination substitutes a dull utilitarianism. Constant created stunning photographs of his steel, wood, and Perspex models, using coloured lighting and its reflections, representing expansive, open spaces, often organized as plateaus, with limited walls and separations, held together by trusses that suggest a spatial frame a-la Yona Friedman.

A few decades later, however, the same claims can be identified in the most celebrated architecture of Western society: in buildings such as the Guggenheim Bilbao or the Jewish Museum in Berlin, or in newly developed urban districts such as Amsterdam's Borneo–Sporenburg. Beyond developing some of the themes present already in the architecture of the late 1960s, the most prominent architecture of the late 1990s was specific in referring to an aesthetic modernism rather than to the modernism of mass housing, of a continuum of building and city, or of city planning – Le Corbusier's villas rather than his Plan Voisin. In such 'aesthetic' modernism, architecture studied its own form in singular, one-off structures. Here, the desired self-realization, creativity and uniqueness could be found, rather than in the architecture that was subjugated to the social or the urban. Thus, architects such as Peter Eisenman, Rem Koolhaas, Zaha Hadid, or Richard Meier could salvage a modernism that addressed the demands now raised by society. Frank Gehry could refer in his 'sculptural' buildings to 1920s expressionism and its focus on subjective creativity, imitating the creative process of early modernist and expressionist sculptors (Kaminer 2011a).

The process that migrated these ideas of spontaneity, creativity, and freedom from the periphery to the centre was a process of *récupération*, in which the ideas themselves transformed in order to enable their integration. The sociologist Henri Lefebvre and the Situationist Raoul Vaneigem were well-aware of the manner in which their ideas were being integrated. Lefebvre lamented that '[t]he established order has a great capacity for adaptation and integration; it assimilates what is opposed to it. It has demonstrated a surprising flexibility, an unsuspected capacity' (Lefebvre 2005: 106); Vaneigem wrote in an introduction to his Traité – *The Revolution of Everyday Life* – that '[a]mong the Traité's readers there were thus some who seized upon my account of a certain mal de vivre (from which I wanted above all to free myself) as an excuse for offering no resistance whatsoever to the state of survival to which they were in thrall' (Vaneigem 2006: 8).

The demands voiced by the May '68 students – freedom, creativity, spontaneity – are precisely the 'empty signifiers' of which Laclau writes. For the members of the ultra-Left, they had a specific meaning. Freedom, for example, meant collective freedom. '[S]ocially the term [creativity],' Lefebvre explained, 'will stand for the activity of a collectivity assuming the responsibility of its own social function and destiny – in other words for self-administration' (Lefebvre 2000: 204). But in order to transcend the specific demands of the ultra-Left, these ideas had to become terms emptied of their specific meaning. Once emptied, they could assume a symbolic role, and become adopted by a wide segment of the public. Yet the success of the dissemination of the demands of the '68 protests also meant their undoing: the very condition which allowed their spread – their 'emptiness', their generality and abstraction – also allowed their co-optation.

Society responded to the demands, but not by the terms of the ultra-Left. It could portray its retreat from the Fordist compromise, from the welfare state and from Keynesian economy as a means of offering self-realization, freedom and creativity – though individual instead of collective freedom and creativity: mobility in the workplace, consumption as a means of self-realization, individual rather than collective work contracts.

The social theorist Axel Honneth describes the process in which, on the one hand, socio-structural changes in the post-war years broadened the options of individuals to develop their own identity and individuality according to their desires, while on the other, socio-cultural changes meant that individuals were themselves drawn to what he terms 'experimental self-realization'. This process had its counterpart in changes in the workplace and management, with greater emphasis on the autonomy of the employees and their ability to adapt and contribute via their own persona. Initially a response to demands raised by employees, the demands for self-realization were, in effect, institutionalized, and were consequently re-directed to the employees: an expectation for original identity and individuality, alongside a legitimation of the implementation of 'flexible working conditions' and other aspects of the neoliberal order:

> The inclination of individuals to think to an ever greater degree of their lives as comprising the experimental exploration of their own identities, does not merely provide legitimacy for a series of restructuring moves in the economy which aim collectively at deregulating industry and the service sector […] rather, the new individualism is also being used today as a productive factor directly, in the sense that by calling upon their apparently changed needs, more is now required of workers, in terms of involvement, flexibility, and individual initiative, than has been the case under the conditions of the regulated capitalism of the welfare state.
>
> *(Honneth 2004: 473–74)*

Honneth offers further elaboration of the process in which demands for self-realization have been absorbed into the contemporary workplace, and re-directed to the employees:

> The claims to individual self-realization which have rapidly multiplied, beginning with the historically unique concatenation of entirely disparate processes of individualization in the Western societies of thirty or forty years ago, have so definitely become a feature of the institutionalized expectations inherent in social reproduction that the particular goals of such claims are lost and they are transmuted into a support of the system's legitimacy.
>
> *(Honneth 2004: 466)*

And in post-Fordist society, creativity became an important source of surplus profit – the growing symbolic economy driven by the 'creative industries'. Art, architecture, and, more generally, culture, were deployed as a means of increasing real-estate value, aiding in the gentrification of inner city neighbourhoods, in urban renewal projects and in adding 'content' – and spectacle – to dour new urban developments (Kaminer 2010). 'Freedom' and 'creativity' were therefore offered in the architecture of the late 1990s and 2000s in a different sense than that demanded by the critique of the 1960s. They were primarily centred on the creative process of the architect rather than the user, yet a tacit belief that unique, one-off, singular buildings can project their latent creative freedom on the users and contribute to the users' self-realization is nevertheless present. Ultimately, such a projection is key in city branding projects, suggesting that singular public buildings symbolically represent their city's vitality and uniqueness – always with emphasis on 'innovation' and 'creativity'. In this sense, the signature architecture of the 'starchitects', the implementation of creativity and freedom on the level of the architect and the singular building, were all aspects of the co-optation of the demands of the '68 generation in the built environment.

The process of *récupération*, then, meant 'filling' the empty signifiers with new meaning that subverted the original meaning. But it also meant establishing a new equivalential chain – absorbing some of the demands of the protest movement into a new set of demands that was no longer the equivalential chain of a unified alliance of discontented, but a set that was allied with neoliberalism. In this sense, the integration could take advantage of the fact that the adversary of the protest movement was the centralized Keynesian, Fordist state, the status quo that neoliberalism also desired to destroy.

PART TWO
The Architecture of Radical Democracy

THE POST-FORDIST CITY

Park Hill

> A building can be taken as the tip of the design iceberg; not least in the sense that it can help us read the larger (socio-economic, political and legal) conditions that underlie it.
>
> *(Fran Tonkis 2013: 8)*

Perched above Sheffield's main railway station, overlooking the city from its hill-top position, is Park Hill, the notorious complex of honeycomb-shaped council housing slabs. After decades of neglect, degradation and decay, the complex finally entered a process of regeneration in the 2000s. The project has been led by the urban regeneration specialists Urban Splash. Despite a backlash by some Sheffield residents and politicians who preferred demolition to regeneration, the project has been favourably received.[1]

Urban renewal projects often follow a period of divestment, an identification of the area as one of deprivation, of 'blight', and in need of radical redevelopment. Locals often object to such a portrayal of their neighbourhood, but end up split between pragmatists desperate for redevelopment in any form, and those fighting the redevelopment. The type of process of regeneration Urban Splash initiates is unusual in Britain but common practice in government-led regeneration projects in northern European countries such as Denmark or the Netherlands. It is distinctive in applying art, design and 'creativity' as a means of urban transformation.

This type of cutting edge regeneration project begins by the demolition of the 'dullest' among post-war slabs in the area. A significant number of social tenure residents are sent away. New buildings are built – cool, smart, even witty designs, though also inexpensive apartments tailored for the lower middle class, a social group with limited choice regarding the purchase of property. As described by Nick Johnson, the current deputy chief executive and previous development director of Urban Splash, the new buildings express 'a variety of architectural styles reflecting the city – a little bit messy here and there, because that's what cities are like, not standardised – with lots of colourful structures and water' (Hetherington 2002). The new housing is accompanied by an investment in culture, whether by organizing street parties, art exhibitions or other events, in order to transform the image of the area in question by infusing it with vitality and vibrancy. Once a substantial number of lower-class residents move out, the lower middle class moves in, and the image improves via cultural content. Then the more expensive luxury housing, which offers the developers wider margins of profit, is built. The process described here exemplifies one form of gentrification: the banishing of the working class, the migrants and the poor from areas with real estate 'potential', and their replacement with a stronger social group, achieved here by a savvy deployment of 'culture'. The specificity of the project depends on local conditions, and diverse variants of this culturally-infused urban regeneration have become common in cities such as Stockholm, Copenhagen and Amsterdam, whereas in Britain they are still considered cutting edge and risky.

The regeneration of Park Hill is a particular case, and is marred by several contradictions. As much as it is a paradigmatic gentrification project of the 2000s, it is also an anomaly because of the Grade II★ listing of the complex in 1998 by English Heritage. The listing, carried out despite vocal objections by Park Hill's antagonists, meant the obliteration of the welfare state could not follow straightforward demolition procedures, as in the case of London's Heygate Estate, and had to take a very different form. Urban Splash had to figure out what aspects of Park Hill prevented its real estate value from rising, and how to remove these 'nuisances' from the complex. Thus, the tensions are positioned within the project itself: between the demand, on the one hand, to conserve the listed council housing complex, and, on the other, to increase its real estate value by transforming it into something very different. Park Hill had to remain the same, yet it also had to change. The conclusion, it seems, was that the more social tenure residents are removed, the better; that the dour greyness of the concrete and grime-covered bricks had to be relieved; that the monolithic aspect and horizontal repetition of the blocks needed some treatment; and, most visibly, the robust heaviness and sobriety required some lightness and brightness. The solutions provided:[2] the concrete frame, the skeleton of the original, was kept, the rest emptied; shiny, colourful anodized aluminium panels replaced the sober brick walls infill (Figure 2.1); the amount of glazing was doubled to add light and (visual) permeability; the elevated streets were severed from the streets below; some additional height for lobbies, particularly a four-storey 'cut out' at the north-west corner, and shiny spiral staircases added vertical features breaking the horizontality of the blocks; many council apartments – two-thirds in the first regeneration phase – became free-market apartments. All this was accompanied by investment in culture and lifestyle. The show apartment displayed all the characteristics expected for an apartment of the culturally savvy professional middle class. Art spaces were created and exhibitions were organized.[3]

Park Hill's regeneration unabashedly destroys the ideas that animated the original architects, Jack Lynn and Ivor Smith (with Frederick Nicklin) in the 1950s, such as 'truth to materials', or a simplicity that is about 'the man in the street' and the experiential. Socially and economically it transfers council flats to the free market and replaces collectivity with individualism. Historically, it annihilates the memory of the welfare state.

In the context of 2000s Britain, the Park Hill complex had few alternatives. As a listed building, it could escape demolition, but in all likelihood would not have undergone a large-scale renovation, being left to decay. City councils, with limited financial resources, could not carry out such projects without the involvement of private capital. Private capital, in turn, including non-profit developers, requires a means of financing projects. Hence, the necessity to substitute council housing with free-market apartments and adjust the building in order to increase the value of such apartments in the market. The post-Fordist 'solution' to urban deprivation is revealed here in its totality: an inferred, though rarely stated, understanding

FIGURE 2.1 Park Hill, Sheffield, 2015. Remodelled section on the left, non-refurbished section on the right. Photograph courtesy of Stephen Parnell.

that a mere physical renovation is too limited a solution for deprivation; a lack of interest, or will, or ability to address the social malaise and long-term unemployment; hence, the need to remove the 'problem' population in order to facilitate the area's rejuvenation. In this sense, the Park Hill endeavour by Urban Splash can be considered both courageous and symptomatic: courageous because of the risk involved (there are, after all, safer ways for developers to make a profit), and symptomatic, because the only alternative for the listed complex was slow death – a typical choice between two evils, or, rather, not a choice at all.

The project demonstrates, then, the destruction of the welfare state – not just symbolically, but in a very concrete manner, by transforming council housing to free-market housing, hand-in-hand with the transformation of the architecture itself to suit the market's demands. It enables identifying the specific elements of the architecture of the welfare state era that are no longer acceptable in a post-industrial, neoliberal order. It explains the relation of architecture to political economy, to a worldview and ideology, and to a specific society at a specific moment, unfolding the precise economic and ideological differences between 1950s and 2000s Britain, and delineating the manner in which these economic and ideological differences materialize in architectural design and built form. It also serves as an example of one form of transformation required of the built environment in order to adjust to the demands posed by contemporary society.

The New City

The Western city, following a panoply of experiments, failures and partial successes, discovered by the mid-1990s the suitable response to the structural transformation society had undergone in previous decades. The process of reinventing the city, which began hesitantly in the 1970s, was long and painful. The previous era of Keynesian economy and strong centralized governments had destroyed the industrial city but offered no alternative. The Fordism of that era had led to the relocation of factories from inner cities to the periphery. Outside the cities, land was cheap and large single-storey factories could be built to accommodate the new sprawling assembly lines. Skilled labour, integrated into the middle class by the late 1950s, relocated to suburbia, in some cases to housing built by their employers (P. Marcuse 1988). Cities were no longer the locus of industrial production, and consequently lost their role in society. Inner cities' ghettoes expanded, inhabited primarily by unskilled labourers, cast aside by growing automation. Real estate markets collapsed, crime and poverty spread. The riots in North American cities in the late 1960s and later in West European cities made the crisis of the city apparent and palpable.

The initial responses to the aporia of cities failed to identify the core causes, targeting, instead, the symptoms. Projects were aimed at attracting businesses and the middle class back to downtowns and inner cities. The 1980s were consequently a period of experimentations, such as the introduction of free enterprise zones, public–private partnerships, and the encouragement of large-scale megaprojects in order to revitalize cities. The latter were mostly developer-driven though required significant investment of public money, focused on programmes such as retail and sports, and designed by the most corporate of architects.[4]

The Docklands project, arguably the most ambitious of such megaprojects in Europe, was paradigmatic of the period's experiments. It perfectly reflects the passage from an industrial to a post-industrial society, from the London Docks as an entry point for raw material and exit point for mass-produced commodities, to the Docklands, a central business district (CBD) modelled on American CBDs, and home to finance capital. The London Docklands Development Corporation (LDDC) was an experiment with public–private partnership (PPP)[5] and with American-style 'enterprise zones'. It expressed the economic transition from industry to finance capital. The Enterprise Zone status meant freedom from planning controls, exemption from development land tax, exemptions from diverse Building Regulations and health and safety provisions as well as 100 per cent capital allowance against tax and a ten year rate-free exemption. The retreat from promises regarding affordable housing and public spaces and amenities exemplified much of what has happened in Britain since. The Docklands project, instigated by Prime Minister Margaret Thatcher, was born to prove the capacity of private capital to produce urban development with only limited governmental intervention, and thus epitomized the era of 'roll-back neoliberalism' (Figure 2.2).

While the Docklands demonstrated the significance of high-end CBDs and finance capital to the new city and new economy, Guggenheim Bilbao presented the importance of high-end programmes rather than popular sport arenas or shopping malls, and refined rather than corporate architectural design. Such landmark buildings were a means of branding cities as places of vitality and relevance and competing for international investments. Associated with the later era of 'roll-out neoliberalism', the Guggenheim and similar projects vied for media attention and publicity, leveraging symbolic capital to produce real capital – making cities more attractive as the locus of the headquarters and hubs of multinational corporations and

FIGURE 2.2 A poster of the layout of the London Docklands being shown to Prime Minister Margaret Thatcher during a visit to the area, 1987. Photograph by Peter Jordan/The LIFE Images Collection/Getty Images.

other forms of investments. The investment in CBDs and landmark buildings demonstrated that the emergent city was no longer a regional capital, but a global city.

Culture and professional 'creatives', in turn, have proven to be useful in reclaiming inner cities from the poor, the migrants, and the unemployed. The process of gentrification has become part and parcel of urban regeneration strategies, a means of bettering an area by replacing a significant segment of the 'problem' population. Members of the middle class with limited economic leverage, particularly artists and students, are mobilized as the foot soldiers of gentrification, 'urban pioneers', entering inner-city neighbourhoods that were previously undesirable in order to find cheap housing (Smith 1996; 2008; Slater 2011). In this sense, the process includes both a return of capital to inner cities and a return of the middle class. The urbanist Peter Marcuse highlighted the specificity of the process of gentrification to the transition from industrial to post-industrial, with growth in white-collar employment at the expense of blue collar, and gentrification as a response to disparate demands: first, a means of motivating the white-collar employees of diverse finance and service firms via culture and lifestyle opportunities; second, a means of removing the no-longer needed unskilled labourers from inner cities, and, third, a means of realizing the real estate potential of these neighbourhoods – taking advantage of what geographer Neil Smith termed 'the rent gap' (Smith 1987; 1996; P. Marcuse 1988).[6]

In cities such as Amsterdam, artists are offered subsidized ateliers and students are given temporary accommodation in 'areas of interest'. Art projects and programmes are funded in order to change the areas' reputation.[7] The city council initiated a programme of creative incubators (*Broedplaats*), used to legalize existing squats and to redevelop specific areas of interest by infusion of cultural activities and middle-class 'creatives'. Social housing was reduced to produce 'a better social mix', though there was never a parallel increase in social housing in more affluent neighbourhoods. Increasingly, inner cities are 'rejuvenated' by cleansing them of the unwanted, now transferred to the urban periphery. Real estate has recovered, inner cities have been 'revitalized', and the eyesore of ghettoes and poverty removed to less visible metropolitan areas. The regeneration of Park Hill fits this description perfectly.

In London, an ambitious development near the Leamouth, London City Island, on the border of the deprived Canning Town, is promoted as 'London's new island metropolis, an ultra-connected destination of extraordinary culture and contemporary living' (Ballymore: 4). The development is a joint venture by Ballymore and Malaysian property developers EcoWorld, and the location, at the edge of the Docklands, was until relatively recently the type of service area to the docks where diverse infrastructural overflow was located. The project envisions around 1,700 housing units on the 12-acre peninsula, realized in two main phases. The brochure for potential investors states that '[t]hose who live here have known for some time that the city's action, both creative and commercial, has been shifting down river, towards a new constellation of key eastern suburbs including Canary Wharf, Shoreditch, Hackney and Greenwich. The 2012 Olympics, gathered around Docklands on the Thames and Stratford by the River Lea, revealed London's new centre of gravity to the rest of the world' (Ballymore: 15).

The brochure cunningly exploits and develops this narrative, which intertwines finance capital, culture, and urban vibrancy:

> Attracted by flexible workspaces between Shoreditch and the River Lea, from the 1980s onwards creative professionals moved into the area en masse. This was the stomping ground of the Young British Artists, and it is now home to a swathe of internet start-ups. Here is Europe's densest concentration of artists and creative professionals. There are design and photography studios, architects' firms and digital technology labs, plus a network of galleries, theatres, bars and restaurants that are increasingly a draw for Londoners from all points of the compass. [...] to see how this ancient metropolis continues to reinvent itself in the twenty-first century, you need to look to the financial and creative energy of the East, and there are few better vantage points than London City Island.
>
> *(Ballymore: 21)*

The story is supported by large colour photographs and by visualizations of a 'non place', a slick high-end neighbourhood of professionals and the affluent, with the typical glossiness in which even the artisan shops featured as local amenities are subsumed into a placeless Photoshop artifice. The glimmering backdrop of Docklands' towers and the Millennium Dome are the only sign of location-specificity. The brochure's narrative and selective history is compelling. The East End hipsters appear as the logical extension of the Docklands' financiers, a shared trajectory eastwards comprising of two impetuses, finance capital and the creative industries. 'East London's transformation cemented two distinct personalities,' the brochure continues, 'the luxury life of Canary Wharf, and the cool credentials of the "other" east' (Ballymore: 23). The ragged chic of the East End enhances here the exclusivity of the project, providing it with cultural relevance and vibrancy. The positioning of the English National Ballet headquarters on the island is not intended to sell apartments to ballet audiences, but to produce a civilized, cultured gravitas and image that would appeal to the right investors.

Flats are, expectedly, '[d]esigned with a warehouse aesthetic' (Ballymore: 112) and '[a]ll of the island's residents are members of the exclusive city island arts club' (Ballymore: 94).

Launched in Kuala Lumpur, London and Singapore, the project is directed towards international investors, offering Malaysian residents and investment firms the first chance to buy, and adding to the rampant property speculation in London that has driven housing prices to levels far beyond Londoners' reach. Instead of gated communities and luxuries typical of such high-end developments, its vision is of an urban lifestyle, pedestrianization and bicycle use, high street rather than shopping malls, and culturally-infused public spaces.

Not far away, in the Greenwich Peninsula, an ambitious £5 billion luxury development by Chinese firm Knight Dragon, a microbrewery's hop farm can be found (Figure 2.3) as well as a printing studio and artists' studios. 'The developers are very unusual in bringing a lot of culture into the place,' said Steve Lazarides, who set up the artists' spaces. 'I've spent twenty years being chased off building sites by other developers, now we're being invited on to one of the biggest in the world' (Mount 2014). The developers have supported and celebrated pop-up performances, theatre, culture and art, identifying the role of culture in gaining visibility in media, in producing a positive reputation for an area, and, ultimately, in aiding in selling property.

Gleaming CBDs, high-end landmark buildings, city branding, gentrification and culture as means of reclaiming inner cities: all these became the staples of the new, post-Fordist city, which was, as mentioned above, a global city. Not all cities could be revived by this new formula. Many small or midsize cities that were once industrial powerhouses and regional capitals, such as Newark in New Jersey, could not become global cities. Midsize and small cities, if lacking in revered historical monuments or in specific assets such as proximity to a major global city or status as capital, found themselves unable to compete for international investment with the likes of New York, London, Zurich or Toronto (Kaminer 2011b). Furthermore, the new city, while eager to display its exuberance and prosperity, veiled an

FIGURE 2.3 A hop farm by the artisan brewery Meantime at the Greenwich Peninsula development in south-east London. © Meantime Brewing Company.

underbelly of poverty and marginalization on its periphery. The affluence of the global city was neither shared nor widely distributed. It was against the conditions of the post-Fordist city as much as against the post-political condition, that the new participatory movement in architecture posited itself.

The Return of Participatory Architecture

A booklet produced by students at a 2009 international masterclass at the Berlage Institute in Rotterdam included a quote by the masterclass leader, San Diego-based architect Teddy Cruz:

> While the neo-liberalist idea of the 'free market' operating at a larger scale of the corporate has benefited de-regulation, individual freedoms and illegality, its approach to the small scale of the street market in many cities across Europe has operated as a repressive system of over-regulation and control, eroding the informal manifestations of diversity and social relations that can promote economic sustainability at the scale of the neighbourhood.
>
> *(Berlage Institute 2009)*

Yet the object of study, a street market in Rotterdam's deprived Afrikaanderwijk, was no neoliberal creation. Its 'over-regulation and control' were the consequence of tight state and city regulation, a residue of the previous era of Keynesian economics, welfare state, and strong centralized government. The anti-neoliberal tone of the quote above is supported in the masterclass booklet by a series of projects that propose forms of liberalizing and deregulating the street market. In other words, while unleashing a virulent rhetoric against neoliberalism, Cruz and his students created proposals that would further erode the welfare state and synchronize the street market with free-market ideology and policies.

The logic driving the masterclass appears flawed and confused, but, alarmingly, this is no singular case. Similar misconceptions, accompanied by emphasis on deregulation and liberalization, hallmarks of neoliberal policies, can be found in many of the proposals and designs of a new generation of socially and politically committed architects. Cruz, an earnest and committed architect, is one of the better-established and best-known figures among this group, hence the dissonance of the Afrikaanderwijk case is all the more bewildering.

The socially and politically committed architects and architecture firms include an amalgam of young vanguard architectural practices and schools of architecture-related Community Design Corporations and consultancies. Among others, they include Urban-Think Tank (U-TT), Rebar, Santiago Cirugeda, Studio Miessen, An Architektur, Stalker, Rural Studio, Architecture for Humanity, Center for Urban Pedagogy (CUP), Raumlabor, Elemental and BAVO, to name but a few. This loose movement has led the discipline to a renewed fascination with the political and social roles of architecture, positioning itself against 'starchitecture', signature architecture, the focus on landmark buildings and the emphasis on formal innovation. Against Eisenmanian ideas of disengaged, 'autonomous' architecture posited as 'critical architecture' (Kaminer 2011a), the loose group propagate engagement with local concerns, culture and politics. Against 'architecture for architecture's sake', the committed architects argue for architecture's role in the improvement of society, whether on the level of daily life, of equitability, or of urban politics and governance.

New York's CUP have fostered participatory design and planning practices; Berlin-based Raumlabor have constructed pneumatic structures as community-creating temporal spaces of freedom; Californians Rebar have occupied car parking with temporal, miniature green spaces; Santiago Cirugeda and Atelier d'architecture autogérée empowered locals by organizing the cultivation and appropriation of derelict urban spaces; many of the groups have proposed urban agriculture or community gardening activities as a means of altering the relationship of individuals to community, of residents to urban space, and as a way of claiming the right to the city. Master plans, blueprints and large-scale interventions are avoided as an ideological stance against the excesses of – 'repressive' – governmental power. 'Do not assume the return of public planning as we knew it;' Michelle Provost and Wouter Vanstiphout of Crimson Architecture Historians agitated in an article titled 'Make No Big Plans', 'the playing field of highly decentralised and privatised urban development, planning and policymaking is accepted for now' (Provost and Vanstiphout 2012: 107).

The loose group in question emerged a few years after the anti-globalization movement consolidated in the 1999 protests in Seattle, motivated by the desire to re-establish architectural efficacy in the realm of politics. The formation of this group took place primarily through diverse international exhibitions and gatherings, such as the Camp for Oppositional Architecture (Berlin 2004; Utrecht 2006), or the 'Experimental Architecture' section of the 2008 Venice Biennial, curated by Aaron Betsky and Emiliano Gandolfi. The 2007–8 economic meltdown further emboldened those involved and expanded the movement's reach.

Traditional disciplinary journals and magazines mostly ignored the movement until recently. Participatory architecture in its diverse forms has not featured in the *Architectural Review* in any significant sense. Publishing realized projects selected for their aesthetic value, the magazine has provided little opportunity for showcasing or discussing tactical or everyday urbanism, participatory design, self-build and related interests. Occasionally, some designs associated with the loose movement have featured: Lacaton and Vassal's Nantes School of Architecture and Palais de Tokyo (Slessor 2009; Ayers 2012), for example, or prize-winning student projects displaying affinities with the informal (AJ 2012/1388).

Architectural Design (*AD*), which in the late 1960s had published numerous articles about participation, pneumatic balloons and spatial frames, became by the 1990s the mouthpiece of deconstructivist architecture. A decade later, *AD* was enamoured with digital 'blob' architecture. Consequently, while the participatory movement discussed here began emerging in the 2000s, *AD* unequivocally continued focusing on digital architecture and its satellite preoccupations. An interest in everyday life, in the social or the political was typically limited to the specific issues of the magazine devoted to cities – though this territory was increasingly being colonized, by the 2010s, by 'digital urbanism'.

In a 2005 issue titled 'The New Mix: Culturally Dynamic Architecture', Teddy Cruz published an article titled 'Tijuana Case Study: Tactics of Invasion – Manufactured Sites', a first expression of the emerging movement in *AD* in a context that does not assimilate it into other concerns (Cruz 2005). The first issue to properly introduce the movement was focused, in effect, on the dissipation of architecture theory, the January/February 2009 issue. It included the profiles of CUP (pp. 76–77) and Stalker (pp. 68–69), and an article by Emiliano Gandolfi, 'fresh' from curating the experimental section of the Venice Biennial, titled 'Spaces of Freedom' (Gandolfi 2009).

It was only in 2011, however, that the participatory movement resurfaced on the pages of *AD*.[8] 'Latin America at the Crossroads' discussed many of the themes relevant to the group: the informal city, urban growth and participation. It included an interview with Alfredo Brillembourg of U-TT, an article about the office Elemental, and another article by Cruz. A few months later, 'Scarcity: Architecture in an Age of Depleting Resources', continued the discussion via a different lens, followed a little later by 'City Catalyst: Architecture in the Age of Extreme Urbanisation'. Articles such as 'Localising the Global' by Kyong Park (Park 2012); 'Revolution of the Ordinary' by Daniela Fabricius (Fabricius 2012); and by Crimson members Michelle Provost and Wouter Vanstiphout (Provost and Vanstiphout 2012) expanded the argument.[9] *AD*, it seems, had grudgingly given ground to participatory architecture.

One magazine that did play a role in popularizing the work of the participatory movement was the Netherlands-based *Volume*. A product of the collaboration of Archis Foundation, Koolhaas's AMO consultancy and Columbia University's C-Lab, *Volume* was born from the ashes of the respected *Archis* magazine. The latter was a city-focused periodical that was under threat in 2004 once the Netherlands Architecture Foundation, a key funder, became displeased with the direction the magazine had taken. The chief editor, Ole Bouman, used the opportunity to rethink the magazine, its format, and its contents, marrying the interest in cities with his own fascination with new media and technology, the immaterial, culture and innovation. Thus, *Volume* was launched in 2005.

Participatory architecture in its diverse forms received here the attention it lacked in more traditional architectural periodicals, though in the first years of publication the field was still subsumed under monikers that emphasized an OMA/AMO approach, or more generally the interest in cities, urban growth, and mass urbanization. Already in its second issue, titled 'Doing (Almost) Nothing', *Volume* published an interview with the 1960s pioneer of participatory architecture Giancarlo de Carlo (*Volume* 2005/2: 21–26), as well as an article by Ilka and Andreas Ruby, owners of a small publishing house specializing in books related to the participatory movement. The Rubys' article, 'Reprogramming Architecture', discussed diverse examples, many of which related to everyday life issues, including work by Lacaton and Vassal, Cedric Price, or Santiago Cirugeda (Ruby and Ruby 2005).

In the fourth issue, 'Breakthrough: How Reality Seeps Through the Cracks in Our Myths' (*Volume* 2005/4), the number of related articles had already become substantial. In addition to Bouman's 'Designing to Socialize' (Bouman 2005), the issue included articles by and on Jeanne van Heeswijk, the Association for Community Design, Habitat for Humanity, Emiliano Gandolfi, and Osservatorio Nomade. The participatory movement, its interests and its members continued to feature in many of the following issues, titled 'Power Building' (issue 6), 'Architecture of Power' (issue 7),[10] 'Craft the Agenda for a World to Come' (issue 8), 'Suburbia After the Crisis' (issue 9), 'Agitation' (issue 10), 'Cities Unbuilt' (issue 11),[11] and 'Unsolicited Architecture' (issue 14).[12] Another significant issue was number 16, 'Engineering Society' (*Volume* 2008/16). Here, alongside pieces titled 'User City', 'Seeing like a Society', 'Amateur', and 'Free Urbanism', were contributions by architectural critic Eyal Weizman, sociologist Justus Uitermark, Urban-Think Tank, Vanstiphout, and Pier Vittorio Aureli.

Consequently, while some architectural magazines such as *Volume* offered the emerging movement a platform, most ignored it, and the consolidation of the diverse groups, individuals and firms into a loose movement took place primarily through exhibitions, meetings, conferences, and other modes of collaboration. Many of the early endeavours were led by artists and art curators, and aided in generating discussions and exchanges among the diverse participants, forming a discursive base and a continuity. The second Camp for Oppositional Architecture, for example, was hosted in Utrecht in 2006 by Casco, an art initiative, and included BAVO, Markus Miessen, Dennis Kaspori, and Miguel Robles-Duran, and the presentation of papers such as 'Detect and Paste City', 'Do It Yourself

(Together!)', 'Daily Utopias', 'A Communism of Ideas', and 'Architecture and Activism' (Casco and An Architektur 2006).

Increasingly, participatory architecture has been invited to the major disciplinary institutions. In 2008, the work of Estudio Teddy Cruz took centre stage in the United States pavilion at the Venice Architecture Biennial. In the same year, the Curry Stone Prize was established to 'promote and honour designers who address critical social needs' (Curry Stone). The Museum of Modern Art (MoMA) in New York exhibited in 2010 'Small Scale, Big Change: New Architectures of Social Engagement' (October 3, 2010–January 3, 2011), an exhibition curated by Andres Lepik, displaying work by Teddy Cruz, Elemental, Lacaton and Vassal, U-TT, and Rural Studio. 'Spontaneous Interventions: Design Actions for the Common Good' was the title of the official U.S. presentation at the 2012 Venice Architecture Biennale, with MoMA's 2014 'Uneven Growth: Tactical Urbanisms for Expanding Megacities' exhibition (November 22, 2014–May 25, 2015) including specially commissioned work by Atelier d'architecture autogérée, Cohabitation Strategies, MAP, and others. In 2015, the British collective Assemble won the prestigious Turner Prize, followed by Elemental's Alejandro Aravena receiving the 2016 Pritzker Prize. All this meant the maturing of the loose movement and its increasing domination of the discipline.

The diversity of the groups involved means that the movement defies easy categorization. 'Tactical Urbanism' (Lydon et al. 2012), 'Everyday Urbanism' (Chase, Crawford, Kaliski 1999), 'Guerrilla Urbanism' (Hou 2010), 'DIY Urbanism' and many other titles have had limited purchase, as each highlights one aspect and interest at the expense of others (Wortham-Galvin 2013; Lydon et al. 2012: 1). Here, the loose movement will be referred to as 'the participatory movement', because the issue of participation is at the centre of this particular study. Yet not all the members of this loose movement actively pursue citizen participation, nor necessarily approve of it.

Many of the 'activist' architects have turned to theories that had been central circa 1968 but were marginalized or co-opted following the demise of the radical movement: theories of participation (Davidoff, de Carlo, Arnstein), of everyday life (Lefebvre, De Certeau), of radical democracy (Mouffe, Habermas, Negri and Hardt, Ranciére), of 'anti-statism' (Negri and Hardt), and 'the right to the city' (Lefebvre, Harvey). While there are many overlaps of interests between the previous generation committed to participatory practices and the young architects in question, the latter are distinctive in bringing together these parallel 1960s interests, in their unsettled approach to issues of state, economy, and politics, in the predominance of contingent practices, in the significant exchanges with artists and other 'creatives'; and in a more pronounced anti-statist position (Wright 2002: 1).

The work of this movement has been studied and theorized so far primarily in two forms: a type of 'operative criticism' (Tafuri 1980: 141), which provides theoretical legitimacy to the participatory movement (e.g. Chase, Crawford, Kaliski 1999; Hou 2010; Cuff and Sherman 2011; Lydon et al. 2012; Oswalt, Overmeyer, Misselwitz 2013), and more recent, critical research, focused on measuring the demonstrable impact of specific case studies. In contrast to the 'operative criticism', the analyses and critique developed from case studies is often sharp and poignant. While the former offers a theoretical means of framing the movement, the latter questions aspects of its practice. In the following section, another route will be taken: a close study of the political theory which sustains the work of these politically and socially committed 'spatial practitioners'.[13] This study will lead to an examination of the relation of theory to praxis, highlighting some challenges in transposing abstract political theory to concrete urban and architectural practices. Certain contradictions posed by the diverse ideas and theories that are labelled here 'radical democracy', as in the case of the aforementioned Berlage masterclass, will be brought to the fore, inadvertently also highlighting important questions and issues that the new participatory movement has mostly avoided addressing, questions that could compromise the entire project of transforming the city and society.

In particular, the question addressed here is whether the theory and practice of the diverse 'spatial practitioners' involved in the new participatory movement should be seen as part and parcel of the contemporary neoliberal order or as its antagonist. While this question, as will be demonstrated, cannot be answered with strong affirmation or rejection, it will become clear that the major antagonist of the movement is not neoliberalism, as some of the statements made by the protagonists suggest, but the nation state.

The following chapter, 'Theories of Participation', will discuss the discontents regarding planning processes and consultations, and delineate political theories which foreground participation and deliberation. At the centre will be the question of urban and social transformation through agreement and consensus. 'Theories of Contestation', the subsequent chapter, will look into political theories that emphasize conflict and contest, as well as at the attempts to transpose the theories to urban practice. The last chapter, 'Praxis', will study three firms associated with the participatory movement: Lacaton and Vassal, Atelier d´Architecture Autogérée (aaa) and Assemble. It will end with the argument that personalization is an instrument of satisfying some of the discontents animating participation while circumventing some of the conundrums of participatory practices.

The purpose here is to study this contemporary movement at a point in which it is still mutating and developing, to assess its successes and failures, its potential to radically transform society and possible pitfalls. There is no intention to produce a critique of practice by theory, but, rather, to assess the work's efficacy in order to prevent co-optation in the future, to promote practices which support the steering of city and society in the most positive sense, and to avoid practices that expand neoliberalism and its negative effects – urban poverty, spatial segregation, and the curtailing of dissent.

THEORIES OF PARTICIPATION

Participation and Agency

> [P]articipation needs to transform architectural planning from the authoritarian act which it has been up to now, into a process.
>
> *(Giancarlo de Carlo 2005: 16)*

'What do we understand by public participation?' the group Laboratorio Urbano asks rhetorically:

> We formulate it as the ability and right of the inhabitants of a certain place to analyse, criticise and transform the environment in which they live. The processes of decision making usually occur without taking into account the people who will be affected by its consequences, and therefore many of these decisions do not correspond to their real needs.
>
> *(AAA and PEPRAV 2007: 178)*

Such demands for citizen participation in decisions affecting the built environment have figured prominently in the discussions of the new, politically committed movement. The return to participatory architecture and urbanism has often blurred disciplinary boundaries between activism, art, architecture and urbanism. Whereas 'artistic models of democracy have only a tenuous relationship to actual forms of democracy', as art critic Claire Bishop has argued convincingly (Bishop 2012: 5), in the realm of the built environment, the relation of democratic models to architectural and urban practice is less haphazard, though certainly requires much elaboration and scrutiny.

There is a twofold argument driving participation: the first, and major, is that the empowerment of citizens in decision-making regarding the built environment is a value – is *just* – in its own right, which is a moral argument focused on process, while the second suggests that the involvement of citizens guarantees better quality of built environment, focused on product (Jenkins and Forsyth 2010: 9–22). The former argument addresses the political aspect of participation: the demand for furthering democratization by expanding the territories under the direct control of the public (Dryzek 2000b: 83). The latter has a technocratic rather than political overtone – participation as a 'best practice' of sorts, a technical issue, a means to an end.

To a certain extent, the current *artistic* participatory movement is the logical progression of the original ideas of the historic avant-garde: merging art with life. This idea, applied very differently by 1920s Dada (Duchamp) and Constructivism (Tatlin), mutated by the 1960s to the desire to enrich and elevate daily life via art (Beuys, Kaprow), and a little later to a profound interest in the ephemeral, the fleeting, and the everyday (Kawara, González-Torres) (Kaminer 2011a: 117–28). Participatory art thus takes the additional step of reducing the role of the artist to a facilitator of life, to an enabler instead of creator, focusing on the issues that are central to 'mundane' daily life and eschewing the expectation that art transcends life.

The parallel contemporary movement within architecture is more directly related to its artistic sibling than to the architectural avant-gardes of the 1920s and 1960s. The latter understood the merging of art and life as a merging of building and city, of architecture and urbanism, creating a continuum of building and city in order to rectify a fragmented society and city. The dissolution of art into life in the contemporary movement is echoed in the aforementioned desire to dissolve architecture into 'spatial practices' with little or no disciplinary distinctions and specificities (Miessen and Basar 2006), as well as in the intense focus on everyday life – on architecture that is not first and foremost functional or symbolic, but creates a very different mix of the cultural, the aesthetic, the utilitarian, and the representational.

In contrast to the historic architectural avant-garde, here the singular building is not undermined. Its formal autonomy is preserved as an expression of pluralism and diversity – hence the fascination with the informal city, self-build and the 'unplanned'.[14] Despite these diversions from the historic avant-garde, a shared position is evident in the modus operandi of the architects in question, active in small firms, as cutting edge, committed practitioners operating, at least until recently, on the margins of disciplinary recognition.

The basic argument at the heart of participation, however, undermines the logic of the avant-garde. Developed from the ideas of Henri Comte de Saint-Simon, both artistic and political avant-gardes exalt a condition in which an enlightened elite leads society's progress by steering it in the right direction. Hence Leninist and similar ideas regarding the role of the Communist Party as a vanguardist party of experts who steer the revolution. '[M]ass democratic practice […],' emphasized political theorists Ernesto Laclau and Chantal Mouffe, 'shuns vanguardist manipulation' (Laclau and Mouffe 2001: 58). The vanguard position is thus antithetical to the demand for empowering the people via democratization. Saint-Simon's conception of an enlightened elite of artists, architects, scientists and the like who can identify society's needs and the means of addressing them, derives from a deep suspicion and doubt – 'elitist', in populist jargon – of the ability of 'lay' citizens to identify their own needs, priorities, and the adequate means of satisfying them.[15] The contrasting argument appears almost benign in its logic and common sense: why not let the citizens decide for themselves? Why dictate top-down instead of empowering the citizens? Why should individual and collective sovereignty be delegated to an elite?

It should be of little surprise, then, that the avant-garde shares with technocracy a rejection of democratic principles. Saint-Simon's elite was, after all, not only the origins of the idea of the avant-garde, but a technocracy: enlightened experts, making the right decisions for society's progress and betterment – suggesting not merely a lack of democracy, but the expulsion of the political. 'The administration of things', the phrase originally used by the Saint-Simonian Auguste Comte, and later deployed by Engels and others (Kafka 2012), perfectly captures the apolitical character of such technocracy. Participation is thus posited against technocracy and the avant-garde, delegitimizing both, and attempting to politicize and democratize spheres of life previously outside popular control.

In the negotiation between expert and amateur, which is at the centre of the participatory process in architecture, the architect typically attempts to steer the process by controlling the issues discussed. Most importantly, the process is aimed at avoiding the discussion of issues related to taste. Taste can hardly be discussed rationally. It reflects identity – first and foremost class rather than individual identity, consolidated through family socialization. 'Architects' values are often very different from those of the public', commented Amos Rapoport, stating a truism (1968: 300). Taste also reflects other factors, as Pierre Bourdieu argued in his seminal study (Bourdieu 2003), including level of education and type of education, themselves, to no small degree, reflecting class. These are significant in pitting the architect against the lay person regarding preferences that cannot be reduced to rational functional or technical considerations, and therefore cannot be 'deliberated' rationally.[16]

Yet the difference in 'taste' between architect and citizen, and the difficulty to reconcile this difference, is not the only issue here. Non-experts tend to affirm the existing: typically desired are the aspects of the built environment that function as signs of high social standings, signs that communicate social 'respectability'. Such signs are culturally, socially and collectively produced, and are therefore subjugated to society's imaginary, to its self-image and aspirations. Experts, occupying a key stratum of technical specialization, also tend to affirm the existing: they accept the limiting framework within which they operate, treating it as a 'given'. In effect, then, the positions of both experts and lay citizens tend to affirm current conditions. What is affirmed by these groups, though, are very different secondary symbolic forms, as Bourdieu called those forms derived from a primary symbolic form, such as capitalism, dependent on it and supporting it. The difference between the secondary symbolic forms that are affirmed by local residents and experts derive from the same issues identified by Bourdieu as responsible for taste: class, family, education, and profession. The differences articulate the diversity of fluid, overlapping, and contingent identities of which societies are composed. It is little wonder that producing urban transformation through collective will and consensus is challenging, particularly when 'change' is understood as substantial, and when ambitions go beyond accepted normative ideas of quality.

Related to the concern regarding affirmation and change is another issue: the presumption that the individuals who make up society reflect its mediocrity and compromise in their ideals as well as their taste. In other words, the proposition that society constructs the individual subjects, their ideals, identities and taste. This line of thought is present in the work of the Frankfurt School, among others, in which autonomy relapses into heteronomy and 'identical thought' dominates.[17] Here, the 'common sense' proposition of participation – empower citizens to make meaningful decisions – appears as a trap of sorts, as a means of merely affirming what already exists by using the veneer of democracy and empowerment. The 'empowered' citizens, it is presumed, would merely select more of the same rather than usher in radical change.

Such pessimism is castigated as elitism by proponents of participation (Fausch 2011). Two contrasting views emerge: the first, a Kantian humanism, suggesting that citizens are autonomous, reasonable individuals, who can exercise their free will and reason and reach a measured decision, and the second, post-humanist, in which citizens lack autonomy, and their supposedly individual, subjective beliefs, desires, and even forms of reasoning are constructed by society through socialization and assimilation. While these are merely caricatures of the actual positions in circulation, arguments fall on one side or the other of this divide: either they overemphasize the autonomy of individual subjects, or they overstress individuals' subjugation to society.

This issue goes far beyond the question of architectural or urban participation, leading to democracy itself: if, in external conditions that include the needed legalities, citizens cannot, in fact, exercise a significant degree of free will, if citizens merely demand what society expects them to demand – what then is the value of democracy? Or, phrased differently: a democracy that provides the legalities that technically enable free voting, but prevents the formation of free thought, is perhaps not a democracy in the first place. The post-humanist critics of contemporary society, ranging from Frankfurt School scholars to Bourdieu and Foucault, have painted a bleak image of a society in which the diverse 'freedoms' it claims are vacuous, a society in which individuals lack any meaningful autonomy, in which true 'free thought', Kantian-humanist 'free will' and 'pure reason' are merely myths. This important question can be furthered, of course, but it is necessary to turn here away from the abyss. The reconciliation of humanism and post-humanism is beyond the remit of this book; rather, a general acknowledgement is required of the condition of participatory architecture in which by sanctioning citizens' opinions it risks producing 'affirmative' architecture and urban development.

The conventional idea of 'lay' citizens being informed by experts and subsequently, after debate and discussion, making an informed decision, is at the heart of the participatory movement, and Jürgen Habermas's 'deliberative democracy', which will be discussed below, is of particular relevance here: the ideal of forming a level plateau for discussion and the veneration of a discussion that focuses on the rational issues that can allow a fruitful exchange and debate (Habermas 1996a; Benhabib 1996a). All this is relevant to the 'common sense' proposition at the heart of participation, that is, that citizens ought to have the power to shape their own cities. But how do non-experts – here, non-architects or urbanists – develop the necessary knowledge to be able to make well-informed, reasoned, meaningful decisions? Such questions form the subtext for this chapter, but at the fore of concern here is the political theory that informs contemporary spatial practitioners. The political theories most widely read by the advocates of participation are by Jürgen Habermas, Chantal Mouffe, Antonio Negri and Michael Hardt, Jacques Rancière, Giorgio Agamben, and, particularly among young Greeks, Cornelius Castoriadis. Political theory is not the only source of theoretical material animating the architects. Other influences include the work of Henri Lefebvre, Michel de Certeau, Isabelle Stengers, J.K. Gibson-Graham, 'Non-Plan' by Reyner Banham et al., and a wealth of 1960s participatory literature ranging from Giancarlo de Carlo to Sherry Arnstein. Theory plays an important part in the discourse produced by those involved in the loose movement. It offers a common language, shared terms, and an intellectual means of developing a discussion that targets the issues that are most important to 'participatory' practitioners. This chapter will specifically look at political theory that advocates and foregrounds participation and ideas of civil society. Such theories interrogate the diverse forms in which an agreement or consensus can be reached through processes and procedures which must satisfy demands for their legitimacy.

Citizens' Will

In the immediate post-war years in which planning enjoyed significant power, planners and planning agencies considered their work to be benevolent, technical and apolitical (P. Marcuse 2013). The harsh critique of planning and urban development that was initiated in the 1960s in the United States by Jane Jacobs and others disrupted this uncritical position. 'Advocacy planner' Paul Davidoff argued in 1967 that:

> City planners and city planning commissioners have not openly avowed a set of political, social, or economic goals. It has been assumed that the professional planner, an expert in the field, would conscientiously serve the public interest. It has not been assumed that the public interest consists of diverse interest groups with competing ideas of what public policy is best; instead, it has been assumed that the public interest is unitary, and self-evident, and that political bias would only distort its interpretation.
>
> *(Davidoff 1993: 443)*

This critique emerged also in Britain, in arguments produced by John Turner, Maurice Broady, 'Non-Plan' and others. Banham and his colleagues argued that 'few of its [town and country planning's] procedures or value judgments have any sound basis, except delay. Why not have the courage, where practical, to let people shape their own environment?' (Banham et al. 1969: 435). The critique exposed planning decisions as inherently political, and called for empowering citizens in meaningful decisions regarding urban development and redevelopment. Planning surveys, which were in common use by government since the early 1950s, fell short of the demands for participation: they were carried out often after the completion of an urban development, were generic and uniform, and appeared to be part of the immense bureaucratic machine rather than a response to individual needs and desires. In August 1968, *AD* dedicated an issue to the 'Architecture of Democracy', with articles about squatter settlements in Latin America, among others. The squatter settlements were commended repeatedly for their 'freedoms'. The articles called for 'self-determination', the 'creative shaping of one's own environment', citizen participation and self-build. Later that year, Alison Smithson commented that '[t]he most popular phrase of the moment is "Citizen Participation",' and continued, disingenuously, '[n]o one knows what is meant by this' (Smithson 1968: 416).

Governments mostly responded to this critique by introducing new planning legislation and procedures. In Britain, the Planning Act 1968 (1969 in Scotland) included a statutory demand for consultation in the preparation of development plans. The Skeffington Report of 1969 proposed that planning authorities inform residents about local plans and hear their comments. But progress was limited. Local authorities were pressed to facilitate development, and had no desire to be embroiled in lengthy, contested processes. Protocols, procedures, and legislation were modified every few years, but the critics of the lack of public engagement were not satisfied, highlighting the shortcomings of the government's responses to their demands.

The United Nations' influential Agenda 21 action plan of 1992, centred on sustainable development, included the demand to enhance citizen participation and control. A key passage in the agenda was devoted to participation:

> 10.10. Governments at the appropriate level, in collaboration with national organizations and with the support of regional and international organizations, should establish

innovative procedures, programmes, projects and services that facilitate and encourage the active participation of those affected in the decision-making and implementation process, especially of groups that have, hitherto, often been excluded, such as women, youth, indigenous people and their communities and other local communities.

(United Nations 1992)

Agenda 21 and other concerns fed into the overhaul of British planning in 2004, with a particular focus on communities (Cullingworth and Nadin 2011: 256). The 2004 *Community Involvement in Planning: The Government's Objectives* was a significant document in this overhaul (BG 2004). Two key points stress that:

> 2.4 It is not enough to focus on providing information and consultation on proposals that have already been developed to the point where it is difficult to take other views on board.
> 2.5 Active participation in the development of options and proposals should be at the heart of the process. The community must be able to put forward and debate options and help mould proposals before they are settled. People need to feel that their participation can make a difference. This is challenging in terms of resources and effort, and means that councillors and planners have to be ready to listen and to adapt their own ideas. It is also important that all sides know just what to expect at each stage of the process, especially when there will be open debate on wide ranging options, or when consultation is focussed on specific propositions.

(BG 2004: 8)

In the spirit evoked by these two points in the *Community Involvement* document, the design 'charrette' has become a key tool for involving locals in the design phase, a means of 'front-loading' participation in contrast to the familiar post-design consultation, in which residents are presented with a fait accompli that they are asked to approve. Design charrettes vary widely, but the most familiar form is a meeting with members of a community, led by a professional – whether a communications consultant or designer – in which the locals face a specific set of questions, to which they respond via 'post it' notes. It is a form of 'controlled' brainstorming, directed to produce specific results and avoid sidetracking, digressing, or ending up with 'useless' reactions and comments. Charrettes are necessarily limited, as they require the investment of time by both professionals and locals, and tend to enable only a specific and narrow set of questions and responses of particular character. They rarely involve the entire community affected. They do not enable questioning the overall framework.

The critique of a democratic deficit within planning processes, then, has yielded some responses by governments, even if only partially satisfactory. Yet the democratic deficit is not an issue limited to planning. It is understood in political theory on one or more of three levels: 'the extent of effective franchise; the scope of issues under popular control; and the authenticity of that control' (Dryzek 2000: 83). In response to the deficits of the dominant liberal democracy, political theorists and activists have posited the idea of radical democracy. The demand for radical democracy has been voiced in the last few years by the *aganaktismenoi* at Syntagma Square in Athens, by the global Occupy movement (Figure 2.4), by the 15M group and *indignados* in Spain, by the Gezi Park protesters in Istanbul, and by the Tahrir Square demonstrators in Cairo – protest movements that have all emphasized issues of

FIGURE 2.4 Occupy Wall Street demonstration on 15 September 2012. Photograph by Paul Stein. Creative Commons: Attribution-ShareAlike 2.0 Generic (CC BY-SA 2.0).

self-organization and self-management, including experiments with direct democracy and diverse participatory practices:

> Assembled under the generic banner 'Real Democracy Now!' the gathered insurgents have expressed an extraordinary antagonism to the instituted – and often formally democratic – forms of governing, and have staged, performed and choreographed new configurations of the democratic. While often articulated around an emblematic quilting point (a threatened park, devastating austerity measures, the public bailout of irresponsible financial institutions, rising tuition fees, a price hike in public transport, and the like), these movements quickly universalised their claims to embrace a desire for a fully-fledged transformation of the political structuring of life, against the exclusive, oligarchic, and consensual governance of an alliance of professional economic, political and technocratic elites determined to defend the neoliberal order by any means necessary.
>
> *(Wilson and Swingedouw 2014b: 3)*

While currently associated first and foremost with the work of Chantal Mouffe, 'radical democracy' is an umbrella term that refers to diverse and competing political theories, all of which are animated by the perception of liberal democracy as flawed. Radical democracy, like the demand for citizens' participation, was significant to many of the May '68 protesters, and has been associated with the ultra-Left. It was also an idea the scholars of the Frankfurt School had deployed against the shortcomings of liberal democracy. More surprisingly, the Italian Communist Party (PCI), when restructuring itself after the Second World War, advocated ideas of radical democracy based on Gramsci's writings.[18] Similarly, Rodolfo

Morandi, a post-war leader of the Italian Socialist Party (PSI), advocated direct democracy (Wright 2002: 17), and Raniero Panzieri, a leading member of the PSI and an early theorist of Italian workerism, argued that the labour movement must be renovated '*from below* and in forms of *total democracy*' (Wright 2002: 18).

The political theory most often identified with architectural and urban participation is participatory democracy, a form of direct democracy, sometimes treated as a specific instance of republicanism or of 'associative democracy'. The republican model is committed to an idea of solidarity, to the formation of an idea of a 'common good' and the creation of a community on such a basis (Benhabib 1996c: 6; Habermas 1996b: 21–26). Sovereignty belongs to the citizens, and cannot be delegated, as in a representative system. Associative democracy, in turn, emphasizes a partial transfer of power from state to diverse associations – advocacy groups and other NGOs, representative bodies for industry and employees, professional bodies and so on, suggesting increasing citizens' active role in organizing and managing their communities. Such associations can enhance democracy, it is argued, by 'providing information to policy-makers; equalizing representation by putting forward the needs of those previously unheard; providing a political education to their members; and by helping to formulate and implement public policies – i.e., providing "alternative governance"' (Carter 2002: 233).

At the more radical end of the scale, the state is reduced to a mere skeleton – managing the field and ensuring fair play, equal access to resources and to the relevant associations (Carter 2002; Hirst 1994; Cohen and Rogers 1992). Associative democracy, therefore, generally weakens the state but does not dispose of it – the state remains a necessary mechanism. Representative democracy is not circumvented, but enhanced via increasing the forms of representation. Citizens are imagined as highly active, though the level of participation required to sustain and provide legitimacy to the system depends on the actual theory and practice in question (Carter 2002).

Whereas most theories of radical democracy privilege some form of civil society, in participatory democracy civil society is specifically understood as constructed by small-scale, face-to-face exchanges. The emphasis is on immediacy and on meaningful participation – that is, directly empowering the public in decision-making. The recent explosion of information technology-related participation, whether Web 2.0 sites or social media, has complicated matters: infused with ideas of participatory democracy, present already at the inception in the 1960s of Silicon Valley, the new technological tools posit the argument that virtual communities can replace the demand for face-to-face encounters, as in town hall meetings or the Athenian agora ideal.

In any case, the implementation of participatory practices in politics and in the built environment follows a logic that allows the broadening of the political field and prevents a clear demarcation of territories as 'political' and 'non-political'. The structures of decision-making that have to be created in order to enable urban participation are necessarily political, and, consequently, experimentations in participatory urbanism are also, beyond question, experiments in democratization.

Consensus and Discontent

Despite the wide implementation of participatory processes in planning, the dissatisfaction and disillusionment among citizens is wide. The spirit of active empowerment embedded in points 2.4 and 2.5 of the 2004 *Community Involvement in Planning*, cited above, is mostly absent in the actual practices of planning agencies. Studies have demonstrated that systems of resident notification regarding development plans in Britain fail to alert many locals, and that the actual effects of citizen participation on development are often minor, and experienced as negligible (Cullingworth and Nadin 2011; Coulson 2003; Edmundson 1993). A member of a local Edinburgh community council,[19] Paul Beswick, commented on developments in the council's area that:

> We engaged at every stage, we made representations and lobbied. However we had no effect on the outcomes of these many developments over many years. Were we just naïve to believe that we could make a difference? The community had a vision but the reality has been determined by the market. [...] The only conclusion to be drawn is that the current planning system pays lip service to community involvement.
>
> *(Symonds 2015)*

'Participation', wrote the editors of *Architecture and Participation* in 2005, 'becomes an organised (and potentially manipulated) part of any regeneration project, in which users are meant to be given a voice, but the process stifles the sounds coming out' (Blundell Jones, Petrescu, Till 2005b: xiv).

The condition in other countries is hardly better. The setting up of local community councils in 1960s France and other measures taken by the Ministry of Reconstruction to widen participation were seen at the time by Lefebvre as a 'mystification of pseudo-democracy' (Stanek 2015: 123). In the United States, the reaction to the critique of planning in the 1960s was to empower the specific advocacy groups that criticized planning procedures. Community Development Corporations (CDCs) were originally created as civil society grass roots organizations, and since the 1970s they have been increasingly empowered by local government. The New Community Corporation in Newark, an example of such a CDC, has since its inception in 1968 provided and managed public housing, retirement homes, day care facilities, retraining programmes and much more (Kaminer 2011b; Choi 2011). But this perfectly suited the retrenchment of government as part of the 'roll-back neoliberalism' of the 1980s, and allowed government to outsource responsibility and liability to the third sector. CDCs and similar organizations were required to compete in tenders for grants, assimilated into a competitive free-market environment. The resources available to such CDCs have shrunk rather than grown, and advocacy groups lost their ability to critique government. In this sense, while citizens' organizations in the United States have experienced a growth in their power vis-à-vis city councils, state, and federal government, their actual ability to produce positive transformation has been extremely limited (Mayer 2011). Hence, a problematic trade-off has taken place in the United States: more freedom and power to locals to self-organize, but at the price of assimilation into a free-market system, a localism that prevents redistribution, and depleting resources that undermine the possibility of significant change.

In Britain, as well as in much of Western Europe, the institutionalization of participation has brought about only increasing frustrations. Consultations are constant, but results seem to locals pitiful. In Edinburgh's Portobello, following success by residents in blocking a development of a mega-supermarket in 2005, a rigorous consultation process in 2007–8 led to the council's 'North West Portobello Development Brief' that restricted retail in the area in question to a corner shop (ECC 2008: 3.8). Yet in 2014 the city council approved a plan for a new supermarket on the site. Locals in Edinburgh's South Side convinced the city to reject a plan for more student housing in the area, only to be overturned in 2015 on appeal by Scottish Government planning. Unable to appeal planning decisions, lacking resources and expertise to fight development, a planning system set on supporting development rather than local concerns – community councils have imploded, rebellious advocacy groups such as Planning Democracy expanded, and the general impression that consultation is mostly a form of 'tokenism', as Sherry Arnstein termed such processes (Arnstein 1969), has taken hold. Rather than empowering the local population, the ubiquitous consultations have created an enhanced experience of disempowerment and anomie, which have, in turn, enhanced the ambitions of the participatory movement.

Dissatisfaction, then, is widespread, and it is not limited to the built environment and to urban development. In reaction to the failures of liberal democracy, the protestors in Syntagma Square and Zuccotti Park experimented with alternative forms of democracy. Much effort was placed on process and procedures in order to guarantee free speech and enable reaching agreements. Predominantly, though not exclusively, these were experiments in forms of deliberative democracy, a theory formulated by the Frankfurt School philosopher Jürgen Habermas.[20]

The conception of 'radical democracy' by the scholars of the 'first generation' of the Frankfurt School remained mostly vague and undeveloped (Chambers 2004). Martin Jay has written that 'Critical Theory's holistic, syncretic outlook prevented it from developing a theory of specifically *political* authority' (Jay 1972: 118). In contrast, Habermas has written extensively about 'deliberative democracy', which is, in effect, a form of radical democracy. The study of deliberative democracy has expanded significantly since the publication in 1996 of Habermas's influential book *Between Facts and Norms*. Political theorists such as Selya Benhabib and John Dryzek have broadened and refined the Habermasian argument, attempting to step closer to a theory of praxis (Dryzek 1990, 2000a, 2000b; Benhabib 1996a). In 2000, Chantal Mouffe commented that deliberative democracy 'is currently the fastest-growing trend in the field' (Mouffe 2013b: 191).

Deliberative democracy shares certain ideas and characteristics with participatory democracy – namely, the argument that the political moment should unfold within society itself, in contrast to liberal democracy, in which the political moment occurs in a secluded territory of institutional politics, by representatives who are legitimized as an indirect 'channelling' of the aggregate of citizens' will. Deliberative democracy shares with Enlightenment understandings the conception of political and state institutions as a technical expression or direct extension of civil society itself, as well as egalitarianism as a prerequisite condition for democracy (Habermas 1996a: 182).

Meaningful exchanges and deliberations in inclusive conditions of relative social and economic equality are central to the creation of such a deliberative democracy. Participation theories often focus on the decision-making process, on the act of public empowerment and will formation, rather than on the creation of a level group for deliberation. In contrast, deliberative democracy remains underdeveloped regarding the reorganizing of the institutional means of channelling the conclusions of the deliberations into concrete actions, to the extent that the political theorist William E. Scheuerman commented that 'Habermasian deliberative democracy remains profoundly ambiguous in its political and institutional ramifications' (Scheuerman 2006: 87).

In further contrast to participatory democracy and its preference for the small-scale and immediate, Habermas's theory can accommodate ideas of global government, a strengthening of the United Nations or similar global institutes (Scheuerman 2006: 91), as its point of departure is the broadening of the ideal of the democratic general assembly or agora beyond the temporal and geographical confines of such meeting procedures. Iris Young and David Held in particular, who have developed their theories from Habermas's work, have focused on the building of new global institutions and the global redistribution of resources necessary for the creation of the prerequisite level field for global deliberation (Young 1996; Scheuerman 2006: 95).

While for many of the participants of the recent protest movements existing institutions of power are seen as hostile, deliberative democracy is more ambivalent in its approach. Habermas can accommodate representational forms of democracy as a pragmatic means of improvement. Yet deliberative democracy sustains suspicions of abuse of power, of power that acts in its own interests rather than as an extension of civil society. Dryzek specifically warned of co-optation by existing formal institutions (Dryzek 2000: 78–81). Habermas has emphasized the anti-statist idea of a decentred society, and has written that unlike liberal democracy, '[t]his concept of democracy no longer needs to operate with the notion of a social whole centered in the state and imagined as a goal-oriented subject writ at large' (Habermas 1996b: 27).

Dryzek chastised deliberative democracy's proximity to liberal democracy, claiming that Habermas's theory merely enabled citizens' influence rather than facilitating citizens' power:

> In [Habermas's] *Between Facts and Norms* we see a model of democracy that is otherwise quite consistent with the liberal constitutionalist model, in particular because a liberal constitution is regarded as necessary to protect and nurture the opinion-formation capacities of the public sphere.
>
> *(Dryzek 2000: 82)*

Habermasian deliberative democracy, Dryzek concluded, is 'safe for dominant forms of politics' (Dryzek 2000: 78). Scheuerman commented that 'deliberative influence does not a democracy make' (Scheuerman 2006: 94). In this sense, Habermas's theory can be described as a pragmatic attempt to rectify the political system by retrieving some of Enlightenment's lost promises. In this endeavour, Habermas's delineation of a democratic horizon has been compromised, to a degree, by his pragmatics, bringing his ideal condition too close to existing liberal democracy.

Dryzek, in contrast, in developing his own proposition for a 'discursive democracy', emphasizes the necessity of a critical dimension – he uses the terms 'argumentative' and 'reflective' to describe the necessary components of such a democracy (Dryzek 2000: 78–79). Argumentation is generally favoured by deliberative democrats, preferred to bargaining or voting – typical of liberal democracy; 'consensus' is not a requirement, as 'agreement' can suffice. Another scholar who has developed Habermas's ideas is Seyla Benhabib. Key requirements for democratic deliberation, she claims, are equality on all levels of participation, coupled by the right of all to question the topics, the rules of the discussion, and the procedures and processes involved (Benhabib 1996b: 70; Scheuerman 2006: 95). The process of deliberation is central to democratic legitimacy, she argues; it is deliberation which forces citizens to think reflexively, to order their thoughts and positions, to develop a rational argument, and to hear and consider others' opinions and positions. Consequently, deliberation itself has value beyond the question of collective will-formation or decision-making.

The emphasis in deliberative democracy on process and procedures enables society to accommodate difference. Benhabib stresses that:

> Agreements in societies living with value-pluralism are to be sought for not at the level of substantive beliefs but at that of procedures, processes, and practices for attaining and revising beliefs. Proceduralism is a rational answer to persisting value conflicts at the substantive level.
>
> *(Benhabib 1996b: 73)*

Benhabib does not suggest deliberative democracy as a large-scale town-hall meeting, but as an ongoing and continuous engagement, discussion, and debate among a plurality of associations and networks, taking place neither at a specific, limited time nor at a specific locus or institution (Benhabib 1996b: 73–74).

Liberal democracy is anchored in legalistic-constitutional mechanisms to ensure minority and individual rights are protected; Sheldon S. Wolin argues that such constitutionalism has acted, historically, as a means of attaining basic legitimacy while limiting genuine democracy (Wolin 1996: 36–37). Deliberative democracy, in contrast, posits that an agreement reached by 'the *freely given assent of all concerned*' necessarily protects the rights of minorities (Benhabib 1996b: 79). In other words, the protection is embedded in the procedure and process rather than being dependent on an external legalistic mechanism.

Whereas Habermas and Benhabib stress the 'subject-less' aspect of deliberative democracy, which suggests an accommodation of real pluralism, Scheuerman points out (Scheuerman 2006: 98) that the model does not necessarily succeed in avoiding the 'repression' of pluralism caused by the inevitable need for a unified voice. Decision-making requires a process that must at some stage reduce the plurality of voices into a specific outcome. Avoiding the formation of a single, unified voice suggests also an evasion of the truly political – deliberative democracy's emphasis on inclusive civic discussion rather than on the mechanisms of power-distribution and self-legislation, its preference for reason as the basis for genuine deliberation, at the expense of the irrational and the symbolic, which are a key to the political moment.

This chapter has highlighted the rancour and discontent of citizens regarding the 'tokenism' of planning consultations and the failures of liberal democracy. It outlined political theories that address the question of participation – participatory, associative, and deliberative democratic theories – and raised concerns about their shortcomings. And it brought to the fore the conundrum of humanism and post-humanism, a conundrum that casts a shadow over the logic of participation.

THEORIES OF CONTESTATION

The Global

> There is nothing, no 'naked life', no external standpoint, that can be posed outside this field permeated by money, nothing escapes money.
>
> *(Michael Hardt and Antonio Negri 2000: 32)*

The desire to channel the needs and demands voiced by citizens rather than 'impose' solutions is at the heart of participatory practices. Not all the committed architects, however, deploy participatory practices, and some are unequivocally opposed to participation. Many related practices, such as yarn-bombing or guerrilla gardening, are carried out without any public consent, whether official or unofficial. And while yarn-bombing or seed-bombing are activities that raise only marginal opposition, if at all, other practices disrupt the consensus and confront public opinion. Jeffrey Hou opens the anthology *Insurgent Public Space* (2010) with a description of 'an eight foot long metal pig that was anonymously planted on a sidewalk overnight' in Fremont. Such individual, transgressive acts display a disregard for or rebellion against public opinion, 'an attack on the official public sphere' (Hou 2010: 1). The placing of the pig was an act that was not legitimized as citizens' will. In the opposition by such actions to consensus, they form a counterpart to practices that are validated through consensus. Consensus-driven participation and anti-consensual engagement, hence, are intertwined, the former perceiving public opinion as the source of legitimacy, the latter perceiving it as illegitimate, a reflection of dominant ideologies. Whereas the practitioners who exalt participatory practices tend to turn to Habermas's theory and see their role as facilitators of citizens' will, those who eschew consensus opinion often turn to theories that highlight contestation, such as the political theories of Mouffe or Rancière, which will be discussed later in this chapter. Hardt and Negri, in contrast, argue that transformation is achieved through contestation 'from within' current conditions, whereas 'popular' sovereignty and its consensual impetus is rejected.[21] The celebration of the global condition that is at the centre of the political project of Hardt and Negri is driven by their animosity to the nation state. The social historian Michael Merrill suggested that 'the central thrust of all their [Hardt and Negri's] work has been an attack on the state and its accompanying conceptions of sovereignty' (Merrill 2010: 150).

The participatory movement has mostly focused on the local – a scale that enables direct engagement, a grounding in place and specificity, a sense of 'the real' and authenticity. Yet, just as deliberative democracy allows scaling up the process of deliberation, the philosopher Antonio Negri, an activist in the 1960s and 1970s and founder of the Italian *Autonomia* movement, has engaged directly with the question of the global in his conception of the idea of a contemporary 'empire'. He has provided theoretical grounding to the emerging protest movement with his popular books *Empire*, *Multitude* and *Commonwealth*, co-written with Michael Hardt.[22] These works have circulated via the protest movements and reached a broad readership, including many of the politically committed architects (Querrien, Petrescu and Petcou 2007). While participatory, associative and deliberative political theories are in many senses closer to urban practices than the work of Hardt and Negri, books such as *Empire* supplied a wider narrative to participatory endeavours, anchoring them in a larger, global movement.

The 1960s 'workerist' group of the Italian Left from which Negri emerged, acknowledged that post-war ('Keynesian') capitalism created better living and working conditions for the working class; that capitalism itself reacted to – and therefore was determined by, to some extent, the pressures and demands of organized labour (Tronti 2012a). Figures such as Raniero Panzieri and Mario Tronti outlined the manner in which capitalism had dismantled opposition by inclusiveness and reformism, to the extent that an 'outside' no longer existed. Throughout the 1960s and 1970s workerism (*Operaismo*) developed and mutated, with Negri leading in the 1970s the radical *Potere Operaio* and breaking with Tronti and his colleagues, who opted to operate within the Italian Communist Party (PCI). The theoretical positions of Tronti and the workerist movement are still present in *Empire*, *Multitude* and *Commonwealth*, though in a somewhat modified manner. The contrasting in this chapter of *Empire* with early workerism serves to argue that *Empire* and its sequels are anchored in ideas originally developed against the conditions of post-war Europe. The argument suggests that the nation state – originally the Keynesian, welfare state – rather than capitalism is the adversary of Negri, and that his work is, in many ways, an ally rather than an antagonist of neoliberal theories and policies.

At the centre of the workerism of the early 1960s was the question of class composition, and the attempt to oppose the PCI doctrine of hegemony through mass movement by a refocusing on workers and the working class (Wright 2002). Tronti perceived Keynesian state capitalism to be a form of 'neocapitalism' in which capital became increasingly dependent upon organized labour. The government, the trade unions, the Italian Socialist Party (PSI) and elements in the PCI were all seen as accomplices of capitalist development – accomplices of the forces dedicated to workers' integration and the prevention of class war by exalting 'development'. The core instrument of integration and development was 'the plan of capital' (hence, 'The Plan'), a term used by Tronti to cover all forms of planning and *planisme* (Tronti 2012b). Tronti envisaged change from within, by workers taking advantage of the capitalists' dependence upon them: exploiting the conditions created by state capitalism. Similarly, already in *Empire*'s opening pages, Hardt and Negri accept the current conditions in their generality, and argue that a radical alternative can and will emerge *within* rather than against the framework of global capitalism: 'the only strategy available to the struggles is of a constituent counterpower that emerges from within Empire' (Hardt and Negri 2000: 59).

The 1960s rereading of Marx in Italy and elsewhere, animated by the crisis of socialism as much as by the recent publication of Marx's *Grundrisse*, faced specific challenges: led by politically involved intellectuals, it was interested in identifying a role for the political, yet it faced the assumption of orthodox Marxism that the structural base determines all aspects of society and the lack of agency in the writings of the Frankfurt School and Althusser (Murphy 2010). Tronti conceived of a theory of 'instances' or 'levels', in which each 'instance' within society enjoys some level of autonomy from the structural base. In later work, he posited 'the autonomy of the political', claiming that politics can take part in shaping society independently of the structural base.[23] This seemed evident enough in the post-war European condition, in which, following the implementation of technocratic planning and Keynesian theory, governments had significant control of society and the economy.

Another issue that emerged from the rereading of Marx in the 1960s was the process of transformation of mode of production. Marx's historical materialism suggested that transformation occurs once the mode of production reaches a stage in which its means of production progress beyond a certain threshold, transcending the existing mode and ushering in a new one. This argument was obscured in the inter-war years, in which the Soviet Union claimed that socialism was an advanced means of speeding the development of the forces of production. Tronti returned to this earlier understanding and reformulated it, claiming that 'the idea of searching for the salvation of the workers everywhere except in the further development of capitalism is a reactionary idea' (Aureli 2008: 32).

In *Empire*, the necessity of the current mode of production, capitalism, is tied to the idea of immanence as much as to the Marxist idea of 'necessity'. 'Necessity' here refers to the conception of necessary historical linear development, such as in the case of transformation from traditional to capitalist to socialist society. 'Immanence', as a concept, goes beyond its literal meaning, and infers a form of 'becoming', a condition in which something – a movement, an idea, a condition – is impregnated with something else that it is about to become. Laclau has pointed out that the idea of immanence first emerged as a solution to the theological debate regarding the existence of evil in a world dominated by a God who is supposedly good and all-powerful (Laclau 2004: 22–23). Scotus Erigena's solution was that there was no evil, but, rather, necessary stages on God's route to divine perfection. Similar ideas of immanence exist also, Laclau reminds his readers, in Hegel and Marx – and, in a more explicit manner, also in *Empire*.

The idea that capitalism needs to be exacerbated in order to transform into socialism typically leads to a fatalistic view of history and to an absence of human agency, culminating in a demand for 'quietism': essentially, the argument suggests that any battle against capitalism and victories over it postpone its demise, and therefore are futile, or worse, a hindrance to overcoming capitalism. In particular, such a conception of change undermines the argument for political action and dissent. For this reason, such 'fatalist' theses have been opposed by figures such as Laclau and Mouffe (Laclau and Mouffe 1985; Valentine 2003: 206).

Hardt and Negri attempt to avoid such fatalism by emphasizing the liberatory operations within the system of global capitalism, fostered by empowered human subjects, operations which accept the basic premise of the global, neoliberal condition, and which have the potential of giving birth to an alternative reality from within the flawed existing one by advancing its causes:

> A new sense of being is imposed on the constitution of Empire by the creative movement of the multitude, or really it is continually present in this process as an alternative paradigm. It is internal to Empire and pushes forward its constitution, not as

a negative that constructs a positive or any such dialectical resolution. Rather it acts as an absolutely positive force that pushes the dominating power toward an abstract and empty unification, to which it appears as the distinct alternative.

(Hardt and Negri 2000: 62)

Hardt and Negri's observation that '[i]n the constitution of Empire there is no longer an "outside" to power' is less controversial (Hardt and Negri 2000: 58). The identification of a systematic dissolution of an 'outside' to contemporary society is an observation made also by figures such as Herbert Marcuse (1969), Hannah Arendt (1960), and Michel Foucault (1991).[24] Negri succeeds in recovering an idea of progress and in circumventing the contemporary Left's dependence on memories of an idealized past, but at the price of a questionable alliance with free-market ideology. Art critic and commentator Malcolm Bull underlines the proximity of Hardt and Negri's thought to neoliberalism, quoting from *Empire*: 'It is our turn now to cry "Big government is over!" Why should that slogan be the exclusive property of the conservatives?' (Hardt and Negri 2000: 349; Bull 2001).

Bull identifies a fissure within the anti-globalization movement, namely, a conflict between the demand for social justice and a demand for freedom. Negri is associated with the latter, and for this reason his work is infused with similar thoughts to the ones that prevail in neoliberal theory, itself typically legitimized via a questionable claim to 'freedom'. Bull responded to Negri by noting that:

> Because Hardt and Negri's version of republican liberty is a theory of power rather than of rights it doesn't easily translate into talk of duties. (Unlike [political theorist Quentin] Skinner, they can't call for laws forcing us to exercise our rights.) Furthermore, their analysis of power is not one that lends itself to judgments about the way it should be exercised.
>
> *(Bull 2001)*

Whereas Marx was an important influence on Negri's early work (Negri 2003; 2005), here Spinoza's philosophy plays a central part (Merrill 2010). Spinoza's 'multitude' replaces the proletariat as the protagonist of the historic transformation; class ceases to be a relevant category. The multitude already possesses the power (*potentia*), *Empire* argues, and consequently, following Spinoza's thought regarding God, also sovereignty (*potestas*). It is in this sense that 'freedom' is embedded already in a state of nature – that is, a basic possession of power by every individual – and therefore power allegedly exists prior to the social formation. Bull argues that Hardt's and Negri's focus on power rather than rights, and their avoidance of judging the execution of power are:

> inherited from Spinoza, whose theological metaphysics dictated that, since all power is God's power, power must be co-extensive with natural right. In a state of nature everyone has as much right as they have the power to exercise, limited only by the antagonistic power of others. The formation of the commonwealth involves no transfer of natural right to the sovereign (as in social contract theory), merely an aggregation of power, and thus of right, that increases the power of the commonwealth over nature and over the individuals within it. Civil right is natural right and natural right is power.
>
> *(Bull 2001)*

There is a significant concern whether Hardt and Negri have indeed overcome the fatalism implicit in the propagation of the 'necessity' of the current mode of production. The authors suggest, after all, that the masses – or 'the multitude' – are already empowered:

> Don't we already possess 'arms' and 'money'? The kind of money that Machiavelli insists is necessary may in fact reside in the productivity of the multitude, the immediate actor of biopolitical production and reproduction. The kind of arms in question may be contained in the potential of the multitude to sabotage and destroy with its own productive force the parasitical order of postmodern command.
> *(Hardt and Negri 2000: 65–66)*

The idea that the multitude is already empowered recalls Tronti's major theory. His 'strategy of refusal' was based on the argument that workers were already empowered, that they had the autonomy to act politically: as capital depended on productive labour, workers could choose to refuse work, and therefore held, in effect, the bourgeoisie and capitalism hostage (Tronti 2010: 346–52). When Hardt and Negri write '[t]he poor itself is power. There is World Poverty, but there is above all World Possibility, and only the poor is capable of this' (Hardt and Negri 2000: 157), the empowerment of the multitude becomes merely a rhetorical device which suggests that a consciousness of the innate power *already residing* in every singular person, however marginalized, is the crucial step forward, and that actions by 'the rich', the powerful, the privileged are completely unnecessary. The conclusions could follow quite a different path than the one Negri proposes: that the poor are 'undeserving' because they already have the power to change their circumstances but have not applied it; that the privileged are not required to aid the poor. The subaltern class needs first and foremost to develop a consciousness of its own power. Nevertheless, for all Negri's propagating of an 'inside', he has never abandoned the idea of contestation in the most diametrical of terms. 'The problem is to know what side you are on,' he argued, 'on the side of the power of life that resists, or on the side of its biopolitical exploitation' (Querrien, Petrescu and Petcou 2007: 291).

In 2009, Negri published an article about the writings of Rem Koolhaas. Koolhaas has served as a model for some of the politically committed architects (Miessen 2010), particularly those located in North America, as Koolhaas offered an alternative to the figure of Peter Eisenman and the autonomous architecture he propagates. Yet Koolhaas's heteronomy is subjugated to the current state of affairs, far more so than Negri advocates. Negri did not fail to identify the resignation embedded in the Dutchman's quasi-objective distanced descriptions of the absurdities and horrors of the contemporary city. 'We are here in a Rabelaisian situation, often full of sarcasm and intense irony, but with no smile,' Negri wrote. 'The architect, demystified, continues to exist as a worldly and bitter witness, a disenchanted accuser' (Negri 2009: 48). And while Negri argues that 'what is revolutionary is excess, overflow, and power' (Negri 2009: 49), exactly those forces with which Koolhaas is fascinated, the Italian scholar is probably unfamiliar with the larger project of Koolhaas – namely, depicting the architect as a 'surfer on the waves' rather than an agent, arguing that architecture is powerless and that critique and resistance are futile – in other words, claiming, like Negri, that an 'outside' position is impossible, but also providing justification for the architect to 'go with the flow' rather than contest 'from the inside'.

Laclau has criticized the absence of politics in *Empire*, arguing that 'within its theoretical framework, politics becomes unthinkable' (Laclau 2004: 22). The book does not proceed beyond a general declaration of basic demands, does not envision a politics, or the manner in which the diverse – and often competing – protest movements can coalesce into a political force. Mouffe commented that Hardt and Negri 'think it is possible to reach a perfect democracy in which there will no longer be any relation of power – no more conflict, no more antagonism' (Miessen 2010: 111).

But perhaps Laclau and Mouffe are mistaken in treating *Empire* as an analytical study. Rather than an academic role, the book has a political purpose. Laclau himself has written of populist movements (Laclau 2005), and about the moment of (political) articulation – the moment in which an abstract idea, a specific demand, or a name of a leader, act as unifiers of an amalgam of differentiated movements, creating a temporary coalition and mass movement as a necessary step towards hegemony. This appears to be the role of *Empire* – creating the moment of articulation, taking active part in the political formation, and precisely for this reason the book must refer to an absence, in the same manner that demands that become symbolic unifiers of a populist movement must remain 'contentless' – 'empty containers' – in order to satisfy the diverse constituencies involved. *Empire* can therefore be seen not as unfolding a political theory in an analytical or programmatic sense, but as the symbol that enables the political articulation of the protest movement.

Conflict

The philosopher and political theorist Chantal Mouffe, following her earlier forceful critiques of Marxist thought (Laclau and Mouffe 2001), articulated an influential critique of deliberative democracy in the 1990s, and proposed an alternative form of radical democracy. Liberal democracy's focus on the aggregation of citizens' demands, according to Mouffe, reflects the market system, while deliberative democracy eliminates power and hence the political in favour of a single morality:

> Since any political order is the expression of a hegemony, a specific pattern of power relations, political practice cannot be envisaged as simply representing the interests of preconstituted identities, but as constituting those identities themselves in a precarious and always vulnerable terrain.
>
> *(Mouffe 2013b: 202)*

Political theories that posit autonomous individuals as constitutive of a political system, overlook the manner in which the human subject is constituted by hegemonic operations, power relations, and society in general, preferring an all too neat and simple model. The liberal idea of mass democracy as merely the aggregate of diverse demands voiced solely in periodical voting, coupled with the desire to exclude irrational, antagonistic issues, transforms politics into a post-political technocracy. She described liberal democracy as 'the reduction of democracy to procedures for the treatment of interest-group pluralism' (Mouffe 2013b: 192).

Attempts to depoliticize political issues, to manage conflict, to force a consensus are thus symptoms of the elimination of the political from the territory of politics. Such a project is bound to fail, according to Mouffe, because it contradicts the political itself. Mouffe bases her argument on the characteristics of the political, which appears as a force that has to be accommodated rather than repressed. She adopts the analysis of the political and the critique of liberal democracy by the political scientist Carl Schmitt. Schmitt, a Nazi supporter in the

1930s, had been previously read by other scholars on the Left who valued his critique of liberalism, such as Herbert Marcuse or Tronti (Tronti 2009).[25] Mouffe writes:

> For him [Schmitt], every consistent individualism must negate the political since it requires that the individual remain as both starting point and destination. Liberal individualism is unable to understand the formation of collective identities, and it cannot grasp that the collective aspect of social life is constitutive.
>
> *(Mouffe 1996b: 22)*

She formulates these ideas as a 'democratic paradox':

> The logic of democracy is a logic of identity, a logic of equivalence, while the liberal logic is a logic of pluralism that impedes the realization of a complete equivalence and the establishment of a total system of identifications […] [liberal democracy] tends to construct each social identity as a positivity and therefore imposes a pluralism that subverts the attempt at totalization that would result from a total equivalence.
>
> *(Mouffe 1996b: 25)*

Mouffe, in reaction to this understanding of the current status quo, calls for a radical democracy that allows strife and positions far from mainstream into the arena of politics, yet accepts some aspects of liberal politics as a means of preventing tyranny and abuse of human rights. Radical democracy, she argues:

> should be conceived as the radicalization and deepening of the democratic revolution – as the extension of the democratic ideals of liberty and equality to more and more areas of social life. The aim is not to create a completely different kind of society, but to use the symbolic resources of the liberal democratic tradition to struggle against relations of subordination not only in the economy but also those linked to gender, race, or sexual orientation, for example.
>
> *(Mouffe 1996b: 20)*

Antagonism and hegemony, the two major terms for Laclau and Mouffe in their 1985 *Socialist Strategy and Hegemony* (2001), are posited as alternatives to both Marxist and liberal theory, inferring strife rather than consensus, political contingency rather than stability. In later work, Mouffe termed her understanding of radical democracy 'agonistic' to emphasize the antagonism she sees at the core of the political.[26]

Mouffe argues against a belief in any form of reason, deliberative or other, bringing an end to strife and disagreement, as the positions held by subjects are only partially based on reason. So both pragmatically – in a sense that avoiding political conflict by rational discussions is impossible – and normatively – in a sense that the desire to eliminate power and the political inherent in such an approach is unwarranted – she opposes the attempt to form what she sees as a lasting 'end of politics'. Instead, Schmitt's friend/enemy dualism, the basis for the German's idea of 'the political', is also the ground for her proposition, in which the binary 'us/them' is at the heart of the political. 'Agonism' is a specific case of antagonism between adversaries – adversaries who accept the legitimacy of the other, yet nevertheless vigorously oppose their ideas and demands (Mouffe 2013b: 202–3). In other words, the emphasis is on enabling of but also containing strife within a non-violent democratic process, which nevertheless is not preconfigured to the formation of consensus, to achieving an end to the us/them condition.

Mouffe, then, intertwines her analysis of 'what the political is' with a normative proposition, i.e. 'what politics ought to be'. She sees liberal and deliberative democracy as failing to understand the antagonistic nature of the political, and admonishes them for repressing the political. Therefore her agonistic pluralism is a correction of sorts to such erroneous conceptions of the political, a call for accepting the political *as it is* within the framework of politics. Mouffe, however, remains trapped within the field of political theory, and her critique is primarily of political theory rather than practice. In fact, she uses the existing liberal democratic conditions to argue the shortcomings of liberal theory in accounting for them. Liberal democracy, as practiced, is in proximity to her own agonistic pluralism, with successful hegemonic operations – such as that of liberalism itself – establishing themselves as 'us', as a partial, exclusive consensus, and undermining their adversaries' arguments with some success. Mouffe deliberately condones the attempt to politically – rather than violently – 'destroy' the adversarial position. The hegemonic and the adversarial are intertwined, yet they represent two polar conditions within the political: while the latter is related to indeterminacy and extreme contingency as well as to unstable identities, the former marks the attempted closure of such a condition, a creation of a temporary stability by hegemonic processes that counter contingency and strife. The condition of adversity, which carries with it the promise of radical differences and pluralism, necessarily produces opportunities for such hegemonic processes that undermine precisely what Mouffe values. Agonistic pluralism is primarily a critique of political theory's shortcomings, and only in a limited sense an alternative radical democracy. At the end of the day, it departs from current political thought but remains problematically close to the reality of contemporary political practices.

Mouffe's agonistic democracy shares certain features with the political theory of the philosopher Jacques Rancière, who argues, similarly to Mouffe, that the desire for consensus is a cause of the democratic deficit (Rancière 2007). The publication of Rancière's *The Politics of Aesthetics* in English in 2004 secured the wide exposure of artists, art critics, and curators worldwide to the work of Rancière, propelling it to the fore of artistic discussions and debates (Rancière 2004; Bishop 2012). Through the close collaboration of artists and art curators with politically and socially committed architects, Rancière's writings entered discussion within architectural circles as well (Boano and Keilling 2013). Consequently, the main discussion of the work of Rancière in the following pages is focused on his conception of aesthetics, yet understanding the philosopher's positions on aesthetics requires placing them within the wider trajectory of his work since the late 1960s, and particularly in relation to his political theory.

A key impetus of Rancière's oeuvre is the attempt to overturn the division of labour. The philosopher believes that the division of labour stands at the heart of inequality, disempowerment and subjugation in society. It presupposes a state of inequality, and hence affirms it. Rancière's position is distinct from critics of inequality or disempowerment within disciplines such as sociology or philosophy. Where Bourdieu identifies the privileges of class in demarcating or legitimizing a specific language and delegitimizing others, the privileges Rancière identifies stem from the disciplines and professions themselves, from the attempts of sociology and philosophy to monopolize the position of power from which only 'experts' are permitted to speak. The lack of agency in the structuralism of Bourdieu or Althusser is criticized by Rancière, yet the main focus is the basic presumption of inequality by disciplines, the systematic preventing of the marginalized to speak for themselves, the denial of 'non-experts' capacity to think and speak (Tanke 2011).

The distribution of the sensible, Rancière's formulation of the division of labour, is the manner in which what is seeable, sayable and thinkable is distributed within society – the specific presumptions, limits, partitions and boundaries that are placed and that determine diverse practices and possibilities of individual subjects and groups. An example is the manner in which the common reduction – carried out by sociology, political science, or the media – of the workers to a single meaning assigned to their class 'character', affirms barriers and limits, and ignores the reality of the diversity and complexity of workers' lives. It ignores their individual subjectivity, let alone their capacities of acting 'outside' or beyond the roles and limits assigned to them: writing poetry, prose, or painting, for example.

Intelligence is a basic human capacity, claims Rancière, distributed equally:

> There aren't two sorts of minds. There is inequality in the *manifestations* of intelligence, according to greater or lesser energy communicated to the intelligence by the will for discovering and combining new relations; but there is no hierarchy of *intellectual capacity*. Emancipation is becoming conscious of this equality of *nature*. This is what opens the way to all adventure in the land of knowledge.
>
> *(Rancière 1991: 27)*

Where Negri presupposes a pre-distribution of power, Rancière suggests an equal pre-distribution of intelligence. Differences in success in deploying intelligence are due to different levels of will, not to capacity. It is of no importance to him whether such a statement is 'correct'. What is important is that such an assertion, if taken as a presupposition, disrupts the distribution of the sensible. 'Our problem,' writes Rancière, 'isn't proving that all intelligence is equal. It's seeing what can be done under that supposition. And for this, it's enough for us that the opinion be possible – that is, that no opposing truth be proved' (Rancière 1991: 46). In other words, Rancière cares more about the possible dissensus effects of such a statement than for its truth value.

Disputes in society arise from equals getting unequal parts, or vice versa, Rancière argues. Existing distributions (and exclusions) have to be anchored in and legitimized by a sense of justice – an argument for the appropriateness of principles of distribution and justice. The *demos*, the excluded, posit the demand for universal equality against the justifications of the current distribution of the sensible. The demand for universal equality is construed as a demand for emancipation – hence Rancière correlates these two competing demands, equality and freedom. The initial achievement of a *demos*, then, is an acknowledgement of equality of freedom – the understanding that everyone has a right to be as free as those with 'worth' (wealth, birth rights, property, etc.). By being forced to legitimize itself, to produce an argument anchoring inequality in justice, equality is, in fact, demonstrated, and 'the principle of superiority' is undermined (Rancière 2007). Inequality, then, relies on a presumption of equality to justify itself; and equality (of intelligence, of access to logos) can be leveraged to question the justice of current conditions and to claim social equality.[27] Hence, the demand for equality is the vital practice that triggers a rupture of the existing order and its dissolution, followed by the creation of a new ordering, a new distribution of the sensible.

The idea of consensus infers inclusion while veiling exclusions, the existence of the 'voiceless'. Democracy, for Rancière, is disruptive and anti-consensual. An excluded group which demands inclusion by claiming universal equality 'separates' the sensible, reinserting the political. The claim for equality is what renders a disruption to the sensible political. In the absence of such a claim, any disruption can avoid politicization, can be co-opted or sidelined, as it does not disrupt the sensible in a substantial manner. The disruption of consensus via dissensus – by the political or by art, as explained below – is a process of denaturalization. The lack of stability and the contingency of the sensible, its lack of grounding, allows dissensus to destabilize the sensible via polemics, poetics, and other disruptive actions.

Aesthetics' Dissensus

According to Rancière, a key aspect of democracy is equality, without which there is no 'political'.[28] 'The police' is the term Rancière uses for the condition of inequality that represses the political. In such a condition it is the police that determines and manages the distribution of the sensible, and erects a fiction of an inclusive democracy. To police the distribution of the sensible, to prevent challenges of universal equality disrupting the existing order, specific practices are deployed, such as the framing of issues by politicians and media, the deployment of specific terms that convey and affirm identities. In these operations, the excluded become invisible. The policing of the valid topics for discussion, of who has legitimacy to speak, and in what senses, are all part of defending the current distribution of the sensible and preventing radical equality. The police creates inequality by implementing divisions, inclusions and exclusions, by erecting partitions. The police is thus the means of creating a unified worldview, a series of presumptions and assumptions that determine much of society itself, depoliticizing and naturalizing political issues, reducing or removing opportunities to dispute the current conditions and order. Consequently, undermining the divisions and limitations, acting to produce a new 'distribution of the sensible', is for Rancière the ultimate political act.

The process of politicization is one of subjectivization – the emergence of political subjects by questioning the 'naturalness' of the current conditions. Subjectivization is not a process of subjugation, in which identities are forced upon individuals by the police, but the active formation of a subject that is at the heart of the political. Like Laclau's 'hegemony', an important aspect is the openness of the class or subject group created in the process – it is not restrictive but attempts at universalizing. The political 'requires […] the creation of an actor not reducible to one part among others' (Tanke 2011: 71).

Rancière ends up criticizing the concept of class, which increasingly appears as a fabrication created by the privileged assigning others the position of an underclass. This reversal, in which the scholars operating against the repression of labour are presented as conduits of repression, raises some concerns: does this lead to a question of will, that is, whether a belief in an equal capacity combined with strong willpower are indeed all that is needed to usher in significant change, to emancipate and empower the underclass? Does this reliance on 'will' return Rancière not to Kantian humanism, but to the territories of Victorian liberalism, the era of the 'undeserving poor', to the belief in individual self-responsibility, that 'where there's a will there's a way'?

In contrast to critics such as Bourdieu or Peter Bürger who identify the aesthetic disposition and Kantian aesthetics with bourgeois society, characterizing aesthetics as a field of privilege, Rancière identifies an emancipatory potential in art. The aesthetics of politics emerges from the centrality of the distribution of the sensible to Rancière's work. The identification of certain sounds ('sonorous emissions') as legitimate speech and delegitimization of others is equivalent to aesthetics' differentiation between 'music' and 'noise' (e.g. Attali 1985). The aesthetics of politics are very much about the fundamental issues – partitions – that precede and govern politics, fundamental issues that are at the heart of the distribution of the sensible: whose speech is legitimate and whose is not; where can speech take place, and what forms are considered legitimate. Such policing of the field pre-inscribes into politics its exclusionary character and heralds inequality. It is, in essence, an aesthetic framework, and it has to be denaturalized, delegitimized, and called into question by the political.

Rancière discusses three 'regimes of art': the ethical regime, the representative regime, and the aesthetic regime (Rancière 2004: 20-30). A regime is 'a series of axioms that arrange art and position it in relation to other practices,' philosopher Joseph Tanke writes (Tanke 2011: 74). The ethical regime of images subjugates art to the interests of the community. For Rancière, art does not exist in such conditions. Such art is expected to affirm society, to strengthen the community, and is prevented from disrupting society. The art of traditional societies such as feudalism is subjugated to the interests of the community.

The representative regime focuses on the mimesis of making (*poiesis*) and effect (*aisthesis*). It is narrative- and action-driven, and hierarchical: appropriateness of genres and subject matter is of primary concern. It is best represented by the absolutist era, in which the system of fine arts was consolidated. Speech and painting were understood to correspond, meaning that representation was seen as unproblematic and central.

The aesthetic regime of art emerged in the late eighteenth century. The idea of 'equality' regarding the subject of painting, the content, meant an indifference, rendering content obsolete and hence allowing the development of abstraction once painting could be about painting rather than an external subject matter. The aesthetic regime undermined the representative regime's insistence of correspondence between a (given) content and a specific means of representation. Mimesis no longer linked a specific effect to a particular manner of making. The aesthetic is highly reflexive. Aesthetics, as a clearly demarcated field of philosophy, emerged following the dissipation of the representative regime, filling the 'void' created by the dissipation of the rules.

The three regimes correspond to familiar narratives from art history, and the categorizations of major artistic periods based on issues such as representation and content are commonplace. The literature critic Peter Bürger, for example, in his *Theory of the Avant-Garde*, provided a Marxist explanation to the changes in art by highlighting the transformation in the production of art brought about by the emergence of the art market and collapse of the aristocratic court. He too offered a similar periodization, but explained the replacement of 'content' by 'form' as the result of the freeing of art from direct commissions, with aesthetics developed in order to explain the need for art once art has no longer a clear role in society.

But Rancière's regimes of art are not precisely periods, they co-exist and overlap, even though there is some sense of periodization, of correspondence to specific moments. The regimes are sets of principles and axioms, not periods. Moreover, Rancière, by altering the categories and their descriptions somewhat, modifies, in effect, art history to better suit – on the level of its overall logic as well as terminology – his political theory. With relatively modest tampering with accepted and well-disseminated art history, Rancière demonstrates how aesthetics are part of the distribution of the sensible.

Rancière argues that the dissipation of the representative regime's hierarchies and emphasis on representational relationship between life and art, heralded by the aesthetic regime, meant not a disjunction between art and life but the reverse, an intermingling of art and life: the choice of everyday subjects, endowing such subjects with profound symbolic meanings, often meanings that defy complete and direct comprehension. The aesthetic regime is tied up with the French Revolution and the identification by art of its own historical role, internalizing the idea of progress as a progress of art. Rancière claims that the art of the aesthetic regime carries a promise of a profound revolution that transforms life in manners far more radical than anything brought about by the political upheavals of the era. The aesthetic disposition, by 'bracketing' the reception of art from other faculties of the mind (reason and utilitarianism, ethics and morals) enables the rise of new conceptions of life.

> The politics of art in the aesthetic regime of art, or rather, its metapolitics, is determined by this founding paradox: in this regime, art is art insofar as it is also non-art, or is something other than art. [...] There is no postmodern rupture. There is a contradiction that is originary and unceasingly at work. The work's solitude carries a promise of emancipation. But the fulfilment of that promise amounts to the elimination of art as a separate reality, its transformation into a form of life.
> *(Rancière 2009: 36)*

All this is somewhat different from the diverse Kantian derivatives – and distortions – found in the arguments of, among others, art for art's sake, Clive Bell or Clement Greenberg. Yet Rancière's aesthetic theory, as Foucauldian as it may seem, is surprisingly similar to that of Theodor Adorno. At the core of the German philosopher's argument regarding modern art is a conception of an art that is, at once and the same time, part of society as well as society's Other. 'Whereas art opposes society,' wrote Adorno, 'it is nevertheless unable to take up a position beyond it; it achieves opposition only through identification with that against which it remonstrates' (Adorno 1997: 133).[29] Rancière emphasizes contingency, instability, and infuses a sense of constant movement into his description of aesthetic art's position vis-à-vis society, but the basic Adornian duality of an art that is at once part of and opposed to society, is also, despite the staticness of this description, the Frenchman's. Adorno's theory attempts to balance the excesses of art for art's sake's emphasis on the autonomous with the demand for artistic engagement. Such a balance, albeit in a more contingent form, is also struck by Rancière.

The problem with the similarity of Rancière's theory to Adorno's is that the latter's theory was considered for good reasons, by the 1970s, outdated and untenable, no longer reflecting the contemporary condition of art and its relation to society. To claim, in the 1880s or 1920s, that art that manifested its autonomy from society was also critical of society appeared sensible. The era in which society consistently attacked modern art for its autonomy – its lack of morality or utility, for its deviance – necessarily endowed aesthetic art with the power of negation. Yet, once bourgeois society accepted and began revering aesthetic art in the twentieth century, as contemporary, non-representational art began selling for high prices and enjoying admiration and adoration by the rich, the media, and the political elite, Adorno's position appeared increasingly to be anchored in a bygone era.[30] Rancière's return to a Kantian aesthetics appears less baffling only when considered as an integral aspect of his political theory – a logical extension of the latter into the territory of aesthetics in order to demonstrate its applicability in a field which necessarily matters for the distribution of what is seeable, sayable or thinkable.

Rancière's aesthetics attribute political efficacy to all forms of autonomous art, whether political or social in their content or not, yet his commitment to giving a voice to the subaltern and to collapsing disciplinary partitions makes his work relevant to the contemporary spatial practitioners. The project of citizen empowerment via participation, of 'letting others speak', of transgressing disciplinary boundaries suits Rancière's own ambitions perfectly. Offices such as Atelier d'architecture autogérée assist locals in developing and consolidating their communities by collective actions such as community gardening. Yet Rancière's argument that equality already exists means that the philosopher, in effect, rebukes precisely the type of work carried out by artists, architects and other experts who attempt to empower the subaltern. Such endeavours presuppose, according to Rancière's logic, inequality. Instead, Rancière imagines emancipation achieved by the subaltern through self-empowerment, miraculously taking place without the need for expert intervention.

Mediating Theories

The interest in participation has played out primarily on an urban scale: addressing residents' involvement in development plans, empowering residents to initiate community projects or intervening in public space. It is led by artists and architects, and for the latter in particular, it is a form of alternative urbanism, an anti-planning form of urbanism in which planners are sidelined. In this territory, the interest of architects in the late 1990s in the work of de Certeau or the Situationists, ostensibly the type of work that cannot be transposed to architectural practice without undermining its temporal and contingent logic, can be accommodated.

Contemporary urbanists and architects interested in participatory practices include a significant number of practitioners whose approach develops from practical, pragmatic issues and technical know-how and are less interested in the abstract questions (Jenkins and Forsyth 2010). However, more disciplinary attention has been given to those who are positioned between practice as artists and practice as architects or urbanists, or between academia and practice, and who have contributed to the production of discourse through publications and exhibitions. Markus Miessen, an architect, belongs to this latter group. Within this diverse group, which is often at odds about multiple issues related to participation yet also engaged in a lively discussion, Miessen has specifically positioned himself as a critic of 'naïve' participatory practices.

In 2006, he co-edited the book *Did Someone Say Participate?* with Shumon Basar, who, like Miessen, was involved with the Architectural Association in London and with curating and publishing work related to the group of committed architects and urbanists. The book includes an array of texts and projects by academics, artists, and architects addressing a diversity of social and political issues – most involving a degree of citizens' participation. A critique of disciplinary boundaries and a demand for freedom from disciplinary confinements are the major interests of the book's editors.

In 2007, Miessen published *The Violence of Participation*, a book that originated in an exhibition in Lyon. The book includes an interview with Chantal Mouffe in which she unfolds her idea of agonistic democracy. In the 2010 *The Nightmare of Participation*, Miessen attempted to unfold a theory of architectural and urban practice, which spatially applies Mouffe's political theory. Miessen is clear in his rejection of (Habermasian) consensus-driven participation, and argues against majority-democracy as well, claiming that 'not everybody should always be asked or invited to be included in the decision-making process' (Miessen 2010: 41). His argument is for a condition in which 'the individual outsider (to a given inbred political structure) can become a driving force for change by forcefully entering an existing discourse rather than opening it up to the floor' (Miessen 2010: 15). Miessen calls this 'the will to act without mandate' (Miessen 2010: 17). In effect, Miessen resurrects the role of the vanguard – political and aesthetic – by legitimizing the non-consensual and the right of certain individuals to intervene and contradict the consensus, the demands of the people. This position rectifies one of the problems of participation – its tendency to affirm the existing and prevent rather than enable radical change. Relegated, in this process, is the idea of democracy, whether radical, liberal or other, as the voices of citizens become secondary. Instead, Miessen appears more concerned with action that leads to change:

> One cannot – and should not – introduce and incorporate the notion of democracy as if everyone can take part in all areas, professions, and practices. It seems dangerous to only ever submit to democracy as the ultimate tool for solving problems or situations in a politically correct manner.
>
> *(Miessen 2010: 84)*

Miessen sketches a projective optimism, arguing against 'the discourses of loss', and calling 'to enjoy and celebrate' the existing (Miessen 2010: 30). Beyond a typical attempt by a practitioner to bypass the pessimism and passivity caused by hyper-criticism, and despite his own qualifications, such a conception hardly disguises a pragmatic undercurrent, which reveres a compromised 'everydayness' rather than the more radical Lefebvrian 'everyday', a territory that is not yet compromised by capitalism. Miessen, then, celebrates the 'free', 'uncontrolled' city; he articulates a preference for small-scale operations and rejects large-scale planning; he emphasizes the possibility of change via micro-interventions (Miessen 2010: 68–69).

Locating himself somewhere between the amateur and the professional in *Did Someone Say Participate?*, the initial figure of the 'crossbench politician' mutates into 'the uninvited outsider', the dilettante, the agent provocateur. The crossbench politician Miessen evokes is highly individualistic. Miessen writes that crossbench politicians 'do not subscribe to the nailed-down membership books or party platforms of other consolidated politicians' (Miessen 2010: 243). Crossbenchers form temporary political alliances for specific issues, avoiding long-term commitment and the creation of movements that can compromise their individuality. The scorn of political alignment inferred by selecting this figure reflects the contemporary condition, in which card-carrying membership of political parties has declined,[31] and a general cynicism towards politics prevails. In this, the fear of compromising one's own identity by allegiance to a specific party or movement, the rejection of the requirement of compromise necessary to achieve a singular, hegemonic collective voice, is apparent. It also reflects, however, Mouffe's rejection of political consensus. So while Mouffe advocates the active political participation of collectivities including movements or parties in politics, her insistence on maintaining a radical pluralism and avoiding consensus means that such collectivities, if democratic, are necessarily fragile, fleeting, and temporary.

Miessen's crossbench politician develops into the 'uninterested outsider'. This figure, 'who is unaware of prerequisites and existing protocols, entering the arena with nothing but creative intellect and the will to provoke change' (Miessen 2010: 103), is uncannily similar to the ideal character of neoliberal management literature (Boltanski and Chiapello 2005: 76–79). And this reappearance of the figure of the vanguard artist is also a reminder of the manner in which so many historic avant-garde postures, positions, tactics, and practices were co-opted and absorbed by postmodern mainstream practices (Kaminer 2011a).

The vanguard or neoliberal figure of the 'uninterested outsider' takes on the position of the consultant called in to merge or downsize a company (Miessen 2010: 170). Miessen writes that the outsiders 'must not be indifferent to risk-taking, and have to be detached enough not to fall in love with existing structures or protocols' (Miessen 2010: 184). The outsider is heroic, different, free, a maverick. It is perhaps helpful to recall the description of the new managerial figure of neoliberalism, as described by Boltanski and Chiapello, in a book cited by Miessen:

> Neo-management is filled with exceptional beings: proficient at numerous tasks, constantly educating themselves, adaptable, with a capacity for self-organisation and working with very different people. [...] The *manager* is a network man, His principle quality is his mobility, his ability to move around without letting himself be impeded by boundaries, whether geographical or derived from professional or cultural affiliations, by hierarchical distances, by differences of status, role, origin, group, and to establish personal contact with other actors, who are often far removed socially or spatially.
> *(Boltanski and Chiapello 2005: 76, 78–79)*

The 'uninvited outsider' is thus the neoliberal figure *par excellence*.

Miessen bemoans the loss of 'difference', in a society that reveres and integrates difference, and while he criticizes 'romantic' and 'naïve' views of participation, seems enamoured with the romantic idea of the clairvoyant outsider 'who can see' what others – *the blind masses* – cannot, due to their indoctrination. There is little of the idea of a (Mouffian) chain of equivalence here, or the need to create a collectivity and hegemony, but, instead, a rejection of existing institutions, of an idea of a society with a common ground – a common ground that is depicted as a prison of thought, a chain, a dogma, a limit to individual freedoms.

A previous generation of architects – Peter Eisenman, Daniel Libeskind, Bernard Tschumi and others – claimed to reproduce post-structuralist theories in architectural form. Yet these endeavours, despite the arguments forwarded by the architects, ended up merely symbolizing the theories of Deleuze or Derrida (Kaminer 2011a: 108). Architecture seemed unable to apply the abstraction and generality of such theories. In contrast, the relation of radical, and particularly participatory political theory to architectural and urban praxis is tighter, more consistent and clear. The process of decision-making and citizens' involvement engages architecture, urbanism and the political in an unquestionable sense. Here too, however, there is an abstract element that prevents an easy transposition from one field to another – the abstract character and lack of specificity and programmatic proposals in the political theory in question: what precise institutions are necessary for radical democracy? How will these institutions operate? How does society reshape itself as a result of or in order to accommodate such a political order? What role ought the 'expert' have in collective decision-making regarding spatial organization?

Claire Bishop has described political theory as the 'abstract reflection of political philosophy' (Bishop 2012: 7). Miessen has written that 'I have [...] been interested in the writings of Belgian political theorist Chantal Mouffe for a long time, but was always missing a concretized form of, or specific approach toward, the issue of direct engagement, inclusion versus exclusion, and how to become an actor in a force field of power relations' (Miessen 2010: 19). The lack of specificity has meant that much of the work of implementing participatory ideas in design practices in the city has been driven by contingency and pragmatics, with solutions tailored to circumstances, and in the absence of a bigger picture, strategy and vision. While the avoidance of strategic thinking is certainly related to the privileging of tactics and contingency, it also places at risk larger ambitions regarding society and change, increases the threats of co-optation and of enhancing social and economic polarizations.

The abstraction and lack of specificity of radical democratic theories is acknowledged by the political scientists and philosophers who initially proposed them. Habermas argues that his deliberative democracy ideas 'leave more questions open because it entrusts more to the *process* of rational opinion and will formation' (Habermas 1995: 131). The political scientist Ian Budge commented, regarding deliberative democracy, that '[c]oncentrating on deliberation to the exclusion of the procedures under which it operates, however, runs the risk of ignoring the really central questions about democracy in favour of others that are frankly more peripheral' (Budge 2000: 195). In contrast, Dryzek pointed out that it is not the role of political theorists to offer a precise operative programme (Dryzek 2000b: 80).

Abstraction has its advantages. It allows radical democracy to function as a symbol, uniting fragments of discontent into one populist movement, in a sense Laclau described (Laclau 2005). It leaves room for very different groups to attempt to fill it with content, as the protesters have done. Yet if radical democracy is to function not as a unifying symbol but as a realizable project, including a project for a new *cité*, then a proper programme is necessary. At the moment, what is on offer is limited in scope. A gap exists between a very theoretical discussion, then, and the bottom-up experimentations of activists. In other words, a mediating theory that can allow a tight theory–praxis relation is missing. Architects and urbanists such as Miessen have contributed as conduits of sorts between abstract political theory and practice, standing in for an absent 'mediating theory'. Georg Lukács wrote that:

> If the theory is juxtaposed to an action without mediation, without it becoming clear how its effect on the latter is intended, thus, without making clear the organizational links between them, then the theory itself can only be criticised with respect to its immanent theoretical contradictions.
>
> *(Habermas 1974: 34)*

The distance separating Mouffe, Negri and Habermas is vast. Their approaches are so irreconcilable that these political theorists – and their followers, such as Benhabib and Dryzek for Habermas or Joshua Cohen for liberal-democrat Rawls – appear unable to find a common language to enable meaningful exchanges. Habermas's point of departure is the question of a just society; hence the ability of a liberal democrat such as Rawls, committed to a normative idea of justice, to appreciate Habermas's proposition. Neither Habermas nor Rawls actually suggest their proposals as a finite form for politics; rather, their proposals are designated as an ideal. Such a moral outlook is anathema to Mouffe. Her point of departure is not the quest for a just society, or for a legitimate form of governance, but to correct the errors of political theory by observing *the reality* of the political. Her ambition is to provide an explanatory theory rather than a model to emulate: 'I think there is a crucial role that political theory can play in helping us to understand our current predicament,' she explains (Miessen 2010: 106). Mouffe's critique of the theories of Habermas (and Rawls) is developed from identifying them as erroneous explanatory theories rather than as models – though a critique of their actual ambitions is inherent in the critique of the alleged inadequate understanding of the political. Basically, Mouffe fails to recognize the intention of deliberative theories that, instead of being interpretative, articulate a horizon, an ideal condition that steers the process of democratization to a warranted, even if unachievable, end. Nevertheless, agonistic pluralism also acts, to a degree, as a normative model – but the argumentation for it provided by Mouffe is closely developed from 'what the political is' rather than what politics ought to be. Her ideal is a condition in which politics absorbs into it the political in the most expansive sense, a politics which accepts the irrational, contingency and indeterminacy: a condition in which 'politics' and 'the political' are one.

The shortcomings of the debate surface when identifying the proximity of the diverse propositions to 'bourgeois' ideals, on the one hand, and to the existing conditions of liberal democracy as practiced, on the other. A reconfigured version of the Enlightenment ideals of a civil society and a set of notions that reproduce in political and urban theory the ideas that originate in and belong to the free market: consumer choice as pluralism; contingency, lack of stability and fixity as determining features of the high-risk aspects of cyclical capitalism, now exalted as values; a managed conflict as a means of societal integration of the most destabilizing alternatives; managed conflict as a means of co-optation by attempting to preserve the *cultural* vitality of the antagonist but without the political, social, or economic threat – i.e. by reducing the conflict to a cultural plateau with limited effect, and thus encouraging 'quietism'. When Miessen writes that 'if you set up a situation in which people can produce a set of relationships and productivities that take the situation further than the conventional understanding of disciplinary or interdisciplinary practices. The logic of change is always based on the notion of exception, while unpredictable acting is the enabler for something "new" to emerge' (Miessen 2010: 100), he effectively reproduces an argument that animates neoliberal theory.

PRAXIS

Community Gardening

> That's game changing – that's not a plant on wheels!
>
> *(Amica Dall, Assemble)*[32]

Atelier d'architecture autogérée (aaa; Studio for Self-Managed Architecture) is a Paris-based design firm, established in 2001 and led by Doina Petrescu and Constantin Petcou. It operates contingently, setting up temporary collaborations with other architectural firms, artists, art organizations, NGOs, city councils, or universities. Despite a focus on France, its reach is global, and Petrescu's and Petcou's anchoring in academia, at the University of Sheffield School of Architecture, provides a direct link to teaching and research. The global, contingent, collaborative and academic aspects of the firm are features shared with many participatory architects, though in aaa they are particularly present. The ECObox (2001–6) and Passage 56 (2006) projects in Paris, in which aaa led locals to appropriate derelict spaces and turn them to community gardens, the stream of publications with which Petrescu and Petcou have been involved (Blundell Jones, Petrescu and Till 2005; AAA and PEPRAV 2007; Petrescu 2007b; Petrescu, Petcou, Awan 2010), and the contribution of the atelier to the Uneven Growth exhibition at the MoMA have been important in positioning aaa at the fore of the participatory movement.

Petrescu and Petcou emerged from the activities of the Form-Trans-Inform group of architecture students in 1980s Romania (Stratford with Petrescu and Petcou 2008). The actions, performances and exhibitions of Form-Trans-Inform were primarily transgressive, in the sense of committing acts that expanded the individual and group's freedoms, yet in the context of the extreme repression of Ceausescu's Romania such transgressive acts were necessarily also subversive. The agenda of aaa is focused on the expansion of architecture beyond issues of architectural form, space (in the conventional sense), type, or materialization. The interests of aaa include environmental sustainability, politics, society and community. Self-management of residents by enhancing citizen participation and empowerment is a key aspect, as are recycling, urban agriculture, and autarky. They write that 'the citizens' right to the city does not only mean the right to occupy space in it, but also means to decide how it is developed, managed and used […] a right to be informed about, decide, act upon and manage the future of cities' (Petcou and Petrescu 2015: 250). 'It is not the power of making things *for* the community, of representing it (which is the architects, planners and regeneration officers' privilege),' Petresco stated, 'but of participating in *making the community* itself, through discrete spatial interventions' (Petrescu 2007a).

Their recent project R-Urban, a collaboration with the city council of the French town of Colombes and the London-based architecture group Public Works, 'aims to empower urban residents to propose alternative projects where they live, and to foster local and greater networks, testing methods of self-management, self-building and self-production' (Petcou and Petrescu 2015: 256). In Colombes, R-Urban included in the first phases the setting up of self-managed 'collective hubs' – temporary structures containing information or facilities regarding housing, economic or cultural issues. Sustainability was enhanced via recycling ('RecycLab' hub) and food manufacturing in an urban agricultural hub ('Agrocité') that included a chicken coop, beehives and community gardening. A significant objective here is to create a co-operative land trust, which would further empower locals. Appropriately, aaa's ambition for the land trust is that it would forego property ownership and instead negotiate temporal and long-term land uses, preferring the idea of the commons to a public–private understanding based on ownership and property.[33]

Urban agriculture and community gardening stand at the centre of the work of aaa, as R-Urban's Agrocité, and the ECObox and Passage 56 projects demonstrate (Figure 2.5). Such community gardens have become a staple of the participatory movement. Anne Querrien, a sociologist, planner and researcher, and one of the founding members of the 1970s radical research group CERFI (Centre d'Études de Recherches et de Formation Institutionelle), wrote that:

> Everywhere artists of a new genre are making use of this opportunity of spaces where you take your place, enter into a dialogue, persuade, feel pressure, experience the possibility of democracy in which each one encounters the other in their sameness and difference. The garden is made for this particular, new urban game: a material pleasure, circumscribed, tangible.
>
> *(Querrien 2007: 309)*

At the heart of the argument for urban agriculture is the concern for environmental sustainability: the idea that by growing local food and thus reducing energy consuming long-distance supply chains, by emphasizing autarky and a localized cycle of production and consumption, by adding green lungs to a concrete city, a meaningful contribution is done to the ecology of the environment (Petrescu 2007a; Pescou and Petrescu 2015). Yet, as the ecological footprint of cities such as London is equivalent to the entire land mass of Britain, urban agriculture's 'impact on urban food systems remains limited' (Bell and Cerulli 2012: 35).

Two experiments with local currencies, both involving the New Economic Foundation (nef), demonstrate some of the difficulties in self-sufficiency and autarky relevant also for urban agriculture and similar endeavours. The first was the introduction of the Brixton Pound in the early 2000s. The purpose was primarily to reduce economic 'leakage' from a deprived area – encouraging the local spending of money made in the neighbourhood and the strengthening of locally owned independent shops. The difficulty the scheme encountered

FIGURE 2.5 Passage 56, an 'ecological interstice' by atelier d'architecture autogérée (aaa) in St. Blaise area, Paris, 2006. Photograph courtesy of aaa.

was that the retailers had to convert the currency back to Pounds Sterling in order to purchase (from beyond the neighbourhood) the products being sold to locals (Taylor 2014: 307). Learning from the limitations of this initial experiment, when introducing in 2012 the Bristol Pound, nef and their partners followed distribution routes to many of the sources of the products, incorporating into the scheme the Bristol region rather than just a city neighbourhood. This eliminated the type of 'bottlenecks' that occurred with the Brixton Pound, but, in the process, the specific role of such currencies in strengthening deprived communities was lost once both affluent and struggling communities were all included in the scheme.

The ambition to create today an autarkic, self-sustaining community faces significant challenges in the contemporary conditions of global flows of capital and products. Even in the inter-war years, Mussolini's propagation of an autarkic Italy remained an empty promise (Avilés 2009), and the 1929–30 scramble for autarky in many of the nations that were badly affected by the crisis – first and foremost raising import barriers via quotas and taxes – was hardly effective. Rather than the antagonist of globalization, the local is today anchored in the global – hence the use of the term 'glocal'. Small-scale interventions often end up with marginal or even negligible efficacy – a community garden hardly alters the huge imbalances in production and consumption in existence in Western cities today.

Yet the limited impact urban agriculture has on sustainability and autarky does not render the investment in community gardens and the like superfluous. The Brixton Pound, even if limited in preventing 'leakage' from the area, contributed to local self-esteem, identity and pride. It had a symbolic role. It encouraged residents to notice and appreciate the independent retailers. A study of the effects of the Bristol Pound claimed that it 'has a beneficial effect on both social and community bonds by shaping interactions, feelings of trust and how users feel about the social and community bonds they hold with their co-users' (UoB 2015). Similarly, community gardens strengthen community cohesion, in some cases aid in community formation. They enable and encourage interaction between residents of diverse social and ethnic backgrounds, create bonds, and bolster engagement with the environment. They provide activities and space for activities that otherwise would not take place. Community gardens often form the basis for expansion of such communal activities to cultural or political spheres.[34] Petcou has commented on the ECObox garden that 'there were people who came to garden, then they started taking part in the debates, and in the end they were in front of town hall with billboards' (Querrien, Petrescu, Petcou 2007: 293).

The focus of aaa on 'micro-interventions' in the urban fabric is specifically calibrated to 'activate' the broader public who shun familiar forms of activism and politics. 'We're exploring an everyday "soft" or "weak" activism that everybody can put into practice,' said Petcou, 'starting with the opposition to consumerism, to unwanted local urban projects […] and to which the activists (in the strong sense of the word), who are more interested in global problems, aren't committed' (Querrien, Petrescu, Petcou 2007: 291). A term Petrescu and Petcou frequently deploy is 'interstices', used to describe the fissures and gaps they attempt to occupy. It is associated with the work of the feminist philosopher Isabelle Stengers (Stengers and Pingarre 2011), providing an insight into the process of transformation 'from inside'. The 'cracks' within compromised society are the existing contradictions within it, the small territories that enable something new to arise that is in minor yet in decisive ways not the same as the system in which it materializes. Interstices can be expanded, adapted, and are highly unstable and contingent. They offer a form of praxis: the aim is within the action itself, rather than being fully subjugated to an external logic or force. The small-scale and containment of the interstices generate a reflective, even reflexive approach, enabling a level of understanding that is impossible on a larger scale where social and power structures become complex and opaque. Most interstices exist for a limited period before their promise is undermined by co-optation, by being absorbed into neoliberal society. Beyond offering an experience of freedom or collectivity and a means of testing innovative, divergent practices, meaningful transformation can emerge directly from such cracks that avoid compromise and grow in scale, ushering in a changed society.

The interest is in transformation driven not necessarily by those individuals invested in and committed to political action, or 'top-down' by people in positions of power, but by transformation developing from unforeseeable quarters, often by individuals or groups with no particular larger agenda, by groups that do not necessarily see themselves as political. There are some echoes here of Lefebvre's conception of practices and spaces of everyday life that are markedly different from compromised everydayness. For Lefebvre, these 'oases' provide a model for an alternative society to come, a possibility and hope, a model to emulate. But perhaps more fitting here are Lyotard's 'small narratives' as a contrast to metanarratives. Whereas for Lefebvre the 'uncontaminated' everyday was often produced by lay citizens rather than political activists, in Lyotard's 'small narratives' such a production of alterity by the unassuming protagonists of history is exalted, and partaking in traditional political activities becomes superfluous.

For aaa, community gardens are such interstices, an opportunity to develop alternative practices within the system, a praxis that can be appreciated by immediate results such as community solidarity and cohesion, spatial quality, and ecological betterment. At the same time, the ambition of Petrescu and Petcou is larger, expecting an aggregate effect in which a large number of such interstices accumulate to produce a significant change on a grander scale. Such a process in which change from 'inside' occurs, is disparate from a linear trajectory of political activism. The praxis of and in the interstices is necessarily loaded politically and ideologically only in a relatively indirect or covert manner. Petrescu and Petcou attempt to steer a political project with a broad ambition via the small-scale of the interstices, working with political consciousness where change is expected to be produced via circumstance and opportunity, with a limited cognition of the wider picture. Or, in other words, to 'activate' the cracks as part of a larger plan, no matter how contingent, dispersed, and decentred such a plan is. Precisely how such an accumulative effect would occur remains vague.

There is, however, another issue. Community gardens can be a site and cause of resistance to capitalism and to government, as the battle to save New York City's community gardens in 2000 demonstrated (Schmelzkopf 2002). Yet the broad and diverse coalition assembled to fight mayor Giuliani's plan to sell the gardens to developers, attests to the consensus surrounding the gardens and suggests that it was Giuliani who was out of step with public sentiment. The inclusion by developers – rather than as response to residents' demands – of community gardens in for-profit high-end housing developments in cities such as London suggests that such urban agriculture activities are well within consensus, a stimulus rather than threat to capitalism (Figures 2.3, 2.6).[35] The temporality of the permission to use the land is often a source of contestation, of desire by cities to redevelop when the opportunity arises, and of resistance by locals. The interest to redevelop the sites may itself, in some cases, be encouraged by the existence of such 'civil' activities as community gardening. As in the case of many other means of bettering an existing neighbourhood, community gardens can increase the threat of gentrification.

FIGURE 2.6 A visualization of communal rooftop gardens in the Elephant Park development in south London. Courtesy of Lendlease.

Petrescu and Petcou are well aware of co-optation. 'The important drive for participation that was originated by critical practices in the 1970s,' Petrescu writes,

> has now become the Government's mantra. In the UK and most European countries, urban policies and regeneration practices encourage 'community participation', but by lacking specificity they generate stereotypical approaches and reiterate fixed notions of 'community' and 'public space'. The existing frameworks of both governmental and local participative programmes are organised in the same way, without taking into account the particularity of each situation.
>
> *(Petrescu 2007a)*

Elsewhere, aaa describe their contribution as a supplement to government activity, as in associative democracy:

> Local authorities and public institutions are integrated in the strategy as equal partners, assuming the roles of enablers, sponsors and administrators. In addition to urban residents and civic organisations, public institutions (e.g. city councils, regeneration offices, public land trusts, schools and cultural agencies) are also invited to take part in this experimental utopia, and to challenge their routines.
>
> *(Petcou and Petrescu 2015: 256)*

Community gardens and urban agriculture do not necessarily support or undermine capitalism or gentrification. At the end of the day, they are a means of improving a neighbourhood and strengthening its community via consent and consensus. The specific effects, whether detrimental or positive, depend on the particular conditions of the neighbourhood and project in question. Some gardens increase gentrification, aid in selling luxury apartments, others do not. Some have palpable positive effect on communities, some have limited or no effect whatsoever. They do not alter the relations of production.

Expanding the Role of the Architect

A somewhat different route to socially affective design has been pursued by the young London-based collective Assemble. The group gravitated from a self-initiated project in London, Cineroleum, to fully fledged commissions, ranging from a temporary music venue for Café Oto to an art gallery for Goldsmiths College. The group itself – its size and composition – fluctuated before settling at a core of about 12 to 18. Many of the group members had just graduated from the Cambridge School of Architecture or were in the process when the initial commissions were received, while other members are from diverse backgrounds such as literature, philosophy, or African studies. Once confronted with commissions, the loose group required some structure. 'Everyone argued about everything,' said Amica Dall, one of the founding members, 'it's not about a consensus building project' (Kaminer 2015). Registered as a community interest company (CiC), and with contingent and developing structures for decision making, pay, and work distribution, Assemble is experimental first and foremost as an architectural firm.

The collective received unexpected recognition in 2015 by winning the Turner Prize for their contribution to urban renewal in Liverpool's Toxteth. Awarding an urban regeneration project the prestigious art prize was unprecedented (Wainwright 2015).[36] 'They don't occupy the realm of the single genius, solitary artist,' said a Turner jury member. 'This is collective activity working in society' (Brown 2015). Assemble have not introduced particularly new methods of designing or working. The idea of an architecture collective was not only significant in the 1970s, but includes a number of well-established contemporary firms, such as the Glasgow-based Collective Architecture, owned by an employee-run trust since the beginning of the century. The intermixing of art, architecture and design is likewise not just the bread and butter of small vanguard firms, but the very territory occupied by financially viable firms such as muf or Publica. Similarly, the focus on crafts or on participation is not novel territory. What is remarkable about Assemble, however, is the manner in which diverse streams coalesce and come together in their work, arguably more so than in any other contemporary firm, and the redefining of the role of the architectural firm and the architect as a result of their practice. The potpourri of interests that animate Assemble include crafts, DIY, phenomenology, art and design, play, ephemerality and temporality, participation and engagement, social responsibility and enterprise, and collectivity. The group shuns the OMA-inspired 'trash' aesthetics deployed by their American counterparts such as Teddy Cruz. Their interest in crafts and a phenomenological approach are distinctively British.

Many of Assemble's commissions have been, in effect, temporary structures related to exhibitions, performances or screenings: the self-commissioned Cinerolium, The Folly on the Flyover, Theatre on the Fly, OTOProjects, Lina Bo Bardi: Together exhibition, Big Slide, The Playing Field, and Bell Square Pavilion, among others. The Folly on the Flyover was a temporary venue under a motorway in London's Hackney Wick, a small industrial and ex-industrial area of workshops – increasingly a workplace of 'creatives' – in the River Lea Valley, located between the residential area of Hackney and the Stratford site of the 2012 Olympic Games. The folly's awkward positioning, emphasized by the structure's pitched roof protruding between the west and eastbound motorway lanes, is recognizable from conditions of high density in cities such as Tokyo. Similar to many buildings in such conditions, the structure opportunistically occupies a 'spatial gap' under and within a zone of infrastructure (Figure 2.7). Assemble describe their positioning of the folly and its formal resemblance to a house by imagining a 'nail house' on site.[37] The house form, constructed from an interwoven bead curtain, contrasts in its warmth, fragility and detail the abstraction and brutality of the urbanscape of infrastructure into which the folly is inserted.

Assemble's interest in 'play' is not limited to temporary follies for time-based events, but includes also playgrounds such as the Baltic Street Adventure Playground in Glasgow's Dalmarnock or an ongoing project based on 'play' in Bristol. The Baltic Playground, developed as part of the 2014 Commonwealth Games, is a participatory project of a particular type, in which local children take an active part in developing the site via their play. The group itself, in collaboration with other artists, carpenters, professionals, and, in some cases, volunteers, is directly involved in physically constructing many of its designs. Such an involvement in the crafts of building allows Assemble increased control of the quality of work down to the level of the detail, and enables immediate response to unforeseeable situations. It facilitates better cost-efficiency, and can, when needed, offer high-end labour at an affordable price. The delicate bead curtain of the folly, or the colourful 'pixelated' concrete tiling of their Yardhouse, exemplify the experimentations made possible by Assemble's 'hands on' involvement in crafts.

FIGURE 2.7 Assemble, Folly on the Flyover, London, 2012.

The feasibility of a crafts-driven approach is restricted to the type of commissions the collective has received so far, but their provision of both 'idea' and 'product' allows Assemble to shift focus in the future. Nevertheless, at this stage the members appear content with the type of commissions they have undertaken. They have avoided taking on unsuitable projects in the past, and intend to do so in the future, shunning undertakings that would compromise the work (Kaminer 2015). As a group originally created within the voluntarist sector, Assemble faces some challenges to its integrity in gravitating towards a more conventional office. Whereas young designers often invest in unpaid work, whether as interns or in design competitions, their labour is construed as a self-investment. Here, the voluntarist aspect places Assemble within the domain of public interest. The firm's function as a social enterprise is embedded structurally in its legal status as a CiC. The British Government demands that community interest companies 'create an "asset lock" – a legal promise stating that the company's assets will only be used for its social objectives, and setting limits to the money it can pay to shareholders' (BG undated). Assemble's 'defence' against being drawn in to projects that could undermine its integrity and reputation is therefore twofold: a legal 'lock', on the one hand, and the ability to reject projects, on the other, enabled by their relatively small financial burdens as a collective that employs only bookkeepers.

When it comes to the issue of gentrification, namely, the potential of projects to further social cleansing, the collective is more limited in preventing the exploitation of its work by greater forces. The Folly on the Flyover and the Baltic Street Adventure Playground were both commissioned as part of larger urban redevelopment projects with problematic outcomes. The redevelopment of the River Lea Valley, not long ago a site of activities such as sports, illegal raves, or squatting, and particularly the redevelopment around the site of the 2012 Olympics, was pursued as an ambitious transformation of the (supposed) *terrain vague* of the

River Lea, as well as of the adjacent residential areas of Hackney and Stratford, both of which have a history of deprivation. The redevelopment of Dalmarnock was a feature of the preparations for the Commonwealth Games, and included the mass demolition of housing in the deprived area. The folly and the playground, as positive as their contributions may be on a small scale, can thus easily be assimilated into larger and nastier redevelopment projects. The ability to reject a project, and preference for clients such as government agencies or community organizations rather than for-profit developers,[38] provides only limited defence against exploitation by such grand redevelopment, particularly when driven by the government itself.

The voluntarist work of artists and architects in territories associated with social care is often condemned for enabling government retrenchment and retreat from responsibilities. 'The danger of projects like theirs [Assemble's]', wrote art critic Adrian Searle, 'is that it will be seen to replace government intervention, leading to further withdrawals of public funds and further atomisation' (Searle 2015). aaa responded to such criticism in defence of their R-Urban project:

> R-Urban could hence be suspected of aligning itself opportunistically with the 'Big Society' principles recently proposed by the UK's Tory prime minister, David Cameron, to implement 'the idea of communities taking more control, of more volunteerism, more charitable giving, of social enterprises taking on a bigger role, of people establishing public services themselves' (Cameron, 2011). But the essential difference is that R-Urban is not responding directly to the onset of the financial crisis and is not embracing a program of economic resilience in which the state is absent: such a program would explicitly promote the reliance on unpaid work to mask the disappearance of welfare structures and the massive cuts in public services. The R-Urban strategy is not relegating economic responsibility to citizens because the state is unable or unwilling to assume it any longer, but claims the social and political right to question the state's power in terms of its role and responsibility.
>
> *(Petcou and Petrescu 2015: 256)*

In contrast to what appears as a desire to remain small and avoid large-scale commissions, Assemble's Dall discloses greater ambitions. 'I think I find the glorification of things which are actually only quite modest [...] quite troubling,' she commented on the ubiquity of community gardens, 'you can't diffuse responsibility just by doing things small or for other people' (Kaminer 2015). Consequently, the question Assemble faces is how to expand the ambition to produce a significantly better society and environment without losing, en route, the qualities of their work, many of which are dependent on small-scale, immediate, and hands-on production.

The French architecture firm Lacaton and Vassal, in contrast to aaa and Assemble, is a typical, 'everyday' architectural firm. Established in 1987, it has completed widely acclaimed projects such as the Palais de Tokyo (2002, 2012), Tour Bois le Prêtre (2011, with Frédéric Druot), both located in Paris, and the Nantes School of Architecture (2009). The firm's principles Anne Lacaton and Jean Philippe Vassal avoid grandstanding and do not offer the type of radical statements typical of many of the protagonists of the participatory movement. Instead, they eruditely describe their work in a language more familiar to architects, discussing spatial and functional concerns, the user, environment, context, and poetics. Their work is consequently published in magazines such as *Architectural Review* that eschew the participatory movement, inferring that their designs can be assimilated into an aesthetic discourse on architecture. The absence of radical statements means that taking on projects such as a five star hotel or villas for the affluent does not appear contradictory as it would for a Teddy Cruz, aaa or U-TT. In many ways, Lacaton and Vassal are a 'normal' practice.

Architectural form, as architectural critics eagerly emphasize (Ruby and Ruby 2002: 5–6), is not at the fore of Lacaton and Vassal's concerns. Form is the result of other conditions and interests, such as space or programme. Their work is identified with the retrofitting of existing buildings such as in the Tour Bois le Prêtre, and with a 'greenhouse aesthetic', namely, the use of 'everyday' temporary and inexpensive materials such as timber for shuttering or polycarbonate panels for closures. In describing their work, Lacaton and Vassal emphasize the manner in which constraints and opportunities determine the project's outcome. While not unusual in an architectural practice, the architects turn the typical contingent aspects of the design process into its main driving force. The work of the firm, however, does more than peddle an everyday aesthetic: its importance lies in the architects' abilities to expand architecture to areas of the building process that have previously been off limits.

Four major issues predominate the work and thought of Lacaton and Vassal: space, the brief, the building process and costs, and materials. All these issues shape the social efficacy of their projects. Their approach to the question of spatial organization and distribution opposes functionalism in the sense of tailoring spaces for specific uses, preferring to create spaces which can be modified, changed or appropriated by the users for the widest range of social practices possible. '[L]oose spaces that were constantly in flux,' the architectural critic Andrew Ayers wrote in the *AR*, 'redefined by their users with temporary, often virtual boundaries' (Ayers 2012: 51). The result is abstract space, which the users are expected to appropriate and personalize according to their needs and desires.[39] This approach to space suggests a development of Le Corbusier's *plan libre*, Tschumi's 'event architecture', and Lefebvrian conceptions of space as the product of social practices. Hence, in the Palais de Tokyo, the architects create as much abstract, open space as possible in order to allow the institution and its visitors the freedom to appropriate it as necessary.

The architects deploy the term 'luxury' in order to describe the quality of space they intend to create. While 'luxury' is first and foremost associated with expensive materials, and consequently Lacaton and Vassal's use of the term ostensibly subverts its meaning, space has indeed become a form of luxury in contemporary society. Double- or triple-height entrance lobbies, generously sized rooms, ceiling heights above the minimum – all these signify affluence, a luxury, as opposed to minimum standards, maximum floor use and so on, typical of social housing, of speculative or low-end housing and offices. Lacaton and Vassal attempt to provide a generosity of space in all their projects, arguing that 'luxury has seemed to us to be the same everywhere: a question of spatial grandeur' (Goulet 2002: 124).

Departing from typical architectural practice, Lacaton and Vassal often question the client's brief. In the case of a square in Bordeaux, Plaza Léon Aucoc, the architects responded to their commission to redesign the square by reporting back to the city council that the public space is fine as it is and requires no transformation whatsoever. Instead, they proposed to use the available budget for ongoing maintenance. In Dunkerque, they proposed to avoid filling in an existing hangar with exhibition spaces and facilities for the contemporary art organisation FRAC, as suggested by the client. Instead, the architects proposed to build a new structure, a replica of the existing hangar, allowing the vast and impressive space of the existing hangar to remain unobstructed for diverse temporal uses (Figures 2.8, 2.9).

FIGURES 2.8, 2.9 Lacaton and Vassal, FRAC, Dunkerque, 2013, view from inside refurbished hangar (top) and external view of refurbished and new hangars (bottom). Photographs courtesy of Philippe Ruault.

The other important subversion Lacaton and Vassal perform is by intervening in the process of building and in the budget and costs. In the Tour Bois le Prêtre the architects coordinated the process to ensure residents remain within the building during the retrofitting, taking advantage of available flats within the tower and thus avoiding dislocation during the process. A typical intervention is by rethinking the costs and the budget, as in the Mulhouse project for social housing, the Nantes School of Architecture (2009), or the Palais de Tokyo. Architecture critic Robin Wilson, discussing the redirecting of the Plaza Léon Aucoc budget to the plaza's maintenance, wrote that '[t]he principle of maintenance links the project tangibly to its economic conditions, articulating economic ties between the architects and the commissioning body in such a way as to prioritise the flow of resources directly from the city government to its citizens' (Wilson 2013: 47).

The use of cheap materials, the reduction of finishes and other techniques, which is the fourth main concern of the architects, is not intended as a 'counter principle to established culture' (Ruby and Ruby 2002: 5–6), as a 'Koolhaasian' flattening of 'high' into 'low' culture. Rather, it is a means of producing outdoor qualities and impressions indoors, of creating an inside–outside continuum, of suggesting lightness, and, most importantly, of reducing the cost of construction. In for-profit projects, the developer usually pockets such savings, reaping higher profit and producing lower quality buildings. The ingenuity of Lacaton and Vassal is in directing the use of this 'liberated' budget to specific causes by negotiating in advance with the client – whether to enable the generosity of space they preach, or other. The Rubys describe it as a 'miraculous transformation of *surplus value* into *surplus space*' (Ruby and Ruby 2002: 6). In Dunkerque, the additional structure of considerable size, absent in the original brief, could be afforded thanks to the architects' smart rethinking of the budget and of cost-efficiency.

'It is a question of where to stop, where to finish the project, how much freedom you give the inhabitant,' Lacaton commented on the 'openness' of their designs:

> The space should not impose a particular way of life. You don't have to conceive of everything; you just must give him or her the potential space to be used and appropriated. If you give enough qualities and a range of capacity, then you provide maximum opportunities for everybody and the project will assume to be changed, transformed and re-appropriated.
>
> *(Diaz Moreno and Garcia Grinda 2015: 11)*

The logic deployed here surpasses the idea that savings on inessentials allows spending on essentials: it is not just a quantitative achievement of more space for the same price, but a particular type and quality of space – abstract, open, 'undefined' – that enables habitation, appropriation, and personalization. Budget is thus transferred from materials to producing spatial quality and quantity.

'We feel it is our duty to start from scratch with each new project,' explained Jean Philippe Vassal. 'That can also mean fundamentally questioning our own profession – and, with that, the way architecture is practiced' (Wellner 2012: 13). It is the expansion of architectural considerations and practice into territories such as cost-efficiency that marks the major contribution of Lacaton and Vassal. The actual achievements of the office, in offering social tenure residents larger and better apartments for example, or in advocating refurbishment instead of demolition (Druot, Lacaton, Vassal 2007), may be dwarfed from a larger perspective by the relentless march of neoliberalism and the scale of gentrification and impoverishment taking place in cities, but are not insignificant. The substantial achievement in their work is in demonstrating how architects can gain agency by intervening in supposedly 'non-architectural' areas. By actively pursuing such an agenda, they counteract the process by which design has been reduced to surface treatment, by which design is no longer expected to account for content, only for form, a process that has taken place in industrial design and other fields as much as in architecture, and has reduced the field to a purely cultural form of expression.

Anti-statism

The anti-statism that animated the 1970s *Autonomia* movement and Negri's early writings is still a major force in *Empire*, as it is in the contemporary protest movements. The discontent and protest has been directed at the political institutions of the nation state, and has generated radical extra-parliamentary populist movements on both right and left. Among the architects, the anti-statism is expressed as anti-planning, as a demand for participation, and as a rejection of large-scale and top-down projects led by government or developers alike. The government and its planning agencies are no longer seen as representatives of citizens' interests or will, no longer depicted as benevolent, but condemned as a self-serving elite, as facilitators of capitalism, as bureaucrats, as repressive institutions of control, or as the political–administrative arm of the wealthy.

Adopting theories, strategies, and tactics formed in an earlier era, the contemporary architectural dissidents are rattling the disciplinary status quo, aided by the crippling effects of the financial crisis on architectural practice, yet often aiming their critique at phantom adversaries, or pursuing tactics that had already failed the previous generation. Often missed in the return to the theories of an earlier generation is the very different circumstance of political economy and society today, a difference that requires the adaptation and transformation of the theories in question, as well as an understanding of the reasons for a previous generation of architects and radicals abandoning them in the 1970s and 1980s.

The passage to post-Fordism, to a post-industrial society and to neoliberal economics meant, among other things, also the weakening of politics by the transfer of power from national governments to the global economic forces of capitalism. Mario Tronti's 'autonomy of the political', conceptualized in the era of strong, centralized governments, is no longer valid in a post-political period in which economy is free to pursue its own interests with only limited governmental intervention. The withering of the state as a result of globalized capitalism stands, of course, at the centre of *Empire*; the condition recalls Engels' reading of Saint Simon, in which he prophesized 'the subordination, indeed eventually the absorption, of politics into economics and consequently the abolition of the state in the society of the future: the "administration of things" replacing the "government of men"' (Hobsbawm 2011: 29).

Many of the demands of the 1968 generation have, in fact, been addressed, though this took place by co-optation: the anti-state stance resulted in the post-political condition and in the empowering of markets; the demands for freedom ended up in expanded individual freedoms at the expense of collective freedoms; the demand for spontaneity and creativity has been answered by culture, by the rise of 'the creative industries', and by an enhanced emphasis on spectacle. Just as 'economy' has transcended 'politics', so has 'culture' replaced a conception of 'society'. Culturally-based identities have replaced class-based identities, just as 'class' vanishes as a major category in the writings of Rancière and Negri. The inspiring '68 slogans 'beneath the paving stones, the beach' or 'power to the imagination' have been assimilated by consumerist spectacle and the 'enlightened' managerial practices of some of the current cutting edge corporations (Boltanski and Chiapello 2005). An antipathy to ideas of totality and to *planisme*, to top-down decisions, to state power, to expertise; a claim to implement democratic principles outside the official territory of politics, to empower the multitude: such practices and ideologies align with neoliberal practices and thought in their anti-statist positions, in the demand to weaken centralized governments, in their focus on the atomization of society into smaller enclaves. They have, in fact, been co-opted and used to foster free-market neoliberalism at the expense of economic, social, and urban planning, which were specific features of Fordist society, whether in the form of the welfare state or other.

In the city, neoliberal dispositions and practices are not only visible in large-scale developments driven by corporations such as the London City Island project discussed earlier, but also in numerous other propositions and practices. Richard Florida's Creative Class (Florida 2004) and Richard Landry's Creative City (Landry 2008) perfectly express the manner in which the focus on creativity can be absorbed into a neoliberal agenda. Tactics such as 'micro-interventions', 'urban acupuncture',[40] or 'retrofitting', which privilege the small-scale, have been used to raise real estate values in specific areas with only minor investments. They are reminiscent of the 'snowball effect' tactics of the urban regeneration of 1980s roll-back neoliberalism: a pooling together of (very limited) public resources for grand projects intended to kick-start an urban boom in an era of decline, of government retrenchment and the abandonment of 'planning' in its post-war sense. 'Localism', rather than empower the subaltern, can easily increase social, economic and spatial polarization: while central government, with its strategic overview, can redistribute resources according to needs, the animosity of the spatial practitioners towards planning, towards top-down decisions, and to state power jeopardizes such redistribution.[41] Negri, in contrast, has argued for scaling-up the contestation to a supra-state global level. 'There is a moment where one must take the leap,' he has said, 'to pose the real big problem that is behind all these micro-practices of which we are speaking and to think about how to respond to it …' (Querrien, Petrescu and Petcou 2007: 296).[42]

The 2010 UK government coalition agreement between the Conservatives and the Liberal Democrats echoed the anti-statist positions and emphasis on localism propagated by the participatory movement. It stated that:

> We will promote the radical devolution of power and greater financial autonomy to local government and community groups. […] We will rapidly abolish Regional Spatial Strategies and return decision-making powers on housing and planning to local councils […] we will radically reform the planning system to give neighbourhoods far more ability to determine the shape of the places in which their inhabitants live […]. We will abolish the unelected Infrastructure Planning Commission and replace it with an efficient and democratically accountable system that provides a fast-track process for major infrastructure projects.
>
> *(HM Government 2010: 11)*

A pre-2010 elections paper by the Conservatives appropriated the term 'open source urbanism' (Parvin 2013; Bradley 2015):

> The creation of an Open Source planning system means that local people in each neighbourhood – a term we use to include villages, towns, estates, wards or other

relevant local areas – will be able to specify what kind of development and use of land they want to see in their area. This will lead to a fundamental and long overdue rebalancing of power, away from the centre and back into the hands of local people.

(The Conservatives 2009: 2)

These documents as well as Prime Minister David Cameron's pet project the Big Society, proposing self-governance and management – which dissipated within a year of its 2010 launch – highlight the proximity of the ideas animating the participatory movement to those of neoliberals. There is little evidence that the practices pursued by the vanguard architects, like the theories of Negri, are in any fundamental sense disparate from, let alone a threat to the new economy. Many of the '68 protesters understood the binary opposition of communism–capitalism as merely two sides of the same technocratic coin;[43] the promise of '68 was of something radically different, yet today a similar critique can be directed at the May '68 movements and their offspring: their ideas and practices share a worldview with neoliberalism.

In the short time span since the birth of the architectural movement in question, many of the involved practices have shifted from highly critical and radical positions to a more nuanced and professional stance, discarding en route not only some of the naivety and simplicity of the earlier rhetoric, but also much of its radicalism. Urban-Think Tank, for example, have approached projects such as Vertical Gymnasium almost purely as an architectural design question, proposing a prototype, a solution that is generic enough to be repeated in various contexts – Caracas, Amman, New York. While highlighting density in their original proposition of a 'vertical gym' for Caracas slums, the gesture is repeated in the density-lacking Jordanian capital. It is difficult to identify their proposition as more 'social' than any other architectural design of our era, except for those aspects that are not controlled by the architects, such as the brief. So in what sense is the architectural design of the gym *social*?

Urban-Think Tank, like many of their peers and despite their denials, romanticize the richness and spontaneity of the everyday life of the informal cities of the Global South:

> This near-instantaneous, spontaneous creation of housing is highly democratic: the structures are equal in size, equivalent in materials, with little if any distinction in morphology or style. These barrio communities contain no institutional buildings, no representations of formal bureaucracy; they lack such services as refuse and waste disposal, and electricity is stolen. And yet they function: their self-regulating system creates living spaces for millions and entire new cities within the existing urban framework, without government assistance. [...] The growth of street vendors and the establishment of black markets are means both of evading the state's tax system and of self-establishment, revolutionizing the role of public space as a tactic, not a strategy, for shaping the city.
>
> *(Brillembourg, Feireiss, Hubert Klumpner 2005: 21)*

They are either unaware or wilfully oblivious of the manner in which their object of desire, the informal city, was created and exacerbated by precisely the free-market economy the architects supposedly oppose (Hidalgo 2011; Tonkiss 2012; 2013: 91–112). Many of the qualities identified in informal urbanism are associated with post-Fordist, neoliberal ideals: spontaneity, self-help, freedom. Already in 1971, the planner Patsy Healey retorted dryly that 'barrios are not romantic' (Healey 1971: 631). At the end of the day, many of the propositions of the young generation of architects are ridiculed even by Negri, who has written that: 'I almost laugh when my closest comrades talk about alternatives in terms of communes, self-managed gardens and city allotments, multifunctional squats, cultural and political ateliers, enterprises of common *Bildung*' (Negri 2009: 50).

The positions evident in the projects of the 2009 Berlage workshop appear less baffling when placed in proximity to the work of Hardt and Negri or Rancière. More disconcerting is the possibility that, in contrast to the philosophers, many among the architects in question have only a limited understanding of the full implications of their positions.

Personalization

Arguably the most important issue on an architectural scale of participation is mass housing: the emergence in the nineteenth century of mass housing meant also the disappearance of a specific user. In reaction, the 'abstract user' – a 'typical' user, an average who does not really exist – was conceived.[44] The discoveries of the architectural historic avant-garde, coupled by the post-war industrialization of the building industry, meant that post-war architecture drove mass housing to an apex, which was seen by the '68 generation as dehumanising, technocratic, and authoritarian. The sociologist Dennis Chapman wrote in 1965: 'The tenant of the rented house and the purchaser of the new house are rarely able to influence the design of the dwelling, even if they understood their own living habits sufficiently to do so, and as a rule they are not able to recognize the effects of dwelling design on their patterns of living …' (Lipman 1969: 197–98). De Carlo argued that:

> We can opt for an abstract idea of the user: the universal human being, with different symbolic connotations that the purposes and tastes of the dominant cultures of every epoch may attribute to him. In this case the discovery becomes a technical operation which intends to select and classify physiological and perhaps even 'spiritual' needs. An alternative is to opt for a concrete condition of society identifying a particular type of user, for example those belonging to a social underclass, and in this case the discovery becomes a political operation. We know where the first hypothesis, adopted to a large extent by the Modern Movement, takes us: to the illusory formulation of a universal scale intended to include all human needs but which instead, just because of the a priori contraction of reality on which it is based, ends up mirroring the interests, values and codes of the power structure.
>
> *(Giancarlo de Carlo 2005: 17)*

'The major fault of the UK architectural profession, 1945–65,' wrote Cedric Price in 1968, 'can be summarised as follows: UNAWARENESS THAT THE REAL "CLIENT" IS A COMBINATION OF ALL WHO ARE IN ANY WAY AFFECTED BY THE ARCHITECT'S ACTIONS' (Cedric Price 1968). The architect and researcher Amos Rapoport commented that '[p]eople, then, move into housing designed for a generalized type and values alien to them' (Rapoport 1968: 301). Aldo van Eyck called the generic user a 'fake' client. The architectural historian Dirk van den Heuvel summarized van Eyck's position as 'the "real" client has disappeared behind the "fake" client of anonymous government bodies' (Van den Heuvel 2015: 138). He suggested this has fed into the architect's reluctance to take on mass housing commissions. Against such 'dehumanizing' mass housing and loss of individuality (just as the 'user' vanished in a faceless 'typical user'), participatory architecture was offered as a solution (Blundell Jones, Petrescu, Till 2005b: xiv).

Many participatory projects, and particularly those acknowledged as successful, have required the non-experts to invest much time in acquiring the necessary knowledge, and demanded an investment of considerable time by the expert in negotiations and discussions as in the cases of Ralph Erskin's Byker Wall (1969), de Carlo's Matteotti Village (1972), or Alvaro Siza's Malagueira (1977). The Byker Wall project in Newcastle was a regeneration of a nineteenth-century slum. In contrast to post-war urban renewals, the project offered the inhabitants, a tightly knit working-class community, the opportunity to return after redevelopment. Erskin famously opened an office in the neighbourhood itself as a means of increasing the exchanges between the locals and the designers and of developing trust. While these efforts were only partially successful, they were, nevertheless, pioneering and influential (Collymore 1982).[45] The Italian steel conglomerate Treni initiated in the late 1960s the participatory Matteotti Village project, planned to house 3,000 of its workers. Giancarlo de Carlo spent a year – funded by Treni – in a taxing participatory process, in which the future dwellers themselves had to invest significant time in self-education and discussions. It included, as a sociologist involved in the project pointed out, '[t]wo months of daily meetings, one in the morning and another in the afternoon […] This was the most complex task to which De Carlo subjected himself' (Molinari 2015: 265). Yet the need to demolish existing 1930s housing to make way for the new build proved the downfall of the project. Actions by current residents prevented the project's completion.

Malagueira, a post-dictatorship social housing project in Évora, was an exemplary participatory mass housing project in which the local vernacular of unplanned settlements intertwined seamlessly with modernist sensibilities. Alvaro Siza commented on the participatory process:

> I have no knowledge of a project more discussed, step-by-step, more patiently revised and re-revised. At least 450 families, in several meetings, have seen it, listened to its explanation by words, models, sketches, drawings, photomontages; they delivered criticism, proposed changes, approved. Municipality technicians and representatives of the population gave their opinion; technicians from my office, from the engineers' office, from several services, have developed and reviewed it; when necessary, they have suggested changes, analysed the economical and technical viability, and coordinated efforts. Many people have officially approved the project. Others, and sometimes the same, have surreptitiously contested it.
>
> *(Mota, 2011: 50)*

More recent attempts, such as Carel Weeber's 'Het Wilde Wonen' ('wild dwelling') ended up, in the Dutch new town of Almere in the early 2000s, in presenting future owners with limited choices regarding their houses, typical of catalogue housing. Circumventing tedious discussions, such a consumer choice model ends up offering nothing of substance: small front garden and large back garden or vice versa? Blue or black window frames? Habitation and dwelling practices are hardly transformed by such restricted choice.

City councils, developers, and planners have been deterred not only by their loss of control of the process when participation in the full-sense of active decision-making by population takes place, but also by the length, expense and effort of such processes. Newark-based New

Community Corporation, for example, in its first years in the late 1960s and early 1970s, invested heavily in 'educating' the involved citizens, sending them on study trips across the US, involving them in didactic workshops and other activities (Choi 2011). These activities were later dropped.

Participatory architecture, more so than participatory urbanism, can therefore be considered a specific response to mass housing – an attempt to humanize it, to replace the abstract user with a real user. Beyond the question of mass housing, participation has limited architectural relevance, in the narrow sense: affluent individuals who commission the design and construction of their own home, or, alternatively, citizens who buy or rent existing properties, are not the concern of participatory architecture. Community centres, a specific interest of participatory architecture, are relatively limited as a commission in terms of ubiquity.[46] The empowerment of citizens, in this sense, appears less about democratization, and more about bettering mass housing and increasing its appeal to its dwellers, a new form of decorum – of 'suitability', 'fittingness', or 'character'.

The emergence of participatory architecture in the late 1960s followed the discussion of and interest in flexibility, triggered by concerns that architecture is too slow to satisfy a fast-transforming society, that yesterday's buildings are already obsolete by today's criteria. While participation has only a limited debt to this earlier discussion, a parallel discussion of personalization owes much more to the question of flexibility. The idea of a time-based design intertwines with flexibility and personalization, as demonstrated in an argument forwarded in 1968 by Rolf Goetze, regarding the monotony and lifelessness of suburban layout: 'The housing continues to evolve, units develop, change hands, families lose or add members, and the sterile appearing original, with its average family of 2.7 children, has evolved an interesting diversity and variation within an ordinary framework provided by the standardized layout' (Goetze 1968: 365). Amos Rapoport's focus on 'adaptability' in a 1968 article similarly linked personalization to flexibility. 'Architects need not accept the public's taste or design in its idiom. There is a way between the extremes of *laisser faire* and absolute control and that is to provide directed opportunity of expression and change', he wrote, echoing the conclusions reached by John Habraken. 'The designer would give up some of his absolute control and concentrate his skills on the design of "frameworks"' (Rapoport 1968: 305). Rapoport also associated the issue with the nascent interest in 'meaning': 'At each scale the environment and space organization have meaning for the inhabitants,' he commented, 'particularly in the measure that they can give it their *own meaning*' (Rapoport 1968: 300). Personalization can circumvent the need for participation, and consequently bypass the aporia of humanism versus post-humanism.

The argument for personalization in the 1960s developed initially as a critique of the standardized products of industrial society. The lack of specificity, the abstraction, the standardization of the serial products, whether chairs, cars or buildings, was alienating, it was argued. The loss of the specific user in mass production was depicted as the corrosion of humanism brought about by functionalist doctrines. The architectural critic Martin Pawley, in his 1968 'The Time House' article, wrote that:

> [conflict and cerebration] can be identified [...] particularly in the large, impersonal office, where evidence of the presence of individuals is generalized and functional rather than active and particular. To the individual this kind of context can represent a devaluation of the personality by its failure to portray any part of his subjectivity.
>
> *(Pawley 1969: 133)*

The personalization of these products – by colouring them, adding a feature, adapting them, etc. – was therefore a means of resistance to the 'one dimensional' society. Signs of personalization thus were seen as evidence of a lack, of a shortcoming of the mass product, and used as an argument against the logic of Fordism and industrialization. Pawley argued that:

> In the case of the automobiles for instance, where it is not uncommon for over a million identical units to be produced, it could be assumed that the combination of a ruthlessly objective brief with strictly limited conditions of use would provide a whole functional product sterilized against subjective infection. The result is very far from the case: within a week of purchase the vast majority of automobiles are personalized by one means or another. A vast accessory industry exists for just this purpose, with innumerable permutations of gadgetry to differentiate individual means of transport.
> *(Pawley 1969: 121)*

Pawley's adversaries here are functionalism, universalism, objectivism and abstraction. The argument is that 'subjectivity' is inescapable as evidenced by personalization, and therefore should be accommodated. 'If the designer cannot express *his* subjectivity,' Pawley writes, 'the lack is made good by the user: if neither knows how to associate with the object, the seller or advertiser finds a way' (Pawley 1969: 121–23). The impossibility of absolute functionalism is presented as reason to abandon functionalism: 'The ruthless development architect […] holding no truck with subjectivity, may well deny that in implementing his redevelopment plan he is exercising his subjective will, personalizing an impersonal process, subjectivizing for his own purposes the applied energy and expertise of others – but his denial is philosophically untenable' (Pawley 1969: 131).

Yet another point of view emerges regarding personalization by the late 1960s. It is obliquely expressed in 'Remedial Housing for Architects or Learning from Levittown', the study carried out in 1970 by Yale students directed by Robert Venturi, Steven Izenour and Denise Scott Brown, which led to the 1976 Smithsonian Institute exhibition 'Signs of Life: Symbols in the American City'. As a sequel to *Learning from Las Vegas*, the Levittown study was likewise directed against prevailing sentiments within architectural discourse – namely, the rejection of suburbia in general, and of catalogue housing such as Levittown in particular. The issue of mass housing is not at the fore of the study, yet it is nevertheless present: 'Social concern was an important part of the early Modern Movement in architecture and mass "social" housing one of its dearest topics,' the text accompanying the studio argued. 'Nowhere have the architect's claims and interest been greater yet nowhere has his impact been less' (Scott Brown 1992: 51).

Levittown offered its residents standardized, repetitive housing types, yet in contrast to more urban mass housing forms with which post-war architecture was preoccupied, here the typology was of a singular, detached house rather than a residential building with shared communal spaces (Figure 2.10). In Trafalgar West, Houston, the study argues, 'what is being "totally designed" is not a mega-structure of "anonymous", industrialised units, but an image and a way of life' (Scott Brown 1992: 51). The 'Signs of Life' exhibition focused on the personalization of the standardized homes of Levittown: the organization of the garden; the 'styling' of the living room by 'Georgian drapery', 'Regency style' couches, or 'art deco' mirrors; the ornamentation of the exteriors with 'Mediterranean grilles' or 'Colonial shutters'. The supposedly culturally 'vacuous' houses of Levittown appear culturally rich and individuated, each with its own identity and expression tailored to the inhabitants' own identities.

FIGURE 2.10 Truck supervisor Bernard Levey with his family in front of his new Levitt-built home, New York, 1950. Photograph by Bernard Hoffman/The LIFE Picture Collection/Getty Images.

Levittown's typology of the singular houses infers privacy and individuation, yet the standardization, the repetition of the type, in contrast, suggests the assimilation of individualism. The Levittown study implies the following: 1. Standardized homes require personalization; 2. Personalization should not be seen as a sign of failure, but of success, as it shows affection and caring for the home, and as an expression of individual identity; personalization is an expression of cultural richness rather than poverty; 3. Levittown, in particular, lends itself to personalization because of the (relatively) high level of individuation present in the singular house type and the ability of individuals to relate to the singular house type in a manner not possible in the residential building.

    A second and similar study is even more significant here. In 1968 Philippe Boudon, from the circle of Lefebvre, published an analysis of Le Corbusier's Quartiers Modernes Frugès housing in Pessac, near Bordeaux. Designed and built in the mid-1920s, it was one of the earliest examples of modernist mass housing, predating the realization of most of the Weimar Republic's architectural experiments. The project, financed by industrialist Henry Frugès, was designed for his employees. From inception, the project was caught between the expectation for differentiation of units by Frugès and his employees, and the demands of mass production. 'Originally,' Frugès reported, 'I had expressed a desire for the greatest possible variety in the designs, which would have meant that, ideally, no two villas would have been exactly the same' (Boudon 1972: 10). Yet in the process of design, he conceded that 'the diversity which I wished to achieve had to be reconciled with the need for serial production, since this was the only way of reducing costs to any appreciable extent' (Boudon 1972: 11).[47] A local newspaper, the *Petite Gironde*, parroted Le Corbusier's argument: 'The idea of building an individual house or group of houses treated as individual units on an economic basis is a delusion. Consequently, the time has come to consider the use of serial production methods in house building' (Boudon 1972: 20).

Pessac was seen as a failure, Boudon suggests, because it was understood as too abstract, too neutral, and too 'new'. A supervision architect interviewed by Boudon stated that '*the failure of the Pessac project* was due to [...] our professional attitude [which] is lamentable because we are producing *architecture in which we impose our will on our clients*; we are in a sense *the fascists of the building industry*' (Boudon 1972: 65). The evidence of this perceived failure was primarily the changes to the housing by the dwellers, adaptations which seemed to undermine Le Corbusier's intentions: addition of external decorations, closure of terraces, alterations to the horizontal window in the elevation, etc. The purity, aesthetic consistency, and cleanliness of the design was lost in the process of personalization and individuation (Figure 2.11).

Boudon carried out the study via a series of interviews, from which he could identify the elements of the housing that were seen positively or negatively by the inhabitants. He compared the layout of the housing to the layout of Oud's housing in Weissenhof, Stuttgart, in order to point out that Pessac's layout, in contrast to accepted opinion, is not 'functionalist'. Regarding the generic user, Boudon perceptively asked '[w]as it really the project that was standardized or was it the *modern family*, the "twentieth-century family"? The use here of the generic singular form would certainly seem to imply a standardized family' (Boudon 1972: 27).

Le Corbusier's 'serial production' in Pessac was a design principle rather than technique of physical construction: an ideology rather than technical innovation, Boudon argues (Boudon 1972: 34). It was about arranging standardized components in diverse forms, a method undertaken at the scale of the singular unit – the components being the kitchen, rooms, etc. – and at the scale of the neighbourhood – treating the housing units as components. Le Corbusier argued that '[r]ational construction based on the use of component blocks does not destroy individual initiative' (Boudon 1972: 35). He referred to the future inhabitant of Pessac in generic terms as Mr. X, 'whom neither of us [Le Corbusier and Frugès] knows but who will become the owner of one of these houses' (Boudon 1972: 35).

Lefebvre commented, regarding the quarter's residents, that '[i]nstead of installing themselves in their containers, instead of adapting to them and living in them "passively", they decided that as far as possible they were going to live "actively"' (Boudon 1972). Boudon's conclusion was that the specifics of the layout of the Pessac quarter and of the housing floor plans, including the abstract, neutral element of the modernist design, the open plan, the organization of standardized components, and Le Corbusier's non-functionalist approach enabled personalization, and were therefore commendable. He wrote unequivocally that 'the modifications carried out by the occupants constitute a positive and not a negative consequence of Le Corbusier's original conception' (Boudon 1972: 161).

FIGURE 2.11 Quartiers Modernes Frugès, Pessac, 2010. Photograph courtesy of Eva Chacón Linares.

The argument that emerges in Boudon's study of Pessac frames a specific understanding of the role of standardized mass housing: the provision of a neutral stage for self-realization. This was not a novel proposition, and reflected arguments that circulated among post-war architects, used, for example, to legitimize the common WBS 70 pre-fab system of the *betonbau* in the GDR (Flierl 1984: 63–67). Boudon's study, however, shifts the emphasis from the neutrality to the act of personalization. Rather than tailored to the specific user, as in bourgeois singular villas, the mass-produced housing has to remain neutral, and this neutrality, dependent upon abstraction, enables the self-realization of the inhabitant via personalization. Hence, the argument circumvents the need for participation, as adaptation to individual needs and desires is understood as a later development of the home, carried out and orchestrated by the inhabitant, and not necessarily incorporated into the process of design.

This logic has recently played out in projects such as the Half House (2004) and Cité manifeste (2005). The latter project, at Mulhouse, by Lacaton and Vassal, consisted of 14 single-family homes, a social housing project. The architects secured an agreement with the developer that a reduced cost for construction would allow additional square metres per unit to the ones allocated by the brief. The reduction of costs were achieved by producing a neutral home – less finishes and internal separations, thus allowing the inhabitants to adapt their homes to their needs, with the benefit of additional space (Figure 2.12). The 'unfinished' aspect of the homes was the interior, yet the entire project infused 'everyday' materials associated with greenhouses and temporary housing into the architecture. '[T]he new user starts to make decisions related to the amount of light or the anomalous dimensions like, "Where should I place my bed or table?",' said Jean Philippe Vassal, '[s]o Mulhouse was very much about making a loft that did not exist before, and transforming it into housing while keeping its spatial qualities' (Diaz Moreno and Garcia Grinda 2015: 13). The 'free dwelling' (*logis libre*), enabled by the open floor plans, perfectly develops the interests of Boudon and Lefebvre half a century ago (Stanek 2015: 115).

FIGURE 2.12 Lacaton and Vassal, Mulhouse, 2005. Interior view of personalized apartment. Photograph courtesy of Lacaton and Vassal.

Elemental's widely published Half Houses project, in Chile's Iquique, offered future dwellers a neutral, standardized, unfinished home – far more raw and 'unfinished' than the Mulhouse housing. This allowed not only a reduction of construction costs and consequently of the price of the properties, but also their adaptation, capitalizing on the typical condition of Latin American informal cities, in which self-build and vernacular are the norm. The investment of social capital, habit, and resourcefulness by future owners demonstrate John Turner's argument from the 1960s and 1970s regarding 'dweller control' and empowerment via self-build.[48] Here, in Iquique, the logic Boudon identified in Pessac is integrated into the design ambition, supplemented by the architectural fascination with the messiness, vitality, and (supposed) freedom of the vernacular. Elemental's and Lacaton and Vassal's projects demonstrate an alternative route to the empowerment of locals, providing some level of control over their dwellings, without necessitating a participatory process.

The current interests in customization as an offspring of personalization, or, more precisely, as the counterpart of personalization in the era of digital production, is rendered a rhetorical concern by Pessac, Mulhouse, and the Half House: the infusion of difference into mass housing via digitally driven customization currently allows differentiation only on a level of inessentials, of minor differences that hardly impact daily life (Baudrillard 2005), whereas the examples of personalization show a far more significant ability to adapt the neutral dwelling to individual needs and desires. The personalization of mass housing recasts in spatial forms the relation of individual to society, avoiding the total fragmentation expressed by singular villas, and the total assimilation of the individual in non-modified uniform mass housing.

What, then, is the logic of 'suitability', 'decorum', or 'character', which is pursued by architectural participation yet achieved in personalization by the dweller? In an early modern sense, Lord Kames wrote in 1762 that 'every building ought to have a character or expression suited to its destination' (Forty 2000: 123). The emergence of 'character' as a specific architectural category in the late eighteenth century took place exactly at the moment in which the fully fledged and psychologically 'deep' human subject formed in theatre and literature, and preceded by only a few years Kant's humanism. Goethe, in turn, suggested that a building's character ought to reflect the character of its maker (Forty 2000: 128). Consequently, the idea of character can easily be extended to suggest that a home ought to reflect the character of the dweller.

The argument that neutral mass housing circumvents the need for (pre-)tailoring the home to the individuality of the user suggests also a critique of architectural participation: the implicit pre-disposition of the demand for participation in housing towards the idea of 'character' and, therefore, of 'a house like me', the idea that the home should somehow represent the character of the inhabitant, that the object ought to communicate the identity of the user, whether formally, materially or decoratively. Such a concern is not at the fore of the participatory discourse, yet it is covertly present in participatory projects in mass housing. When Rapoport wrote that 'visual complexity by itself, even when it is achieved [by design] […] is difficult to personalize and impossible to change' (Rapoport 1968: 301), the design he referred to could be participatory as much as 'top-down'. Difference, in this instance, is produced in the object itself. This approach, on the one hand, returns to eighteenth-century notions of 'character', related to the rise of the individual subject in bourgeois society, and, on the other, to the recent phenomenon of hyper-expressive landmark buildings, precisely the phenomenon against which the participatory movement posited itself. At the end of the day, the demand for participation in mass housing appears to further the incursion of post-Fordism and neoliberalism, of which the 'starchitect' landmark buildings are a direct expression (Kaminer 2011a: 73–111), into daily life, assimilating, in process, dwelling and habitation into questionable worldviews and practices.

PART 3
Languages of Architecture

THE POLITICAL AS THE SYMBOLIC

Architecture and Symbolism

> [O]ne can modify social reality by modifying the agents' representation of it.
> *(Pierre Bourdieu 2002: 128)*

The rejection of symbolism by modernist architecture, whether in Louis Sullivan's work and in the early work of Frank Lloyd Wright, or later, by Le Corbusier, Mies van der Rohe, and Walter Gropius, was supported by a number of overlapping arguments. A key aspect of the rejection was a desire to rid architecture from its role of symbolizing social hierarchy and class, preparing the discipline for a classless society. This was an endeavour supported by progressive architects of diverse political persuasions. Related to this was an implicit understanding of architecture as an autonomous discipline, paralleling and involved in the 'autonomous' development of fine art, and hence the interest in removing everything superfluous to the architectural properties of the design, including all references to an 'outside' meaning. Another argument was related to industrial production and the intention, which underlay the design of Pessac and the Bauhaus experimentations of the 1920s, to synchronize architectural design with the logic of serial production. This necessarily meant a focus on the essential architectural elements at the expense of everything that appeared gratuitous, following ideas of standardization and efficiency widely discussed around 1914–30. The logic of industrial production focused on the quality of the object and its use value rather than on its meaning, rendering the symbolic properties of architecture superfluous.

Critics such as Reyner Banham noted in the 1960s that modernism had, in fact, symbolic content: Le Corbusier's buildings symbolized modernity by emulating, for example, the modern ocean liner rather than by strictly following functionalist principles (Banham 2001). By the 1970s, it seemed clear enough that there was no complete escape from symbolism – or, more correctly, from significations and meanings. Architecture always 'means' something, and at a basic level, at the very least it denotes its function. Numerous publications studying the meaning of architecture argued that architecture's meanings cannot be suppressed or avoided (Dorfles 1962; Norberg-Schulz 1963; Jencks and Baird 1969; Eco 1986). Yet this signification belonged to a different order than the one rejected by modernism – it was certainly more abstract and denotative than the connotative representation of social hierarchy. To a limited extent, it was also more egalitarian, even though underneath the cultural references lay a class-based substratum. Subsequently, postmodernist architecture attempted to re-introduce the representational, via, among others, Charles Jencks's argument that architecture is first and foremost a field of communication rather than a means of spatial or social production (Jencks 1973; 1977). Yet despite a short infatuation with the symbolic, by the late twentieth century the discipline of architecture appeared to retain its disavowal of representational content. Symbolism has been mostly limited to public discourse regarding the architecture of public or quasi-public buildings such as Foster's Bundestag or Libeskind's Freedom Tower.

The following section does not intend to return to the 1970s discussions of language, of meaning, and of representation. Rather, it will selectively study three areas related to the linguistics of architecture, beginning with the symbolic, continuing with the language of urban form, and ending with an argument regarding the poverty of architectural language. The first of the three will outline the symbolic core at the heart of the political, and will discuss the least controversial correlation of architecture to society; that is, the contribution of architectural design to the symbolic manifestation of society. The second chapter will study the argument that the morphological language of built form is determined by, and therefore also shapes to some extent – societal organization, whereas the last chapter will outline the reductive character of architecture as a strength rather than weakness.

While the 1970s discussion of these issues is not at the centre of this section, the particular lens through which historic work was assessed in the 1970s is highly significant: the architecture of 1920s Weimar Germany discussed here in the second chapter, for example, is read via the writings of Tafuri from the late 1960s and early 1970s. The three issues interrogated here, the symbolic, urban form, and language, are addressed in this section because they do not receive adequate attention in the contemporary discussions of architecture's efficacy. This oversight is cause for concern, because the symbolic, as will be argued later, *is* the political, and the consideration of urban form as a means of societal organization brings to the fore an issue that is architectural in a sense that many of the issues currently featuring in the architectural discourse of agency are not. Significantly, the discussion of urban forms shifts the focus of this book from the political to political economy and social forms. And finally, the limitations of architecture as language are, arguably, responsible for the difficulties architects and architectural critics have faced in describing architecture as political, but also enable a correlation to the political, characterized similarly as an imprecise field of communication.

The Symbolic Constitution of Society

In the work of Laclau, the epicentre of the political is the moment of 'articulation'. 'We will call articulation any practice establishing a relation among elements such that their identity is modified as a result of the articulatory practice,' wrote Mouffe and Laclau in 1985 (Laclau and Mouffe 2001: 105). Where Mouffe, in her own work, highlights strife as the core of the political, here the understanding shifts to an emphasis on framing. Articulation ties together disparate demands and ideals and sets others apart. Articulation can create, strengthen or undermine an equivalential chain, it creates synergies across very different social and identity groups and is vital to hegemony. It is necessarily correlated to ideology.

If ideology, as Louis Althusser argued, is the shared lens or filter through which individuals and collectives interpret reality, 'organize' it in a mental sense of relating and distinguishing diverse aspects of reality and attaching to them explanatory causes, then ideology is necessarily involved in identity formation of individuals and groups (Althusser 1969; 2001).[1] Ideology thus contributes to the formation of individual identities as well as their socialization in larger groups, and is constituted or affirmed by the identities themselves. In other words, ideology and worldview are key aspects of individual and collective identity formation, a key aspect of the political. Bourdieu has written that political action:

> aims to make and unmake groups – and, by the same token, the collective actions they can undertake to transform the social world in accordance with their interests – by producing, reproducing or destroying the representations that make groups visible for themselves and for others.
>
> *(Bourdieu 2002: 127)*

Lefebvre wrote that '[s]ymbolic representation serves to maintain these social relations in a state of coexistence and cohesion. It displays them while displacing them – and thus concealing them in symbolic fashion – with the help of, and onto the backdrop of, nature' (Lefebvre 1991: 32). The process of forming the collective identities, which become a base for (politically) raising collectively shared demands, includes a continuous battle over creating and severing associations and links between the (ideological) interpretations of diverse aspects of reality in a constant attempt to formulate a coherent and consistent worldview, a process to which articulation is central. The aim of the battling factions is to create worldviews that can be robust enough to resist critiques and attempts from 'the outside' to undo the links and correlations of which they are formed. The symbolic is here the means of holding together the diverse elements that form the identities of collectives, it is an instrument of according cohesion among disparate elements. Rather than superfluous to the political moment, the symbolic is the ground zero of the political.

Already in the work of sociologist Émile Durkheim in the late nineteenth and early twentieth centuries, the symbolic emerges as the substance that ties together a collectivity. Durkheim's writings on religion (Durkheim 1915; 1998b), developed by the study of anthropological work on the Australian aboriginal clans, identified a role for the sacred in the social formation of collective identities. Durkheim understood society as a body that has its own consciousness, which is more than a simple aggregate of the consciousness of the individual subjects who compose it. Collective consciousness steers individuals more profoundly than individuals shape society (Giddens 1971: 67). Morals and ideals emerge as a key aspect of the continuity of society, though they too transform over time. The process of the division of labour is explained as a rational process related to the growth of human population and density, and the social fragmentation associated with this process as well as with rising individualism, is not seen as social disintegration per se, but suggests a transformation of ideals and morals rather than a nihilistic abandonment of morals (Giddens 1971: 72).

As traditional society transforms into a modern, complex and mass society, the collective consciousness becomes increasingly diffuse, abstract and general. This abstraction enables a wide range of diverse 'applications' or 'interpretations' of it by subgroups within society (phratries or moieties) and by individuals (Durkheim 1984: 172). Durkheim claimed that 'society is both the source and repository of human ideals' (Giddens 1971: 107). Society is formed by these shared ideals, beliefs and morals, to the extent that society and its collective consciousness are hardly inseparable.

Politics, according to Durkheim, requires some level of separation between the governed and government, a separation absent in more simple social structures such as the Australian tribes. 'We should then define the political society,' argued Durkheim, 'as one formed by the union of a greater or lesser number of secondary social groups [such as families or phratries], subject to the same one authority which is not itself subject to any other superior authority' (Durkheim 1957: 45). As these secondary groups develop from phratries, clans and families in more simple societies to more diversified social groups in modern societies, the necessary defence of individuals from the power of government and the emergence of civil society becomes evident. Yet Durkheim did not correlate the symbolic to the political. Politics, for him, was merely the territory for the 'administration of things', a separate sphere to that of morals.

Religious systems in all forms of society, according to Durkheim, create dichotomies of the profane and the sacred. Religion is thus a form of solidarity between members of a defined group of followers and believers, based on shared ceremonies and rituals (practices), and shared morals and worldview (beliefs), all conceived as a reaction to what is perceived by the group as the sacred (Durkheim 2015; 1998b). The totem is an object which embodies the sacred and is separated from profane daily objects to avoid its 'contamination' and to enforce the dichotomy. What makes an object sacred is not its intrinsic characteristics. The sacristy of the totem is expressed in its representation, which is often perceived as the most sacred of all, and by members of the relevant clan, who are themselves 'sacred' and share the sacred properties. Hence, group identity and unity emerge via the sacred, with the totem being merely one aspect of this. Rituals and ceremonies develop around the totem and its sacred representation. The ritual and ceremony enable detaching the individual subjects from their profane daily life. They not only prevent the contamination of the sacred by the profane, but also enhance the sacred moment by containing it in a specific time. All collective moral beliefs have a sacred character.

Durkheim writes that 'the totem is above all a symbol, a material expression of something else':

> Because the clan cannot exist without a name and without an emblem, and because this emblem is constantly before the eyes of every individual, it is towards this and towards the objects of which it is the image that the sentiments which society awakens in its members are directed. As a result, men are forced to imagine the collective force whose influence they experience in the form of the thing which serves as the flag of the group.
> *(Durkheim 1915: 236)*

Durkheim calls the force that operates on the clan members, uniting them and steering them, *mana*. It is a force that is universal and indefinite as much as it is pervasive. The totem represents the clan, understood here as society, and differentiates it from other clan-societies. In effect, the totem principle and society are one, and individual subjects within society, who are dependent on society in numerous manners, submit to this higher force of the collective, the *mana*. Obedience to the collective force is necessary in order to belong to society and to enjoy the advantages of community, whether regarding marriage and reproduction, social standings, security from other clans, defences from nature, or other shared means of existence – regarding, among others, food, health, heating, and shelter. As the collective forces act on individuals via 'mental' rather than material pressures, they are felt yet are not perceptible to clan members as social forces. Hence, these forces are explained by a transfiguration, as sociologist Simoneta Falasca-Zamponi calls the process: the understanding of the social force as a mythical force, the *mana* (Falasca-Zamponi 2011: 38–39).

Marcel Mauss, Durkheim's nephew, argued that 'there are no symbols unless there is communion, and the fact of communion creates a bond which might give the illusion of the real, but is in fact already the real'(Falasca-Zamponi 2011: 50). Representations are not to be judged as true or false, Mauss argued, but rather, must be understood as a vital aspect of community-creating. Mauss furthered Durkheim's understanding that societies are systems of (shared, collective) representations, by arguing that representations and acts, the ideal territory of symbols and the material territory of praxis, are intertwined: a complete separation and differentiation is not possible, as one feeds into the other. Mouffe and Laclau argued, years later, that 'the problem of the political is the problem of the institution of the social, that is, the definition and articulation of social relations in a field criss-crossed with antagonisms' (Laclau and Mouffe 2001: 153).

For Mauss, like Durkheim, politics belonged to the state, and for both sociologists, the separation of spheres in modern society was a fact they accepted. Nevertheless, for Mauss, in 'primitive' societies, in the absence of 'state', politics and morals were one. Comprehending the 'total social fact', the term he coined to characterize rich and complex social phenomena such as 'the gift', required overcoming, in the sphere of sociological research, the modern division of labour (Mauss 1970; Falasca-Zamponi 2011: 56–61). Mauss, consequently, prepared the ground for an ambitious endeavour for sociology: unfolding the machinations of totality.

Architecture's Political Symbolism

The symbolic content of architecture typically refers to a shared worldview or symbolic order. Familiar examples include skyscrapers, which are understood to represent corporate power in a very literal sense. These straightforward and generally accepted modes of symbolization fit into narratives of power contestation, as in the story of the development of the Manhattan skyscrapers delineated as a fierce competition between local publishers, driven by the belief that dominating the Manhattan skyline with the tallest building of all, projects prowess, which in turn would be rewarded by larger circulation of the newspapers. This familiar trope from the history of 1920s Manhattan demarcates a transition between two conditions. In the first, economic success and affluence lead society to the investment in culture, in the arts, and in spectacular buildings that express society's achievements. This expression is literal, because of the cost and effort (technical or other) of the endeavour, as well as symbolic, by projecting an image of the affluence and prowess. In the second and more recent condition, a landmark building is used to symbolically establish the prowess, relevance and vitality of a city as a means of attracting international investment. In this second condition, associated with Guggenheim Bilbao and city branding, affluence does not precede such architecture, but is created by it (Zukin 1995). Such a process is reliant on the collective association of high-end landmark buildings with affluence, and hence, on past experiences.

Another argument regarding the architectural symbolic relates to the passage from Fordism to post-Fordism, and has already been discussed in this book, albeit in other contexts. Here, the architectural avant-garde's implementation of Fordism, as in the work of Ludwig Hilberseimer, did not only apply the principles of efficiency and standardization in the spatial organization of buildings and cities, but also signified these ideas. In more recent times, the spectacular architecture of the landmark buildings of Gehry, Eisenman, Hadid, Morphosis and others perfectly represented freedom, creativity and difference, all of which are part and parcel of the worldview and self-image of post-Fordist society as much as efficiency and equality belonged to a previous era: *zeitgeist*, the spirit of the epoch, in built form.

All this is familiar territory and hardly controversial. Yet these symbolic representations are necessarily political, as they coincide with society's self-image, the shared values that society venerates and sees as 'sacred'. They are abstract and general; they lack specificity. But this is also the condition of Laclau's empty signifiers, and of the 'new' values Durkheim associated with modern society. The rebuilding of Ground Zero in New York brings to the fore the interweaving of the symbolic and the political with the architectural. This high-profile project and the battles surrounding it, disseminated via much media debate, demarcated political positions and highlighted fundamental questions regarding the role of the political economy vis-à-vis politics and the political.

As high-profile carriers of symbolic content, the status of the Twin Towers was surprisingly hazy. Their tenants were a multiplicity of companies ranging in scale and power, and irrelevant to the importance of the buildings themselves. The buildings' familiarity to the international public was significantly overshadowed by the iconic status of the Empire State Building or the image of the Chrysler Building. The Twin Towers were erected by the Port Authority of New York and New Jersey (PANYNJ), a quasi-governmental company, yet the Twin Towers' office spaces were within the free rental market, and the buildings were leased to developer Larry Silverstein shortly before the attacks. The 'World Trade Center' was a generic name, used as a marketing device for buildings in many cities, including Brussels, Amsterdam and Rotterdam.[2] Rather than their short reign as tallest buildings in the world, it is the domination by the Twin Towers of the view of Manhattan from the south-west that made them a spectacularly familiar sight, appearing as the most iconic of structures within an iconic image of New York City.

After 9/11, the Lower Manhattan Development Corporation (LMDC) was created as a subsidiary of the Empire State Development Corporation, which is controlled by the governor of the State of New York. LMDC commissioned the architecture firm Beyer Blinder Belle and engineers Parsons Brinkerhoff to prepare a master plan for the reconstruction of the area. These schemes, alongside others by Peterson/Littenberg, Cooper Robertson, and David Childs (SOM), were presented at a public consultation event in the Javits Center in July 2002. They were rejected following a public outcry and media outrage. The outcry, and the popularity of non-official competitions for the redesign by the *New York Times* and *New York* magazine, which solicited entries by 'starchitects', led the LMDC to withdraw the schemes and announce its own competition. Seven invited teams took part, with Libeskind declared in February 2003 as the winner (Figure 3.1) and the THINK team as runner up.[3] Initially celebrated as a great moment for New York and for architecture, Libeskind's proposal was soon marginalized by the developer Silverstein, the leaseholder and the main funder of the rebuilding via insurance money. Silverstein forcefully steered the project towards more standard corporate architecture, developed by his own architect, David Childs of Skidmore, Owings & Merrill (SOM).[4]

The Political as the Symbolic 141

FIGURE 3.1 Ground Zero/World Trade Center winning competition entry, the Freedom Tower on the left, Studio Daniel Libeskind (SDL), 2003. Courtesy of SDL.

Rafael Viñoly and Suzanne Stephens attributed the setbacks in the process to a mix-up between architectural and urban design (Viñoly 2003; Stephens 2004). The initial schemes presented by Beyer Blinder Belle were all master plans, and were attacked for lacking architectural specificity, identified as 'banal' by a media and public that presumed the generic envelopes represent the actual buildings. The ensuing competition, in turn, was presented as an 'innovative design study' while asking for master plans from the selected teams. Here, however, the responses were decidedly more architecturally elaborated than the original master plans of Beyer Blinder Belle and company. The appeal of Libeskind's entry was architectural rather than urban. Hence, the qualities that needed to be preserved in the passage from competition to realization and from master plan to architecture were architectural rather than urban – a misconception, and a cause of disappointments, as argued by Viñoly and Stephens.

There is, however, a more glaring conundrum at the heart of the reconstruction project. Silverstein, a private developer, was expected to produce a highly symbolic building on a national as well as international, public level. Such demands are typically placed on high-end public buildings, such as parliaments or national libraries, not on private enterprise focused on profit-making. Libeskind's original design for the Freedom Tower (now named One World Trade Center) ended up as a typical corporate skyscraper. In the process, much of what was striking and spectacular, that is, much of what captivated Governor Pataki and the public in Libeskind's original design, was eliminated. In this sense, the rejection of the original schemes by Beyer Blinder Belle should not necessarily be seen as a misreading. The master plan schemes were indeed bland and technocratic. Their purpose was to respond to specific quantitative and utilitarian questions, primarily regarding the positioning of transport and circulation and the allocation of 11 million square feet of office space – a familiar marriage of the utilitarian with the economic. In all likelihood, because of the economic pressures on the project, the building envelopes would be completely filled by the developers to maximize profit, making the form of the elements within the master plans not a guidance, but a final result.

Missing from the initial schemes was symbolic content. The commissioning, with the most standard of briefs, of master plans which address functional and economic considerations while ignoring the symbolic for such a contested site, led to the humiliating retreat of LMDC and Beyer Blinder Belle. The participants of the 'innovative design study' competition were smart enough to identify this condition, and to overdevelop the architectural content of their proposals at the expense of the master planning aspects, providing first and foremost powerful imagery with symbolic content. Libeskind's imagery, addressing memory, formal innovation and creativity, providing both literal and abstract symbolism as well as spectacle, proved to be a perfect response to public expectations. The political–symbolic triumphed, temporarily, over the technocratic–utilitarian–economic.

The victory was short lived, however, because of the power of the economic forces involved and the limited power of the public and its representatives. The efforts of mayors Giuliani and Bloomberg, who could not be suspected of being anti-business, to argue against deploying the logic of economic development faltered. The centrality of Silverstein to the reconstruction process meant that the corporate vision tamed and reduced the symbolic–political, an outcome that emphasizes the dominance of economy over politics in contemporary society (Figure 3.2). The architect and critic Michael Sorkin succinctly argues that a key moment of the derailment of the process was a mix-up not between urban design and architecture, but between the memorial and the reconstruction of the towers: a shift of expectation for a public symbolic value from the memorial – a public structure par excellence, and hence suitable for such a role – to the new tower, a commercially driven enterprise, and hence unable to fulfil the expectations (Sorkin 2003).

Yet it can also be argued that Silverstein and Child's corporate vision was short-sighted. The entire economy of the skyscraper is built, after all, on symbolic economy: the ratio of rentable area to utility areas is notoriously bad for tall buildings, and the construction costs are considerably higher than for low buildings. The symbolic power of the skyscraper, as a

FIGURE 3.2 One World Trade Center, Skidmore, Owings & Merrill (SOM). Photograph © James Ewing | OTTO, courtesy of SOM.

landmark building that projects corporate might, however, allows higher rents, and renders the 'problem' of bad ratio and high construction costs irrelevant. The World Trade Center project necessarily carries a greater symbolic weight than any standard skyscraper. Such symbolic weight, expressed via a highly symbolic design, could easily have led to higher demand for spaces and higher rents. Silverstein and Child failed to fully take advantage of the conditions of post-Fordist society and of symbolic capital, missing, by 'playing safe', the potentials to maximize profit.

The expectation for symbolic form in the design of the new World Trade Center was for a symbolism that expresses the American consensus: a broad and inclusive symbolism. This is the type of symbolism expected from architecture – particularly in public buildings – and the one promoted by Jencks. It is affirmative, services dominant power and ideologies, and corresponds to the type of symbolic order studied by Durkheim. By symbolizing prowess, affluence or ideals, the architectural design also affirms the social stature and hegemony of the represented ideals or institutions.

Collège de Sociologie

In July 1937, the renegade Surrealists Georges Bataille, Roger Caillois, Georges Ambrosino, Pierre Klossowski, Pierre Libra and Jules Monnerot announced on the pages of their journal *Acéphale* the formation of the loose study group the Collège de sociologie. The group would study in the following two years the relation of aesthetics to politics via the work of Durkheim. The sociologist Falasca-Zamponi characterizes the questions the group addressed in contemporary terms: 'Is it possible to reconcile affectivity with democracy, emotional unity with openness and tolerance, aesthetic concerns about expressive form with democratic decision-making?' (Falasca-Zamponi 2011: 5). The group itself announced that:

> The precise object of the contemplated activity can take the name of Sacred Sociology, implying the study of all manifestations of social existence where the active presence of the sacred is clear. It intends to establish in this way the points of coincidence between the fundamental obsessive tendencies of individual psychology and the principle structures that govern social organization and are in command of its revolutions.
>
> *(Ambrosino, Bataille, Caillois et al. 1988: 5)*

The key figures animating the Collège were Bataille, Caillois and Michel Leiris (Merle 2012: 118–20; Falasca-Zamponi 2011: 5–7). The small group of intellectuals assembled once a fortnight for lectures on and discussions of diverse topics such as Carnival, the army, and shamanism. The topics were selected for their role in community formation and in the creation of solidarity via the sacred. Caillois characterized the endeavour as the interrogation of 'the problems of power, of the sacred, and of myths' (Caillois 1988: 11).[5] Durkheim's study of religion and social formation in primitive societies enabled the group to study the forces of the irrational undercurrent in contemporary society, infusing the sacred with ideas of contingency and violent contestation. The Collège identified the manner in which fascism deployed the sacred in order to enhance collective unity, and rather than identify the sacred with fascist 'irrationality', it perceived the successes of fascism to be facilitated by contemporary society's – and liberal democracy's – weakness and fragmentation, caused by its utilitarian rationality and rejection of the sacred. Hence, the project of the Collège was to restore the sacred as a generator of a new collectivity that is radical and progressive. The sacred emphasized the collectivity, subsuming the individual into the collective in a total sense, impossible in the hyper-individualistic liberal democracy, yet with different and lesser cohesion than imagined by Durkheim or practiced by fascism. The Collège termed this territory 'sacred sociology'.

The Collège perceived society to be construed by autonomous spheres. Politics were, as in Durkheim's work, associated with the profane utilitarian, whereas aesthetics with illusion. Instead, rituals and symbols were at the heart of the sacred, and hence of society. Bataille claimed that the myth 'cannot be separated from the community whose creature it is and that ritually takes possession of its authority' (Bataille 1988: 22).[6] Falasca-Zamponi highlights the pitfalls of the Collège's analysis: postulating the separation of spheres as understood by Weber or Durkheim prevented the group from identifying the tight correlation of the political, the aesthetic, and the sacred in contemporary society.

What evaded Bataille and Caillois, as it did Durkheim, then, was the notion of the political. Their blind spot replicated the case of the secret societies of the Enlightenment, which developed their ideas in the waning years of absolutist power, unable to conceive of a 'political' beyond the sphere of politics of the absolutist state – a sphere devoid of the political, reduced to administration and policy. If the political imperative of values and morals was veiled, it was partially due to their absence from politics, and partially due to their universal claim. Claiming the universality of these morals was part of a hegemonic process, which entailed de-politicization by their depiction as universally valid, 'naturalized' values.

Durkheim and the Collège were, in fact, preoccupied with the political while considering the territory of the sacred, of morals and values, as external to the utilitarian world of the profane politics of their respective eras. A couple of decades later, Claude Lefort, a founding member of the radical group Socialisme ou barbarie, provided a crucial step in the elaboration of the relation of symbols and the sacred to society and the political (Falasca-Zamponi 2011: 238–52). Whereas for Durkheim and Mauss society and its representations were so interwoven they were inseparable, for Lefort, the symbolic is separated from society: it is a form of alterity, which has to be distanced and different from society in order to be the locus of power. A symbolic order or power that coincides with society, which is the same as society, cannot have power over society in the first place (Doucet 2013: 160–61). Lefort's understanding of the symbolic was inspired by Machiavelli and developed through ideas gleaned from Merleau-Ponty and Lacan (Breckman 2013: 178).[7] Machiavelli's argument that conflict is a key ingredient of any society is blended with a phenomenological position regarding the body politic. It places the symbolic in the specific locus of the sacred: it is 'above' society, it is created by society and creates society – it is both reflective and constitutive. All societies are necessarily political, Lefort argued, not just modern ones that boast a separation of government and governed, as all societies have power relations.

Lefort's work aimed at identifying a force which, while taking part in the formation of a society through unity, requires rather than curtails difference and conflict. The separation of the symbolic from society enables the existence of diversity and heteronomy within a society that is nevertheless united and regulated, in a limited sense, by shared symbolic forms. Power, which is here, in effect, the political, is constituted by (and is) symbolic form, and is elevated above the real – the latter being the territory of social conflict driven by diversity of competing interests. Yet despite the seeming externality of political and symbolic form to society, they are by no means superfluous. Society would be impossible without the political – a society without such symbolic form would not become a society in the first place, and would not be able to conceive of itself as such. The gap separating the symbolic from society is manifested in the fact that the symbolic is never a precise representation of society – there is always an excess, which prevents the creation of the perfect symbolic image.[8]

Lefort demonstrated his thesis by studying three forms of society: the absolutist Ancien Régime, the democratic, and the totalitarian. In the case of the Ancien Régime, Lefort argues, the figure of the sovereign was at the heart of the symbolic order, which explained and legitimized the sovereign's power as the place of transition between the divine and the secular, the sacred and the profane, representing knowledge, law and power. The body of the monarch, or, in effect, the image of the body of the monarch, is the symbolic vehicle that produces the pre-modern society (Flynn 2005). In contrast, in the democratic order the symbolic place of power remains a void, as no singular figure can assume such a powerful and symbolic position within a democratic society, not even 'the people'. The monarch is effaced, removed, and the place formally occupied by the monarch remains empty. This absence is somewhat different from Laclau's 'empty signifiers' (Laclau 2007). It is a lack, but of a different kind: a headless figure – Bataille's *acéphale*. In a democratic society, diverse figures and movements claim to speak on behalf of the legitimate body, 'the people', hence to occupy the empty seat of symbolic power, and their claims to legitimacy are necessarily tested and challenged. The occupation of this 'void', this empty seat of power at the heart of the democratic symbolic by a strong leader, or image of a leader, marks a retreat from democracy, as much as the attempt to collapse the symbolic into society, to create a 1:1 relationship between the social and its image, similarly marks a transition into totalitarianism. In the totalitarian state, the attempt is made to fill the void with a materialization of 'the people', a strategy aimed to rid society of internal conflicts and establish a total unity without diversity. An absence at the heart of the symbolic order is therefore a basic condition of democracy, which, on the one hand, enables difference and contestation, sensed as fragmentation, but on the other, causes instability and contingency. The instability and the absence call for rectifying the symbolic order, yet such a process – not dissimilar to Mouffe and Laclau's 'hegemony' – necessarily reduces democracy. Marc G. Doucet wrote of Lefort's argument:

> Once the democratic symbolic order is in place, it provides a logic for socio-political contestation as a constitutive dimension of the ordering of power. This is not to say that protest will somehow naturally occur, or that all forms of socio-political protest are necessarily 'democratic'. […] In this sense, there is an important distinction to be made between the democratic symbolic order as a particular ordering of power and the traditional principles of democracy, such as autonomy, popular sovereignty, liberty, equality, accountability, and transparency. The former does not guarantee or necessarily sustain the latter. The democratic symbolic order merely provides the necessary conditions to mount social protest against what appears as 'non-democratic centers of power', understood as those that would seek to make themselves one with power.
>
> *(Doucet 2013: 165–66)*

The symbolic, or the sacred, the 'mortar' which constructs a community as much as it reflects it, is therefore no less than the political itself. And this logical sequence leads back to Laclau's understanding of the core political as the symbolic moment, the moment of articulation.

Aesthetics and Politics

Roger Caillois understood aesthetics, literature and taste as the arena of individualist subjectivity, presumed to be removed from any collective understandings (Falasca-Zamponi 2011: 152). They were not, he argued against prevailing opinion, the locus of contemporary myth. Art belonged to the realm of the profane. Collective consciousness merely inspired artistic work. Bataille and Caillois criticized art's distance from daily life; the aesthetic, understood in the sense of high art and Kantian disinterestedness, was seen as an illusion, an expression of individualistic society. In this sense, the anti-art stance of the two reflected the historic avant-garde's criticism of art's disinterestedness (Bürger 1996), but also carried it further, rejecting the historic avant-garde itself as merely 'art'. Yet the aesthetic appears to be, despite the arguments of Caillois, within the territory of the sacred. Walter Benjamin, in 'The Work of Art in the Age of Mechanical Reproduction' (Benjamin 1968), suggested that in contemporary society the political spectacle replaces the religious ritual – and that the political spectacle is created by the convergence of the political and the aesthetic.

The philosopher Jerome Stolnitz succinctly traces the latent relation of aesthetic disinterestedness to morals and values, and hence, also to the sacred and the political. He discusses Lord Shaftesbury's rejection in the eighteenth century of action directed at an ulterior objective, whether 'egoistic' or 'altruistic'. Stolnitz argues that in Shaftesbury's conception of the aesthetic, an understanding is formed in which disinterestedness, the core of the aesthetic disposition in modern society, is necessarily ethical: the appreciation of god, or, alternatively, of beauty, for its own ends rather than for external interests, is, for Shaftesbury, the expression of truly moral existence (Stolnitz 1961; Falasca-Zamponi 2011: 10–11). 'Virtuous Man' was thus marked by an aesthetic disinterestedness. Whereas this formulation was transformed significantly in Kantian aesthetics, the principle according to which such aesthetic disinterestedness is subjugated to moral value, while removed from the fore of the argument, is nevertheless present. The *sensus communis* of which Kant wrote, is a shared 'common sense' of beauty, that is, a collective rather than purely individual or subjective ground on which aesthetic judgements are made.

Hence, the shared capacity to appreciate the 'sacred' in a work of art creates a community. And that shared capacity is the aesthetic disposition, which merges with the characteristics of the works of art that are appreciated – the aesthetic content. The appreciation and what is appreciated through the aesthetic are the sacred. In the era of Enlightenment, with 'society' understood in narrow terms of 'respectable' citizens who could proficiently read, write, and rationally discuss contemporary issues, Kant's inferred community resembles this specific and limited Enlightenment-era civil sphere. So while reason governed certain spheres of life, a shared aesthetic disposition, an 'interpreter' as well as constitutor of the sacred, governed the territory of art. The rejection of 'politics' by Enlightenment aesthetics can therefore be related to the perception, among the rising bourgeoisie and the secret societies to which many belonged, of 'politics' as the realm of the utilitarian, whereas their project called for subjugating such profane territory to the sacred – morality. Aesthetic thought thus echoed the conclusions reached by the secret societies, positing aesthetics as apolitical and moral, and hence as superior to politics.[9] Such understandings were perfectly reflected by Schiller's 'moral stage'.

Consequently, aesthetics, in its Enlightenment understanding, kept the profane world of politics at a distance. Aesthetics and morals intermesh, becoming inseparable, and take part in forming the ground from which a community emerges – albeit an elite, a small 'consensual' civil society. As this restricted 'society' became more inclusive and grew in the nineteenth century to incorporate a larger segment of the population, high art increasingly became a niche field, defining a small elite community of art connoisseurs but falling short of supplying a sacred form for the larger society. Instead, a yet unresolved battle between certain forms of 'profane' mass culture, aspiring to the status of sacristy, and high culture, clinging to the residues of its once sacred status, has been waged since the 1920s. By this time, values and morals, the political, became increasingly, though still to a limited degree, drawn into the arena of politics via an agonistic process of democratization and egalitarianism.

The increasing fragmentation of society became evermore visible by the 1970s, echoed in cultural fragmentation and in the retreat of a state-supported didactic and patronizing 'middlebrow' culture in the face of commercial mass culture. Identity groups no longer foregrounded class, often veiling class differences by use of culture. Subcultures, in particular, as forms of cultures 'filtering up' from lower classes in a reversal of the more standard 'trickle down' of conformist hegemonic culture of aspiration, ended up cutting across class divisions and transcending the issue completely. Rather than an emergence of a new hegemonic culture per se, co-optation by commerce became the established, hegemonic means of countering the threat, of perpetuating the status quo by a *trompe-l'oeil* of constant change. Importantly, though, the illusion of a pluralism of cultures was paralleled by a pluralism of secondary symbolic meanings, not of primary symbols.

Architectural Opposition

The link between the symbol and the symbolized, which is at the heart of the symbolic order, appears as a 'weak' link because the relation seems to be merely associative, a minor improvement to the arbitrariness of the relation of the signifier to the signified. The weakness of the link suggests the easiness of breaking it, inferring that the symbolized is superfluous. Yet the relation of the signified to the signifier, even if merely a cultural code that can be altered and changed, is nevertheless a relation that matters – for it is the relation itself that is at the centre of the political. Maintaining or breaking, reconfiguring and re-establishing such relations is the core of political activity and strife, of political articulation. If the political is an agency that, to a certain degree at least, takes part in shaping society's development, then the relations of symbols to symbolized are themselves central to the shaping of society.

Symbolic relations have a contingent character, and are malleable and prone to reconfiguration. It is precisely this aspect of the symbolic which is of particular value to movements and agents who are committed to producing change via the political: just as much as oppositional equivalential chains can be broken or undone by dominant forces by a reframing of issues and modest alterations to ideological configurations, so can oppositional forces undermine dominant narratives. The great advantage of the hegemonic order here is its ability to frame issues thanks to its dominance of the media and state apparatuses, and, most importantly, the condition in which the dominant forces have already achieved hegemony, meaning that their narratives, their equivalential chains, their worldview, are already widely shared and disseminated. Yet the success of a hegemonic process is also its undoing, as Laclau has argued:

> The chain of equivalences which are unified around this signifier tend to empty it, and to blur its connection with the actual content with which it was originally associated.

Thus, as a result of its very success, the hegemonic operation tends to break its links with the force which was its original promoter and beneficiary.

(Laclau 2007: 45)

Critique, as outlined earlier in this book, interferes with the relation of symbolic forms to states of affairs. It has the capacity to destabilize the links and associations created by dominant ideologies between specific elements in reality and their symbolic forms and explanatory devices. This is the centre of the political operation of critique: dismantling existing equivalential chains and creating new ones by targeting the 'weak' semantic links between the hegemonic symbols and reality.

The American sociologist Daniel Bell argued in the 1970s that culture is divorced from society, identifying a mismatch between the ideas and ideals prevalent within art and culture and the hegemonic ideas of current society (Bell 1996). He not only accepted, in effect, Weber's notion of compartmentalized spheres within modern society, but enhanced it, suggesting a disconnect between signifier and signified, between culture and society. Art and cultural forms were autonomous, even independent of society. Evidence, in 1976, seemed in abundance. Both high and mass culture were extremely critical of society, with transgressive and subversive cultures leading a frontal attack on the conservative, consensual society formulated in the post-war years – the suburban, white, middle-class consumer society.

In a longer perspective, Bell's assertions can be contextualized in the 1970s, the era of societal restructuring. Art and culture were responsible for the destruction of a pre-modern unity of spheres, Bell argued. 'The modern movement disrupts that unity', he wrote. 'It does so in three ways: by insisting on the autonomy of the aesthetic from moral norms; by valuing more highly the new and experimental; and by taking the self (in its quest for originality and uniqueness) as the touchstone of cultural judgment' (Bell 1996: xxi). Yet in these characteristics art appears to express rather than contravene the ideals of bourgeois society. More specifically, rather than being divorced from society, the critical forms of culture and art that were being developed in the late 1960s were related to the new emerging forms of society, precisely the ones Bell attempted to outline in his earlier work on the post-industrial society (Bell 1976). The uneven development of society means that certain sectors advance ahead of others, that change and pace of change are neither uniform nor universal, but achieved in fragmented phases and in hesitant steps. The contradiction was therefore not between culture and society, but between a culture dependent upon a new form of society, on the one hand, and, on the other, the hegemonic forms of society in retreat – those of industrial, Fordist society and Keynesian economies. Bell could not identify these conditions as they were yet to be fully manifested: embedded within the era of restructuring, the complete logic of the transformation could not be perceived in 1976. The relevance here is that Bell highlighted a condition in which culture could lead an onslaught against a hegemonic order, that, while never 'free' of society, culture could nevertheless avoid subjugation to current hegemonic order as long as it could derive its positions from a counter-society, or, rather, counter-set of demands, a counter-equivalential chain: in this case, the forthcoming, emerging hegemonic order of post-Fordism and its emphasis on creativity, difference, uniqueness and individual freedom.

Earlier in this chapter, the role of architecture in representing society's hegemonic order – its ideals, self-image and worldview – was discussed. What is disconcerting for architecture is its difficulty to posit a counter-hegemonic symbolic order, a symbolic that aids in shaping and asserting an alternative equivalential chain to the contemporary hegemonic one. The ideal space for developing such counter-hegemonic symbolic orders is the hypothetical project, expressed in the form of paper architecture. Its autonomy from the pressures of economy and consensus allow the testing in architectural design of ideas that relate to a very different 'sacred' than the hegemonic. Such work does not just express the singular positions of the author, the architect, but is shaped by ideas shared by a group surrounding the author – his or her direct milieu, dominated by architectural peers. Yet paper architecture is extremely limited as a means of forming a new collective consciousness, as it is exposed, mostly, only to architectural practitioners and critics through publications and exhibitions, and tends to focus on the purely 'architectural'. Nevertheless, it has the potential to intervene in architectural debates, steering the discussions, and thus indirectly in wider political discussions – often by associating specific architectural counterparts to positions aired in the wider political terrain. While paper architecture enjoys significant freedoms, its efficacy is pre-limited.

Arguably the best example of a counter-hegemonic architecture was described in Part One of this book: the architecture that was allied to the reformist movements of the late nineteenth century. As the section revealed, the focus on mass housing, on space and its usage and on habitation marked this architecture as distinctive from the hegemonic architecture of the era and its interest in churches and public buildings. The architectural historian Adrian Forty assigned the refusal of the German Kaiser to enter Max Berg's Centennial Hall in Breslau (Wroclaw) in 1913 to the association of the concrete structure with social democracy as much as to the event's programme (Forty 2012: 145). The anecdote highlights the political significance of alternative symbolic orders and their intervention in the political sphere.

Once the reformist movements became hegemonic and dominant, so did the architecture associated with it, ascending from a counter-hegemonic position to dominance, becoming the core of architectural modernism and of the welfare state. And while this architecture, with its Fordist kernel, spoke of efficiency, of utilitarianism, it nevertheless carried symbolic meaning – it symbolized renewal, progress, egalitarianism, all of which echoed the symbolic content of the reformist movements. Similarly, the architecture that in the 1960s took the form of a rebellion against modernism, whether in Rossi's *The Architecture of the City* or in Venturi's *Architecture and Contradiction*, and a little later in Rowe and Koetter's *Collage City*, in the writings of Charles Jencks, and in the designs of the Five 'White' Architects, Rossi, Venturi Scott Brown, Mario Botta and many others, was not simply an internal architectural affair. The symbolic content of such work was allied, often unwittingly, with the post-Fordist and neoliberal order, initially counter-hegemonic before ascending to dominance: difference, creativity, spontaneity, self-realization, individualism, and freedom were the symbols shared by this order and its architecture. Both examples occurred in eras of societal restructuring, and demonstrate the possibilities of counter-hegemonic symbolic orders expressed by architectural design and theory.

How, then, to describe the symbolism of the current participatory movement delineated in Part Two of this book? At the centre of this movement are the same empty signifiers as those of the neoliberal order, described above: difference, creativity, spontaneity, self-realization and freedom. As a form of protest, the movement also posits demands for justice and for new forms of collectivity. The demand for freedom, a reaction to the democratic deficit, seems to be the dominant empty signifier, overshadowing the others. But these signifiers are somewhat subverted by the participatory movement: their meanings are not quite the same as for the hegemonic neoliberal order, and the practices they are intended to legitimize are disparate from those of ('neoliberal') corporations. The proximity of the current movement to neoliberalism was highlighted in Part Two, and it suggests that the battle being waged is not between two competing worldviews or ideologies, positioned in radical antagonism. Rather, the battle is being waged 'from within', on the level of co-optation and 'counter' co-optation, a battle over the meanings of the empty signifiers, over the make-up of equivalential chains and the type of practices they are meant to support and legitimize.

The symbolic, then, is at the heart of the political. Despite the inherent weakness of the links of the symbolized to the symbol, and of architecture to its signified content, or among the diverse demands and positions held together in equivalential chains, the symbolic matters. The core operation of conceiving of a new politics requires intervention on a symbolic level. Architecture, first and foremost, represents society, carries and communicates symbolically the ideals and social hierarchies of society. But in certain conditions it can also communicate an antagonistic or adversarial set of values to those dominating society at a specific place and time. In order to be political, however, such values have to be anchored in political ideas external to architecture itself.

URBAN FORM

After '68

> Social space contains – and assigns appropriate places to – (1) *the social relations of reproduction*, i.e. the bio-physiological relations between the sexes and between age groups, along with the specific organization of the family; and (2) the *relations of production*, i.e. the division of labour and its organization in the form of hierarchical social functions.
>
> *(Henri Lefebvre 1991: 32)*

In France, the events of May '68 took place at the moment in which the old Beaux-Arts school was dismantled, replaced by several *Unités Pédagogiques* (Pawley, Tschumi 1971).[10] In the following years, sociologists, and particularly urban sociologists from Henri Lefebvre's sphere of influence, were invited to different *unités* and took part in radicalizing the students (Violeau 2007).[11] Among the young architects and students immersed in the radical ferment of the period was Bernard Tschumi, who worked at the time for Candilis, Josic & Woods; Candilis was head of UP6, the most politically-committed unit (Martin 1990). Tschumi was familiar with the work of Lefebvre, and knew Hubert Tonka, Lefebvre's assistant and a member of the radical architecture group Utopie. In 1970, the architecture journal *L'Architecture d'aujourdhui* published an ideas competition entry by Tschumi and a work-colleague, Fernando Montés, called Do-it-Yourself-City. The project marries a techno-utopia with radical politics and is indebted to Cedric Price's Potteries Thinkbelt (Ockman 2008: 160). It includes diagrams, tables, collages, and axonometric drawings of small, mobile objects which were designated as urban interventions, functioning as local multimedia information and communication centres. The project expresses interests that can be associated with systems theory, cybernetics, or informatics. The ideas of 'play' and 'event' already appear at this early moment: 'The inhabitant's disposable means,' write the architects, 'permit his choice of diverse degrees: change of his environment, select his informations [*sic*], provoke an event. He is able to visualize and discuss information, active reunions of persons, of artistic manifestations, as well as of games' (Tschumi and Montés 1970: 98–105).

An important section of the project is the identification of 'activities' and the allocation of architectural forms to specific activities – the transition from a radical sociology to architecture. The activities outlined by Tschumi and Montés depart from the functionalist 'needs' that dominated the previous decades. Such 'needs' were embedded in a mechanical understanding of society that reduced life to basic essentials, ignoring communal, social, cultural and spiritual desires of a public that had become more affluent and was no longer satisfied by pursuing the most basic means of survival. In response to the planned society, planned economy, and planned cities of the period, in reaction to the social engineering attempted by the Keynesian welfare state, segments of the public – and particularly the students – demanded spontaneity, freedom, and creativity. In the discussions led by Lefebvre, Chombart de Lauwe and others,

> the concept of need was not only qualified and differentiated (with the introduction of 'fundamental' or 'deep' needs, and with the distinction between 'individual' and 'social' needs) but also replaced by a range of other concepts which were expected to uncover the dynamics of the everyday uses of architecture: aspirations, practices, demands and desires.
>
> *(Stanek 2015: 113)*

Therefore the 'activities' outlined in Do-It-Yourself-City must be understood as an attempt to infuse into the city – through architecture – the social and cultural 'content' that the barren, rigid, and repetitive modernist city did not offer, including the temporal and ephemeral. While many of the radical architecture groups of the period were content with the creation of ephemeral inflatables as a means of inserting spontaneity, diversity, and temporality into architecture and the city, Tschumi and Montés move a step further by developing a series of small architectural objects that are meant to facilitate specific activities which, in turn, suggest self-realization in the sense that the reified and monotonous urban environment of the 1960s did not.

The young Bernard Tschumi searched for the 'environmental trigger' – architectural efficacy. He concluded that knowledge of the built environment, '(not building) can contribute to polarising urban conflicts and inducing radical change' (Tschumi 1975: 93). But, in the early 1970s, Tschumi discovered, through post-structuralism, the work of Bataille (Martin 1990). The writings of Bataille offered the Swiss architect the possibility of developing his interest in radical acts that emphasized transgression, circumventing, in effect, the need for 'proof' of societal efficacy. The series of posters 'Advertisements for Architecture' perfectly highlights the transition in Tschumi's thought: the rot, excrement and decay found in the Villa Savoye, the subject of one of the 'advertisements', comfortably fit Bataille's interest in the obscene and excluded. However, not all traces of radical sociology are absent in the advertisement series. The advertisement that depicts someone falling – or, rather, being thrown – out of a window includes the caption: 'Architecture is defined by the actions it witnesses as much as by the enclosure of its walls. Murder in the Street differs from Murder in the Cathedral in the same way as love in the street differs from the Street of Love. Radically' (Tschumi 1994: xx). What this poster suggests is that architecture is neither the built object, nor the Cartesian space enclosed by the walls, ceiling and floor, but that architecture also includes the specific occurrences that take place in it. This presents an extreme expansion of the architectural field, and reflects Lefebvre's understanding of social practice as a determining factor of space. However, the roles of the building's architect and of the architectural design in initiating the event in question remain opaque.

The events of May '68 in Paris began not in Paris proper, but on the new university campus in Nanterre, in the vicinity of La Défense. The campus, designed by the architecture studio Chauliat, was a typical example of late modernist functionalism, with spatial segregation enhancing social segregation, functional zoning of living, working, and leisure areas, and separation in living quarters between men and women. It was typical of the era and of governmental policy to build new universities on urban outskirts. By the late 1960s this policy was already being questioned by governmental departments. A report in the *Cahiers de l'Institut d'Aménagement et d'Urbanisme de la Region Parisienne* claimed that

> the exurbanization of the universities has accentuated the unbalance of the towns, bringing a degradation of the spirit of the city centre, multiplying displacements, aggravating segregations of all sorts. The internal planning of the University Estate seldom gives a satisfactory way of life – campuses are too vast, [...] the habitation scattered, the utilization of space too rigid, the circulation schemes inarticulate and lacking a welcome centre.
>
> *(Pawley, Tschumi 1971: 539)*

Lefebvre was a professor at Nanterre at the time, and observed the students' remonstrations and the manner in which they spread from the periphery to the centre, to the area of the Sorbonne. In the short book *The Explosion*, written in the immediate aftermath of May '68, Lefebvre argued that the specific conditions of the Nanterre campus had a role in generating the agitation.[12] Lefebvre highlighted the expulsion of the students from the city to the peripheral campus, and emphasized the consequent marginalization experienced by the students of Nanterre as one of the causes of the events; not merely an expulsion to a periphery, but a periphery that included a shantytown and a multitude of social groups that experienced similar anomie (Figure 3.3). In addition to the geographic position, the architecture – its rigidity, its standardization, and particularly the social divisions that it enhanced programmatically, spatially, and formally – was also responsible for the radicalization of students. Lefebvre describes the explosive conditions created by the placing of the different pressures and discontents of 1960s France in one location; the modernist architecture was shaped by the technocracy and standardization which dominated the policies of French government in that era; it turned the students into cogs in an assembly line by its programme and organization – giving form to the Fordist project of reorganizing society as a factory, preferring efficiency and quantity to self-realization and quality of life. The architecture, in effect, exposed the ideology of society by exacerbating it, enabling the students to develop a consciousness of the division of labour, the sexual repression, and other conditions of post-war society that affected their daily lives.

Consequently, the students' reaction to the restriction of desire – the separation of women and men dormitories on campus – was a demand for sexual liberation; the reaction to the controlling and limitations by university authorities was a demand for freedom in society; the reaction to the arbitrariness and opacity of power in university was a demand for participation and transparency; and the reaction to the geographical marginalization was the creation of new centralities and subsequently the occupation of central Paris. The campus – its architecture, its layout, its programme – was, therefore, a microcosm of French society at the

Urban Form **155**

FIGURE 3.3 The shanty town of Nanterre in 1961. Quiet streets and police presence as All Saints' Day coincided with the seventh anniversary of the FLN's rebellion. Photograph by Keystone-France/Gamma-Keystone via Getty Images.

time, and enabled the students to scale their critique of the specific conditions on the campus to that of society at large:

> The students hesitate between two approaches: a parallel university devoted to the critique of the official university, and a permanent critique within the official university. But they accept neither the project of a critical university, nor that of an autonomous university (or department), whether in the guise of co-management or self-management. *They initiate a great contestation of the entire society, its institutions, its ideologies.*
> (Lefebvre 1969: 111 [*my italics*])

In other words, Lefebvre identified a revolutionary role for architecture as a 'pressure cooker', a machine to enhance contradictions in society and generate a popular rebellion. But, when assessing the success of the design of the campus from the perspective of its designers and authorities, it was a failure: a failure to integrate the students into society via architecture and spatial organization. Similarly, the role of the designer of the building in Tschumi's murder poster remains irrelevant. In both cases, the action, the event, appears detached from or even contrarian to the design's intentions.

Lefebvre's conclusions appear somewhat deterministic, perhaps over-influenced by behaviourist material from that era or Amos Rapoport's work, yet similar analysis came from other, less radical circles as well. *The Architectural Review*, in its first acknowledgment of the events of '68, wrote about new British universities and their design that 'their outer-urban, rather than city centre, siting' was a major concern for students (Fisk 1970: 293). It also mentioned the functional zoning of the campuses, though it questioned the role of such spatial organization in students' remonstrations:

> One new university, Warwick, has been designed with all the students' facilities on one side of the campus, all the teaching and administrative areas on the other. In between are several hundred yards of 'no man's land'. The whole arrangement seems to have been laid out to facilitate the out-break of warfare between staff and students; the scheme might have been expected to reinforce feelings of 'them' and 'us', and an alternative layout, with buildings dispersed randomly, should in theory promote a sense of community. But Warwick has notably been free of student unrest.
>
> *(Fisk 1970: 294)*

While Tschumi indicted the building in the murder described in his poster, Lefebvre implicated the campus for generating the student unrest. Lefebvre acknowledged the critical role of architecture in demystifying social conditions in university and society by making apparent what is usually veiled. He further suggested that architecture does not only 'say' what society is, in the sense of symbolic communication, but also 'does it' by exacerbating current social conditions. So architecture, according to Lefebvre, has efficacy, has political agency: it can become political by demystifying social reality by its subservience to the dominant ideology, to political economy, and to society.

Architecture as a means of demystification, of 'raising awareness' and producing a consciousness of social reality, and architecture as a trigger of political agitation were certainly interests of Tschumi. Tschumi identified three possible trajectories for architecture: 1. conservative: subjugated to and representing the dominant ideology and political economy; 2. critical ('commentator'): demystifying the operation of ideology in society; 3. revolutionary: leveraging professional knowledge in order to create new urban and social structures (Tschumi 1975: 95).[13] Tschumi, expectedly, rejected the first, and focused on the latter two categories. Whereas he attempted to discover a critical or revolutionary role for architecture, Lefebvre identified precisely such a role in Tschumi's first, 'conservative' category – in architecture which is subservient to the dominant ideology and political economy. Both Lefebvre and Tschumi identified the possibility of architecture assuming radical political agency, but neither could outline a prescription for the designer interested in socio-political efficacy; rather, efficacy did not correspond to the designer's intentions.

The retreat in the 1970s from the search for a radical architecture is therefore explained by the 'dead end' practitioners, historians and theorists experienced. The pneumatic balloons, the ephemeral structures, spatial frames, and the expansion of the field imagined by Tschumi and others, produced little evidence of the designer's agency, of the control of the socio-political implications of their designs, with forms of radicalism ending up primarily as rhetorical statements.

In order to counter such pessimistic conclusions by identifying the potentials of realizing an alternative architecture before a supportive political economy is implemented, this chapter will return to Tafuri's argument as spelled out in *Architecture and Utopia*. A key issue here is the relation of urban form to social form. Lefebvre's description of the campus of Nanterre is one example of an approach in which urban morphology reproduces in its own spatial organization the form of societal organization. The discussion of urban form, which has a particular traction in Italian architecture, replaces the focus on the political with a question of societal structures. This chapter will thus develop an argument that reformist architecture can precede political economy by focusing on the relation of urban morphology to societal organization.

Spatial and Societal Organization

In his influential essays published in *Structural Anthropology* and in his memoir *Tristes Tropiques*, the anthropologist Claude Lévi-Strauss describes a village of the Brazilian tribe Bororo in terms reminiscent of Durkheim's writings on Australian tribes (Lévi-Strauss 1963; 2011). Lévi-Strauss had attended in the 1930s the Collège de sociologie meetings, and his 'structural anthropology' had some – albeit limited – debt to the Collège's interpretation of Durkheim and Mauss. The village in question had a concentric form, with 26 identical huts lining its peripheral circle. At the centre of this circle stood a much larger hut, the 'men's house'. It functioned as the home of the bachelors and as a quasi 'men's club' for diverse day activities of the male population. The women were forbidden entry – they occupied the peripheral huts, the territory of domesticity. The village was split between two subgroups (moieties): the Cera and the Tugaré, the former located on the northern half of the village, the latter on the southern, a diametrical organization, with the diametrical axis cutting through the men's hut. Membership of a subgroup was accorded by the subgroup identity of the individual's mother. Marriage was restricted to a member of the opposite moiety. The peripheral huts belonged, in effect, to the women and were inherited by the women of the family. The married male would therefore leave the men's house, and join his wife on the other side of the village – the Cera side for Tugarén men and vice versa. 'The men's house mitigates this process of uprooting,' wrote Lévi-Strauss, 'since its central position straddles the territories of both moieties' (Lévi-Strauss 2011: 221).

Lévi-Strauss was pursuing the question of 'dual organization' of such societies, demonstrating that while the local informants described dualist structures and the overall image is of dualisms (men–women, sacred–profane, north–south, two moieties, etc.), the actual structures are more complex, often based on implicit triads. Significant support for the argument was found in a study of the villages' geometries and spatial organization. The use of the village layout as evidence of the social forms of the community suggests a direct correlation between the two.

The village appears diagrammatic: its simple, concentric layout is self-evident, a direct expression of social practices. Lévi-Strauss, however, demonstrates that the social organization of the village is more complex, and that while the village's spatial organization is a key factor, it is not quite as straightforward as it seems. Additional diagrams are required to reveal the underlying social structures and their reflection in the layout.

Lévi-Strauss describes two contrasting depictions of a North American Winnebago village, as recorded by another researcher (Lévi-Strauss 1963: 133). The tribe, like the Brazilian Bororo, was divided into two moieties. Members of one of the subgroups drew the village as a circle containing huts within a larger circle, while members of the other subgroup drew a dividing diametrical line cutting the circle into two, with huts on either side. Slavoj Žižek argued that these contrasting representations of the spatial organization outlined 'a fundamental antagonism the inhabitants of the village were unable to symbolize, to account for, to "internalize", to come to terms with, an imbalance in social relations that prevented the community from stabilizing itself into a harmonious whole' (Žižek 2006: 25–26). For Lévi-Strauss, the two differing depictions of the layout demonstrated the ability to describe a concentric layout in a linear diametrical fashion and vice versa, a slippage from one form of representation into another. It suggested that more significant than the actual form, was the type of relations between elements that the forms 'geometrically' or spatially enabled or prevented.

Certain elements within the villages' spatial layout have secondary rather than primary roles, Lévi-Strauss contended. The external circle of an Indonesian village is the boundary that identifies the community itself, whereas the north–south axis of the Bororo appears to have only limited function, an institution of 'zero value' as Lévi-Strauss calls it. Such 'institutions have no intrinsic property other than that of establishing the necessary preconditions for the existence of the social system to which they belong', he wrote (Lévi-Strauss 1963: 159).

The relation of urban form to society has been a core interest not only for Italian architects, but also for geographers, sociologists, urban historians and others. 'The social life of urban forms', as the sociologist Fran Tonkiss has referred to this issue (Tonkiss 2013: 16), suggests that morphology, as the physical product of a society at a specific time and place, is determined by society, and therefore can be read as evidence of the forces that produced it. Moreover, by enabling, encouraging or limiting specific social practices, morphology and form takes part in the shaping of society. In this, the realized building is a 'total social fact', to use Mauss's term, a rich and complex social phenomenon in which a wide array of social, economic and political forces become 'visible'. Rossi referred to the realized building as *fatto urbano*, urban fact, the urban object that carries with it a wealth of historical, geographic, social and political meanings (Rossi 1991: 22).

Beyond the most obvious relation of urban morphology to technical capabilities, then, and in addition to carrying the symbolic meanings of the community, the Bororo village identifies the correlation of urban form to social practices and organization. An example of a recent analysis of twentieth-century morphology that similarly ties social and urban form, albeit more architecturally, can be found in the study of Red Vienna by the architectural historian Eve Blau.

In the study, Blau highlights the extensive use of the pre-industrial courtyard, the *Hof* of the *Hofhaus*, in diverse 1920s housing forms, and particularly in permutations of the traditional perimeter block. She suggests that these strategies enabled the city council, by assuring permeability, openness and diverse forms of passage, to turn the private internal spaces of blocks into public or semi-public spaces. Blau writes that:

> The *Gemeindenbauten* created spaces that were part public, part private; that were both open and closed; that were available for circulation and public use but also enclosed with the built-up circumference of the city block; that overlapped with the existing urban grid but undermined the logic of its order.
>
> *(Blau 1999: 339)*

Such a spatial policy substantially increased the ratio of public to private space and was therefore aligned with the ambitions of the Social Democrats which ran the Vienna city council. Blau contends that the development of Vienna in the 1920s was shaped by the necessity of compromise with existing building codes combined with a desire to subvert them in order to create new spatial and social conditions. The Karl Marx Hof complex (Figure 3.4) and similar large-scale urban structures were consequently the epitome of Red Vienna's urban strategies, creating a new form of housing and habitation not as utopian fragments or by reorganizing the street layout, but by a constructive yet contrarian dialogue with the existing, historic city. Such a dialogue is not dissimilar to Tafuri's characterization of the members of the Commission of the 1803 Napoleonic plan for Milan, who 'were disposed to operate within the structural terms of the city as it had developed historically, except that they pronounced an explicit judgement on that development' (Tafuri 1976: 22). Likewise, rather than opt for a radical break with the past by embracing the architectural designs being tested in Weimar Germany at the time, the architecture of Red Vienna appears as an evolvement of the historic Biedermeier style in many senses. 'The social values associated with the Biedermeier,' writes Blau, 'domesticity, family, and *Gemeinschaft* (community), combined with formal simplicity and honesty – were deemed by city building officials (and one would assume by the party leadership) in Vienna to be appropriate for the Social Democrats social housing program' (Blau 1999: 348). Change via critical dialogue with existing conditions, or an evolvement of familiar style perfectly expresses the general approach and strategies of 'evolutionary socialism' of the Social Democratic reformists, 'slow growth from within' (Blau 2015: 29). Here, both the form itself and its symbolic meaning are mobilized in an attempt to shape society.

A recent contribution to the discussion of urban form comes from architect and theorist Pier Vittorio Aureli. His work, expressed through publications such as *The Possibility of an Absolute Architecture* (2011) and *The Project of Autonomy* (2008), as well as in the work of his architectural firm Dogma, is a sequel of sorts to the discussions of Rossi, Tafuri, Carlo Aymonino, Paola Vigano and Bernardo Secchi. For Aureli, architecture is political because it addresses separation, composition and counterposition, key characteristics of the political according to Carl Schmitt. The proposition is that formal separation or composition are not only associated with their political counterparts, but that they are constituted by and constitute them.

'Urbanization' is the term Aureli uses for the current dominant order of economic and urban development, described in terms more reminiscent of post-war state capitalism and planism than of post-Fordism and neoliberalism. The process of urbanization and development has the effect of evening out differences and reducing discriminations, Aureli asserts, aiming at the production of a smooth, undifferentiated continuum: total integration. Highly invested in the Italian workerist theory of the 1960s, Aureli's positions recall Tronti and his colleagues' opposition to the state-capitalism of that era and the identification of reformist planism, and state-led 'modernization' and 'development' with capitalism.

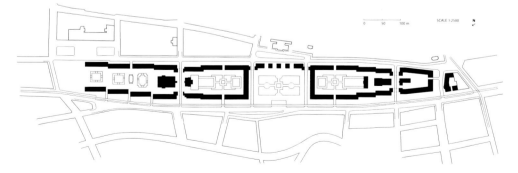

FIGURE 3.4 Plan of Karl Marx Hof, Vienna, showing the permeability of the perimeter blocks. Drawing by Adam Kelly (2015).

The term 'urbanization' is identified with the concept of city–territory, a term used in 1963 by the members of the architectural and urbanism firm Architetti Urbanisti Associari (AUA) – Vieri Quilici, Giorgio Piccinato and Manfredo Tafuri (Viganò 2012; Aureli 2007). Subsequently, city–territory has been a concept widely used in Italian urbanism. It developed from Patrick Geddes's concept of urban conurbation, city–region, allowing discussions of diverse scales and the relationships between them, new polycentric urban and quasi-urban forms, and, importantly for the post-war years, infusing the concept with economic and social issues, enabling a focus on urban processes. Introduced during an era of mass-suburbanization and erosion of 'city' into a seamless urban expansion, later to become urban sprawl, the concept was a vehicle of interrogating the emerging urban conditions. City–territory, then, was involved in the expansion of the concerns of urbanism in those years, in Italy and elsewhere, from issues of land use to an inclusion of a wider array of non-spatial concerns. It is an analytical instrument, though one which necessarily frames modes of conceiving of the city and the urban, and acting on the city.

An example of how the analytical concept of city–territory became deployed in planning practices is the Sicilian Belice Valley, an area devastated by an earthquake in 1968. Planners, reacting to the disaster, proposed the spatial, infrastructural and economic reorganization of the region by conceiving it as a city–territory. The ideas of the planners were driven by a desire to 'modernize' an underdeveloped region by spatial reorganization and new infrastructures, producing the foundations for a process of economic development. The project was 'an experiment in socio-economic engineering, and strictly associated that conception with a particular spatial layout: the "city–territory"' (Parrrinello 2013: 572). The region-scale proposals demonstrate the proximity of the city–territory idea to Aureli's concept of urbanization, as well as their complicity in capitalist development.

Against the ubiquity of urbanization, the continuous development and redevelopment led by the logic of the market, and against the concept of city–territory as an analytical tool complicit with urbanization, Aureli posits architectural form: by creating a boundary between the architectural form and 'urbanization', the architectural object differentiates itself, becomes other than urbanization. The boundary is the locus of mediation between the urban context and the building, between, it is suggested, the undifferentiated, compromised mass, and the singular moment of architecture positing an alternative.

The position of Aureli appears not dissimilar to Adorno's depiction of autonomous art as critical by being different from yet anchored in society (Adorno 1997: 133). Or, alternatively, K. Michael Hays's 'critical architecture', in which autonomous architecture is not completely disjunct from society or the city (Hays 1984). Partial freedom, in other words, which maintains relevance with society by its position towards the city. The terms used by Aureli are different: 'the city', understood as the *polis*, is the desired political community, while 'urbanization' is the current post-political condition. No distinction is made here between Fordism and post-Fordism: the logic of Fordism, for Aureli, continues today, even if its manifestations have altered.

But there is an important difference between the argument that autonomy enables criticality, as articulated by Hays or Adorno, and Aureli's argument. For Aureli, the 'autonomous' is an isolated generic object – one of the serial objects that make urbanization physically manifest is isolated by being differentiated formally from the serial, by, for example, a plinth, a boundary. This condition of partial isolation constitutes the autonomy of the element rather than a formal differentiation of the building itself, and renders it critical of urbanization. One argument made by Aureli, then, is that the isolation of the generic element allows to actually perceive the element, evaluate it, and to consequently comprehend the process of urbanization of which it is a part – a critical process.

A generic singularity is a contradiction, or at the very least creates a tension between the two contrasting conditions. Architecture as 'example', a singularity, though one to be reproduced. While such an understanding excludes the non-generic landmark building, the generic fragment in question, like the landmark, has to maintain its singularity to avoid being absorbed into a sea of reproduced versions. The singular landmark is an auratic 'original' by definition, but the generic fragment is endowed with a similar aura by its isolation, elevated and thus transformed from its generic condition.

Aureli asserts that the isolated element does more than produce a critical consciousness: the assemblage of isolated elements together form a loose whole, an idea of a city constituted by fragments – Oswald Mathias Ungers's archipelago model. The role of the archipelago model is clear enough: to enable maximum autonomy of the parts (architecture) within a minimal idea of a whole (the *cité*). '[T]he archipelago,' writes Aureli, 'envisions the city as the agonistic struggle of parts whose forms are finite and yet, by virtue of their finiteness, are in constant relationship both with each other and with the "sea" that frames and delimits them' (Aureli 2011: xi). The parts are described as competing and adversarial fragments. The architectural theorist Ana Jeinić has argued that such descriptions are politically vacuous (Jeinic 2014), in the sense that what is outlined is restricted to a formal description of a relativist political condition rather than an articulation of political content, of actual positions and values. Aureli limits the expectations from architecture to deliver a transformed society:

> The only program that can reliably be attributed to architecture is its specific inertia in the face of urbanization's mutability, its status as the manifestation of a clearly singular place. If the ubiquitous nature of mobility and integration is the essence of urbanization, the singularity of places is the essence of a city.
>
> *(Aureli 2011: 46)*

The demand for the articulation of place against the non-place of urbanization is not only the same demand posited to architecture by Norberg-Schulz and other Heideggerians, or the focus of dreary 'place making' in Britain. It infers a desire for a lost authenticity, and while strictly architectural in its terms, also the positing of specificity and particularity (even if 'generic') against the global, the universal, and the general. It suggests that the political ambitions expressed in *The Possibility of an Absolute Architecture* are extremely narrow, and primarily provide an architectural avenue to satisfy the desire for authenticity of place.

The Marxist concept of totality is associated here with urbanization and 'despotism', and hence rejected, whereas 'the whole' is supported and approved. Aureli opts for a model in which the whole is particularly vague – even in Colin Rowe's collage city, the whole has a clearer generator, geometric composition. The description of the archipelago model, however, can be read as a precise form of a familiar political community: contemporary liberal democracy, in which the idea of the whole, of society, of community, is reduced to bare minimum to allow each individual maximum freedom, in which the whole is merely the aggregate of individual elements. In other words, Aureli's ideal model is no more than a modified version of liberal democracy. The one important distinction between liberal democracy and Aureli's archipelago is the sea: in the former the sea is merely the 'enforcer' of individualism, of separation, the forces which prevent a cohesive idea of unity or collectivity developing. In the latter, Aureli's archipelago, the sea is urbanization, the sea is the adversary against which architectural fragments are deployed in defiant gestures. Nevertheless, Aureli's emphasis on conflict between the 'islands' and 'sea' does no more than Schmitt's or Mouffe's theories: they articulate the real condition of the political rather than a desired condition. In other words, the archipelago here is already in existence, is the familiar liberal democracy, and visible in the urban fragmentation caused by neoliberal development, the weakness of politics and the dissipation of planning.

Urban fragmentation, up until the 1960s, has mostly been understood negatively. Interpretations of fragmentation typically identified capitalism or individualism as the major causes, an expression of a fragmented society, collapse of societal cohesion reflected in physical form. A contrasting understanding, popular within postmodern theory, suggests fragmentation is a form of freedom, whether symbolically as an expression of more choice and diversity, or practically, as caused by a more pluralistic society. In Aureli's writings, the architectural fragment is exalted. Yet the associations and interpretations mentioned above do not necessarily contradict each other. The urban fragment expresses, indeed, both a freedom (from planning, from government) and pluralism, as well as societal fragmentation (the weakening of government, of civil society, of community). The identification by Aureli of 'urbanization' rather than fragmentation with capitalist development is an oversight of the dual trajectories of capitalism, in which processes of globalization and international trade have strengthened a sense of homogeneity and sameness, on the one hand, and an impression of diversity and pluralism on the other. Just as the idea of a local that is posited against the global is erroneous, so urban fragmentation and homogeneity are parallel and linked processes driven by the same forces.

The emphasis on the generic and on difference created by formal boundaries rather than formal difference, as suggested earlier, allows Aureli to exclude landmark buildings from the status of autonomous elements and building blocks of a *cité*. Some of this is tenuous: surely the archipelago model can be similarly applied to the 'collection' of landmark buildings, formulated to present a city constituted by the aggregate effect of the symbolic enclaves of the landmarks against the generic 'sea' separating these 'islands'?

The main issue here is political economy rather than the political. 'Urbanization' is driven by political economy, by the familiar argument for the necessity of economic development, repeatedly raised in support of airport and city expansions, infrastructural development and much more. Aureli could argue that the move against the relentless 'progression' of economy is political due to the conscious decision it involves and its ideological rather than economic motivation. While loaded with many tenuous assertions and speculations, *The Possibility of an Absolute Architecture* is significant in bringing the question of urban form to the fore of discussion of politics and the political, and in articulating the relation of architectural form to urban morphology as a key issue with societal implications. Aureli's work shifts the discussion here from societal organization to the impact of political economy on urban forms, even while focusing on a political dimension.

Urban Form and Economic Organization

The skyline of Canary Wharf conjures up the image of an American Central Business District (CBD) of glass skyscrapers, and, more specifically, of Manhattan's south-east skyline. The association is hardly surprising. Both are centres of finance capital. The south-east view of Manhattan's Battery Park City is dominated by The World Financial Center (WFC), developed, like Canary Wharf, by Olympia & York (Figure 3.5). The two also share a master planner (SOM) and architect (Cesar Pelli for the One Canada Square tower and for WFC). All these would, ostensibly, sufficiently explain the similarities in appearance. Yet the ability of these agents – the developer, the master planner and the architect – to replicate a Manhattan image would have been impaired were the underlying conditions of the projects significantly disparate.

Canary Wharf's form appears startlingly different from post-war European business districts such as the 1950s Centro Direzionale of Milan. It is necessary to highlight the disparate conditions that underlie these two CBDs, conditions that predetermine much of the outcome. In the case of European post-war business districts, whether in Milan, Stockholm or elsewhere, the government's involvement was central, including decisions regarding the actual urban forms and the spatial organization of the areas. Even in the case of Italy, with its relatively weak planning institutions, the master plan (*piano regolatore*) of 1953 was key in shaping the district. In comparison, the Docklands were redeveloped by the LDDC, a public–private partnership, to which the government seceded control of the process, as outlined in Part Two. Despite offering the corporation significant support 'from the outside', whether politically, financially, or technically, the government's role was secondary to that of the private sector, particularly until the late 1980s. The LDDC did not commission an overall master plan for the Isle of Dogs. Instead, planning, even corporate planning, was replaced by what the RIBA president called 'dynamic contextualism' (Edwards 1992: 137): a contingent, small-scale approach. On an urban design scale, Olympia & York commissioned the master planning of Canary Wharf, exempt from integrating into a larger master plan by government or corporation, and taking advantage of the status of 'enterprise zone' (Figure 3.6).

FIGURE 3.5 Battery Park City, Manhattan, buildings by Cesar Pelli in the foreground, in front of the World Trade Center, 1996. Photograph by Ken Lund, Creative Commons.

FIGURE 3.6 Model of Canary Wharf master plan by SOM. Photograph ©SOM.

The result therefore resembled American CBDs not only purposefully in order to create an image for the Docklands familiar from the United States, symbolizing the presence and prowess of finance capital, but also because the circumstances were similar: exemption from governmental planning; the master plan and redevelopment driven and shaped by large-scale corporations; the similar scale of the project. Manhattan of the 1920s, untypically for that era, was likewise dominated by large corporations, and had no governmental or municipal plan with which to comply apart from the 1916 zoning. The Isle of Dogs likewise reflects the lack of an overall master plan and influence of large corporations: competing enclaves of urban fabric, replicating spatially the division of the territory between diverse large-scale developers.

Compare such conditions to those of London's East End in the mid-nineteenth century, likewise a free-market economic condition, but one in which small-scale developers, typically carpenters with a couple of assistants, would buy a small or mid-sized plot, carve it into three, build a building on one and sell the other two to other, similar, developers. This process, in the absence of planning or large-scale developers, created an informal urbanism, only marginally less 'chaotic' than the self-build East End a few decades earlier or the contemporary informal cities in Latin America, Africa or Asia. In contrast to this informal urban extension, central London of that era boasted of neoclassical robustness, pomp, and symbolism, developed by a powerful imperial government.

These examples identify different formal expressions with different conditions of political economy and governance. London's East End 150 years ago as an expression of free market dominated by small-scale entrepreneurs; Central London of the period as expression of imperial governmental control; the Centro Direzionale in Milan as a product of governmental master planning in the era of Keynesian economics, and Battery Park City and the Docklands as typical products of a free-market economy dominated by large-scale corporations. The major issues here are the level and type of state or private sector involvement and control, the related absence, weakness or strength of planning, and the type of political economy and the stakeholders it produces.

Much nuance can be added to all this, as any close examination would show. The formation of the Docklands included a diversity of stakeholders and multiple actors, each contributing something, and to different degrees, to shaping the outcome. Long before Margaret Thatcher's first government, or the implementation of monetarist policies in the UK, the LDDC's predecessor, the Docklands Study Team, consisting of planners from diverse central and local governmental agencies, supported a redevelopment proposition focused on service sector jobs and a middle class population (Brownhill and O'Hara 2015: 543). The proposal, titled City New Town, was one of eighteen scenarios outlined in 1973, and evidently the favoured option, with 60,000 service jobs versus only 1,000 industrial jobs, and a 50:50 split of public and private housing. Hence, the gravitation away from the provision of public housing and from industry as a means of regeneration was already evident long before the actual political and economic changes took place. Moreover, the ability to characterize an era as sharply free market or its reverse is itself limited, as overlaps, contingency, and transition are a constant. The status of the LDDC and its priorities were never stable or fixed, but, likewise, contingent and changing, an essentially private-interest focused corporation at one moment, and a more public-focused corporation at another. And the importance of the project to Thatcher's government as proof of private capital's ability to lead urban regeneration meant, paradoxically, that the British government ended up being highly invested in the project.

Such detail and much more can be added to expand each case, exposing contradictions and the reductivism involved in rigid characterization of eras or projects according to 'neoliberal', 'Keynesian' or other logics. But the danger would be to obscure by abundance of detail the fact that not all forces operating on a certain project are equal, and that a specific form of political economy dominates at a certain time and place, however nuanced and contradictory such a statement must be. The impossibility of creating a precise index relating formal outcome to conditions should be evident enough, then, as in each case a multiplicity of additional factors play their part in determining an outcome. Yet a significant level of correlation between such key conditions and urban form is also apparent. Here again, as in the case of symbolism, arises the question whether urban form that is not subjugated to the hegemonic order can be created – or, in other words, whether alternative forms of societal organization can be articulated by urban morphology before achieving hegemony.

Reformist Architecture

The social democratic parties that ascended to power in France, Britain, Germany, Sweden and elsewhere in the inter-war years were significantly different than their successors in the post-war period. They were positioned in an ambiguous place between 'evolutionary socialism' and revolution: on the one hand, their not so distant split from the communist parties meant that their ethos was still Marxist and revolutionary and that they fiercely opposed capitalism (Laclau and Mouffe 2001: 73); on the other hand, they had become the political mouthpiece of the sectarian agenda of the trade unions, channelling the demands for higher wages and job security via 'bourgeois democracy'. The economic, social, or political programmes of these parties in the inter-war years was extremely limited. The major proposal was nationalization, but beyond a few minor and isolated cases, nationalizations did not take place in the European social democratic-run countries in the 1920s. Economics historian Robert Skidelsky wrote that the British Labour Party between the wars:

> suffered in those days from a split personality: on the one hand it was committed to constitutionalism; on the other it lacked a social democratic or gradualist programme without which tenure of power was bound to be rather barren of achievement. It thought in terms of a total solution to the problem of poverty, when what it was offered [in 1929] was the limited opportunity to cure unemployment. It was a parliamentary party with a Utopian ethic. It was not fit for the kind of power it was called upon to exercise.
>
> *(Addison 1975: 45)*

The case of the Weimar social democrats (SPD or MSPD) was somewhat different than their counterparts in France or Britain, because of their dominance in the 1920s of the political stage (the SPD took part in the governments of 1918–21, 1923, 1928–30), and because of the association of the republic with this specific political party. Yet, as mentioned above, the actual economic and political programme of the party, like other social democratic parties of the era, was narrow.

The 1920s were, of course, also a great decade for architectural and urban experimentation in Germany. What will be argued here, following Tafuri's position in *Architecture and Utopia*, is that some of these experiments reproduced in architecture and the city the logic of Keynesian economy and of planism before Keynes developed his general theory (published 1936) or Henri De Man (in the years 1931–35) and the Groupe X-Crise (Le Centre polytechnicien d'etudes economiques, active 1931–39) provided an outline of *planisme*, and before such theories were adopted by social democrats and centrist parties. In this sense, architecture succeeded in realizing projects which were not subservient to its contemporaneous political economy or modes of societal organization.

Two experiments of the Weimar Republic can serve here as examples of different architectural trajectories taking place in parallel: the Weissenhofsiedlung by Mies van der Rohe and the 'zigzag' complex at Bruchfeldsstrasse ('Niederrad') Siedlung in Frankfurt by Ernst May. The canonic Weissenhof was composed of suburban homes, *pavillions*, stand alone, singular buildings, with a single slab by Mies (Figure 3.7). Built in the suburban outskirts of Stuttgart and with meandering garden city suburb streets, Weissenhof epitomized the middle-class demand for freedom, privacy, and individuality by allowing the singular building a certain detachment and freedom from the urban whole. In contrast, Ernst May's *Siedlung* privileged the urban block rather than the singular building. In the *zickzackhausen* block, the courtyard became the 'oasis' for the working class, while the block negotiated collectivity and individuality in the urban form (Figures 3.8, 3.9). The relation of the block to the city remained ambiguous: on the one hand, it was not detached from its environment via front gardens or by being raised on columns, yet, by rotating the block elements, its zigzagging mass deformed the typical street. Each element in the block

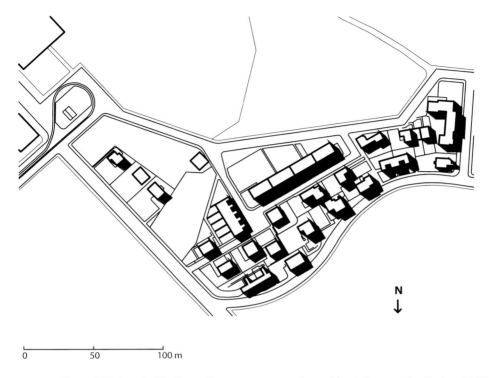

FIGURE 3.7 Plan of Weissenhofsiedlung, Stuttgart, master planned by Mies van der Rohe, 1927. Drawing by Adam Kelly (2015).

was subordinated to the logic of the whole, whereas Weissenhof allowed significantly more freedom to the single building. However, none of these ideas were followed to their conclusion; May's block retained certain independence from the city and allowed each replicated element to be formally articulated. Particularly in perspective view, the elements appear independent, even if repetitive. Weissenhof, in turn, offered, despite the autonomy of its singular buildings, a limited 'wholeness', achieved primarily by Mies's slab 'anchoring' the entire district.

The term *pavillionsystem* has been used, first and foremost, to describe the layout of detached or semi-detached suburban houses. Yet the logic of free-standing, disconnected residential buildings, of which Weissenhof is merely one example, is a scaled application of the same layout principle that allows significant freedom to each architectural element. The *pavillionsystem* was identified by the architectural historian Emil Kaufmann as a reflection of the spirit of the revolutionary period of the late eighteenth century, expressing the position of the individual in the emerging middle-class society by allowing the singular building its own autonomy, just as the elevated place of the human subject in Kant's autonomy of the human will (Teyssot 1981; Vidler 2008). Whereas Kaufmann sketched an associative relation, in which individual autonomy is reflected in a building's autonomy, Tafuri outlined a tighter relationship by arguing that the emergence of the *pavillionsystem* was related to the fragmentation and alienation of society caused by market capitalism, to the breakdown of a totality into alienated fragments, visible in the built environment as much as in society.[14]

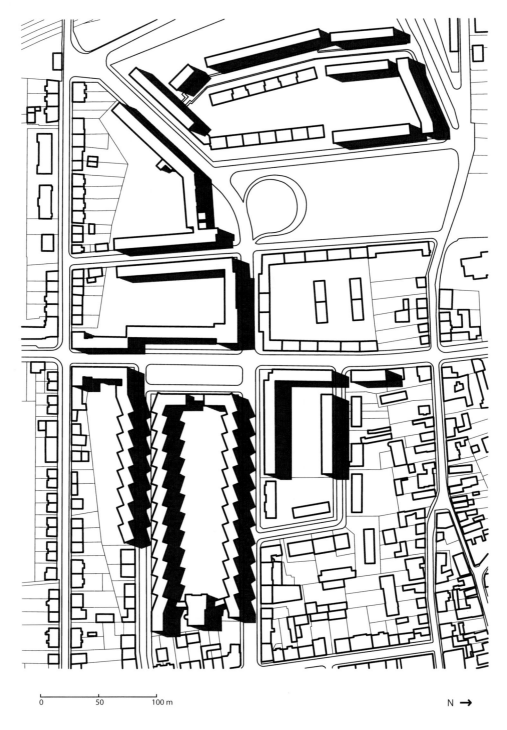

FIGURE 3.8 Plan of the 'zigzag' complex at Bruchfeldsstrasse, Frankfurt, master planned by Ernst May, 1926/7. Drawing by Adam Kelly (2015).

FIGURE 3.9 View of courtyard of the 'zigzag' complex, photograph by Alfred Lauer, 1927. Courtesy of the Deutsches Kunstarchiv (DKA) in the Germanischen Nationalmuseum.

Tafuri described the introduction of the abstract iron grid in North American cities beginning in the late eighteenth century as a decoupling of architecture and urbanism, of building and city, allowing architecture autonomy from the city and encouraging formal experimentation (Figure 3.10). He wrote that 'absolute liberty is granted to the single architectural fragment, but this fragment is situated in a context that it does not condition formally' (Tafuri 1976: 38), highlighting the inefficacy of the autonomous fragment. The architectural critic Louis Mumford identified the American abstract grid with speculation in real estate. 'If the layout of a town has no relation to human needs and activities other than business,' wrote Mumford,

> the pattern of the city may be simplified: the ideal layout for the business man is that which can be most swiftly reduced to standard monetary units for purchase and sale. The fundamental unit is no longer the neighbourhood or precinct, but the individual building lot [...] Such plans fitted nothing but a quick parcelling of the land, a quick conversion of farmsteads into real estate, and a quick sale.
>
> *(Mumford 1989: 421–22)*

The logic here is similar to Simmel's discussion of money, in *The Philosophy of Money* and in 'Metropolis and Mental Life' (Simmel 2002; 2003), as a form of rationalization and abstraction that facilitates exchange by enabling a comparison of commodities that are structurally different: the rational iron grid, likewise, reduces differences (of plot shape, orientation, etc.) to a limited number of categories, which make comparison and hence also exchange easier. But the *pavillionsystem* does not necessarily require an iron grid; meandering suburban layout

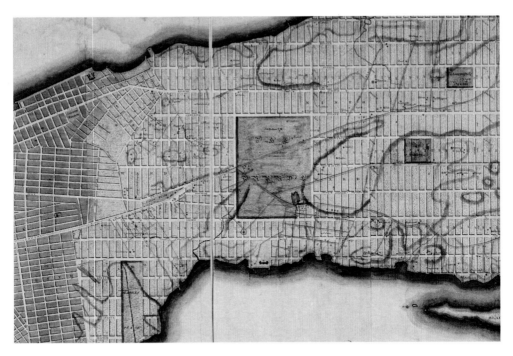

FIGURE 3.10 Excerpt from the 1811 Commissioners' Plan for Manhattan (1807) showing the iron grid layout for urban expansion to the north (right). Courtesy of Library of Congress, Geography and Map Division.

can produce it as well, as in the form of Levittown or Weissenhof. In any case, the *pavillionsystem* privileges the singular structure at the expense of the whole.

The proliferation of the *pavillionsystem* coincided with the rise of the bourgeoisie. It emerged as the small-scale imitation of the country houses of landed nobility by the wealthy traders and aspiring members of the bourgeoisie – the villa in late Renaissance Venice, or, in the case of France, the imitation of the aristocrat's *châteaux*. It was a sign of prestige, class aspiration and social position, and accentuated a town–country relationship of economic dependency (Ackerman 1986). It reflected the importance of individualism and privacy in middle-class society. Initially, the villa was restricted to wealthy citizens, but:

> in the mid-nineteenth century, the privilege has filtered down to those [citizens] of modest financial means [...] Once the villa had been presented as a commodity, it was a short step to its manufacture by entrepreneurs for the open market, and another short step to its mass production on the periphery of great cities and ultimately of smaller ones.
> (Ackerman 1986: 15, 17)

Such a description focuses on the most familiar form of the *pavillionsystem*: the detached or semi-detached houses. The logic of urban organization embedded in it applies also to other scales of detached residential buildings. Free-market capitalism in the urban environment, particularly when practiced by small to medium-size developers, benefits from such a system by allowing developers more freedom from the dictates of any 'civic', 'bureaucratic' or even 'divine' understanding of the city as a totality – in other words, when given free reign, small-scale developers tend to create autonomous singular buildings, suitable in scale from their perspective in investment and effort to their own restricted ambitions, technical capacities, and financial abilities. A correlation emerges, then, between political economy, size of developer, and size and organization of the urban fragments.

Consequently, Mies's Weissenhof can be seen as both a product and representative of the free-market economics and ideals of freedom, individualism and privacy. In contrast, May's Frankfurt *Siedlungen* have been identified by Tafuri with the assembly line (Tafuri 1976), with the organization prescribed by Keynesian economics and planism: a comprehensive approach that emphasizes totality, creating a wholeness, a continuum of building and city, of architecture and urbanism, and of architecture and society, which is the architectural–urban expression of the ideal of creating a rectified society by forming a new totality in which the alienation of the individual from the whole is overcome.

Tafuri described these two competing modernist trajectories as 'the irrational' of formal experimentation and the 'rational' urban-led development – two sides of the same coin, from his perspective: both are capitalist and bourgeois. In order to correlate such definitions to Peter Bürger's theory of avant-garde, the first trajectory, that of autonomy and formal experimentation, will be here considered as the modernist mainstream, and the second, of a continuum of building and city, as the avant-garde. While the former focused on the aesthetic–technical development of architectural design, the latter paralleled the artistic avant-garde's desire to create a continuum of art and life. Two of the examples Tafuri used were Hilberseimer's vertical city and Le Corbusier's Plan Obus: while Hilberseimer's work exposed the underlying ideology of reorganizing the city and society as an assembly line (Figure 3.11), Plan Obus veiled this ideology via its smooth, organic and naturalistic forms. In comparison to the extremity and rigidity of Hilberseimer's 'assembly line', May's Bruchfeldsstrasse Siedlung appears as a relatively humane and benign 'factory'.

May's politics were reformist rather than revolutionary. His early work was highly influenced by the Garden City movement and particularly by Raymond Unwin, for whom he had briefly worked in 1910. His focus was on creating a comprehensive, 'rectified' city, a totality, and on forms of collective housing, socialization and equality, and he penned critiques of individualism and arguments for standardization. Yet his favoured form of housing remained the singular family house with garden. While he tended to integrate singular family houses into cohesive plans and terraced housing, such typologies were never rejected. Rather than 'built socialism', as Anatoly Lunacharsky called Bruno Taut's Hufeisensiedlung (Flierl 2011: 161), May's New Frankfurt, including the Bruchfeldsstrasse Siedlung, was 'built reformism', or, in Tafuri's words: 'Nazi propaganda was to speak of the Frankfurt settlements as *constructed socialism*. We must see them as realized social democracy' (Tafuri 1976: 115).

The favourable political conditions in the 1920s for May's work in Frankfurt included the social democratic federal government, the significant power of a city council dedicated to what it perceived as 'modernization', and a strong coalition of politicians, planners, and architects that enabled the realization of the ambitious project despite the free-market capitalism of the era. Ludwig Landmann, the Frankfurt mayor (1924–33), led the city towards modernization and recruited May. He ruled via a coalition of centre-Left parties: his own Democratic Party, the SPD, and Zentrum. May was allowed to create a strong urban housing office with wide-ranging powers (Mohr 2011). He could recruit the team he needed, including the planner Herbert Boehm, the civil engineer Max Frühauf, the landscape architect

FIGURE 3.11 Perspective view of North-South Street, Highrise City (Hochhausstadt) by Ludwig Hilberseimer, 1924. By permission of The Art Institute of Chicago.

Leberecht Migge, the architect Adolf Meyer, and the graphic designer Hans Leistikow, who produced the New Frankfurt posters and the design of *Das Neue Frankfurt* magazine.

In the 1920s, the precise mechanisms, and particularly the economic mechanisms, which would be put in place in the two decades following the 1929 crash were still unknown. Whereas Scharoun's work or Mies's *Siedlung* can be identified as products of laissez-faire capitalism, the work by Hilberseimer, May and others identified a very different form of spatial organization, which would become hegemonic only at a later moment, together with forms of societal organization typical of the Keynesian era. Therefore the diverse urban and architectural experiments of Weimar – of May, Martin Wagner and Fritz Schumacher rather than Mies or Scharoun – were carried out while there was a sympathetic political condition, but before the realization of The Plan. Or, in other words, in Weimar architecture and urbanism discovered the correct form the Keynesian, Fordist Plan would take in the urban environment *before* Keynes or de Man actually formed their theories and long before their actual implementation.[15]

Keynes had advocated public works and governmental intervention in the economy to stimulate employment long before 1929. Throughout the 1920s, he worked closely with Lloyd George's Liberals, seeking a progressive middle ground between the laissez-faire of the Conservatives and the anti-capitalism and socialism of Labour of those years. The 1929 economic crisis and subsequent Great Depression generated a thought process that ultimately led to his 1936 magnum opus *The General Theory of Employment, Interest, and Money*, whereas the political collapse of the Liberals encouraged Keynes to collaborate with Labour. En route to his magnum opus, he published a series of articles in which some of the ideas central to his theories were first exposed. *The Means to Prosperity*, a 1933 pamphlet, was the most important among them and a first presentation of his multiplier mechanism. These articles were published once the architectural experiments of Weimar had come to their end. Such early endeavours into Keynesian economics fell short, in any case, of the full theory exposed in *The General Theory*: a new macroeconomic model, in which the investment multiplier was linked to monetary policy and government investment.

Whereas Keynes's focus was macroeconomic theory, the Belgian Henri de Man, like Groupe X-Crise in France and the Political and Economic Planning group in Britain, had a somewhat more generalist approach. Before turning to economics, de Man had studied the behaviour of workers and their organizations and national identity. Despite his background in sociology and social psychology rather than economics (Cuyvers 2015), microeconomics dominated de Man's work in the 1930s. A major concern for him was the contemporary question of underconsumption and overproduction, and an important prescription he advocated was the monopolization of capitalist economy. De Man was familiar with the early 1930s work of Keynes, but was not exposed to the British economist's *The Means to Prosperity* before introducing his Labour Plan (*Plan du Travail*) in 1933–35. The Labour Plan advocated governmental intervention, public investment, structural reform and economic planning, 'a pragmatic and technocratic but equally innovative socialist reply to the challenges of the deep economic crisis of the early 1930s' (Cuyvers 2015: 101). The Labour Plan, a key policy proposal of the Belgian Workers' Party (BWP) was influential internationally, and is considered a major contribution to planism.[16] Despite the centrity of economics, de Man's work is also a technocratic theory aimed at producing a planned society. And this theory was not available before 1933, with only hints of it elaborated in a series of eighteen articles on economics for the *Bulletin d'Information et de Documentation*, in the years 1931–35. In Britain, a pressure group called Political and Economic Planning (PEP) was established in 1931. It created research groups on specific issues and published reports on housing, social services, health services, and the geographic-spatial location of industry during the 1930s. The PEP 'was strongly technocratic in outlook, committed to efficiency and modernization' (Addison 1975: 39). Its research groups were led by 'white-collar managers, experts, and professionals' (Addison 1975: 39). Another British pressure group, the Next Five Years, active in the same period, proposed to create an Economic General Staff, a National Development Board, the coordination of social services, town and country planning, and locating industry in deprived areas to offer job opportunities. All this activity aimed at advancing social, spatial and economic planning, however, took place in the 1930s, and particularly in response to the 1929 crash and its aftermath – the growth of unemployment and economic downturn.

So, architecture can precede its corresponding political economy; but some qualifications are necessary. In the immediate aftermath of the First World War, discussions of Fordist efficiency and standardization were common, and their influence on the work of the early modernists is well-documented (Swenarton 2008: 2–3). Thus, the concept of the assembly line was already disseminated and its efficiency was revered. Similarly, the idea of a strong, centralized and interventionist government had been demanded by reformers in diverse European countries since the 1880s, as discussed in Part One of this book, and by the 1920s had gained traction within a significant segment of society. In this sense, Keynesian economics and planism were merely the later consistent and coherent articulation of these ideas in the form of macroeconomic and microeconomic–technocratic theories. May's *Siedlungen*, then, implemented these ideas in urban planning and design before their parallel development in other fields. This is not meant to belittle May's or Hilberseimer's achievements, but rather to point out some of the necessary elements which enabled the realization of their projects. To list the ingredients: a powerful position; a strong coalition of likeminded politicians, planners and architects; a favourable local and central government; an emerging and widely disseminated idea, though still vague and abstract, of an alternative to the current political economy and its societal organization.

This implies that while 'revolutionary architecture' may indeed be impossible in advance of a social and political revolution, as Tafuri argued, 'reformist architecture' can precede economic, social, and political change. Tafuri had indicted the architecture and urbanism of May and others as the ideological vehicles of capitalism, but such an indictment should be understood to be relevant to proponents of a social revolution, not to reformists. In effect, the indictment by Tafuri carries a veiled endorsement: reformist architecture and urbanism determined aspects of societal organization, albeit in limited form, before their ideology and worldview became hegemonic.

This chapter has shifted the discussion to the city, and specifically to the relation of architecture to the city as an expression of 'the position' architecture assumes vis-à-vis the societal organization and political economy of its time. It has gravitated away from the political, introducing the issue of social forms and urban forms, as well as spatial organization as a reflection of the conditions and characteristics of the political economy. In contemporary conditions, after three decades that evinced the advance of neoliberalism, the collapse of radical movements and the retreat of reformism, including the rise of a neoliberal architecture of spectacle, hyper-individualism, and speculation, the rebirth of a 'reformist architecture' would provide a long-awaited alternative and a hope for the betterment of society via architectural practice. However, another concern remains: can architecture appropriately express political positions?

'VULGAR' ARCHITECTURE, 'VULGAR' POLITICS

The Semiotics of Architecture

> [T]he fundamental feature of today's society is the irreconcilable antagonism between Totality and the individual.
>
> (Žižek 2006: 16)

In his essay 'Function and Sign', the semiotician Umberto Eco studies architecture as a language. A utensil, in addition to its use value, writes Eco (1986: 59), '*communicates the function to be fulfilled*'. Moreover, the utensil also promotes and signifies a specific way of use, of doing or making. Signifying the function and a way of doing takes place even while the utensil is not used, and perhaps has never been used, or would never be used. In other word, the signification is independent of the actual use of the specific utensil in question. Eco writes that 'what our semiotic framework would recognize in the architectural sign is *the presence of a sign vehicle whose denoted meaning is the function it makes possible …*' (Eco 1986: 60).

The process of denoting a function is dependent on cultural codes. Eco uses the example of a 'primitive man' who would be unable to comprehend the use of an elevator's buttons to demonstrate how even function depends on cultural codes. This leads to identifying the dependency of codes for new functions on existing codes – one may consider the interfaces of desktop music players from the late 1990s and early 2000s and the manner in which they emulated familiar car radios or home stereos rather than fully adapt to the logic of digital media. By totally subverting existing codes to the level they are no longer recognized architecture becomes a form of art.

Eco is here investigating the ability of buildings and structures to communicate. Eco's unfolding of the communicative aspect of the building, of the utilitarian object, demonstrates why functionalist architecture had symbolic content despite its utilitarian focus, and why architectural critics of the 1970s argued that architecture always had symbolic content. These 'sign vehicles' can be denoted or connoted in relation to additional codes. While utility is Eco's point of departure, he identifies the manner in which building elements, such as windows, can connote a way of inhabitation – a worldview, an ideology – in addition to denoting function and hence also have a symbolic function. He argues that what is at stake here is a different form of utility, in a social rather than functional sense, and that such symbolic value may supersede the functional. Eco describes the functional aspect as primary function, and the connoted symbolic as secondary function, though quite evidently the secondary can in some cases be the more significant of the two, as in the case of a throne.

Eco uses the example of the Gothic ogive, and demonstrates how its connotation transformed over time. By the nineteenth century, the Gothic was identified with high religiosity – by Pugin, Ruskin and others. This meant imposing a new reading, and one which is clearly ideological. Eco suggests that such a 'connotative lexicon' was necessarily dependent on earlier interpretation of the Gothic cathedral. But there is here another aspect – the identification by romantics of the medieval era as one of high Christianity in contrast to their modern era. Hence the architecture of the period was similarly associated with religiosity, despite the persistence of pagan rituals and beliefs throughout the medieval era in much of Europe.

In search for a specific architectural code, Eco encounters certain difficulties. Geometry as a descriptive code for architecture, for example, is not limited to architecture. He suggests three code lexicons. The first is based on technical codes, describing architecture structurally. 'There is at this level of codification no communicative "content,"' he writes (Eco 1986: 73). Then there are syntactic codes: diverse spatial categories such as high-rise, open plan, 'free' elevation, symmetrical section. The third lexicon is that of semantic codes:

> These concern the significant units of architecture, or the relations established between individual architectural sign-vehicles [...] and their denotative and connotative meanings. They might be subdivided as to whether, through them, the units (a) denote *primary functions* (roof, stairway, window); (b) connote *secondary functions* (tympanum, triumphal arch, neo-Gothic arch); (c) connote *ideologies of inhabitation* (common room, dining room, parlor); or (d) at a larger scale have typological meaning under certain *functional and sociological types* (hospital, villa, school, palace, railroad station).
>
> *(Eco 1986: 74)*

Yet Eco points out the poverty of such codes: their ability to create new meanings by establishing diverse relationships is significantly limited. He writes that: 'One could take a verbal language as a *field of (nearly absolute) freedom*, in which the speaker is free to improvise novel messages to suit unexpected situations. And in architecture, if the codes are really those indicated above, that does not seem to be the case' (Eco 1986: 75).

Eco describes how Le Corbusier's designs were tailored to specific social exigencies and argues that the result would be three systems – architectural forms, functions, and social exigencies or an anthropological system – which can each be read independently. Basically, he identifies the looseness of the relationship between the architectural forms, the functions, and the social, to the extent that the relationship is tenuous.

Eco emphasizes the dependency of architecture on its externalities – on other fields, whether sociology, anthropology or other. 'Forced to find forms that will give form to systems over which *he has no power*, forced to articulate a language that has always to express something external to it' (Eco 1986: 82). Eco suggests two possible conclusions from his findings: (a) that architecture can be understood as powerless, subjugated to other concerns; (b) that 'architecture has the power, through the operation of its system of stimulative sign-vehicles, to determine what those functions and values are going to be' (Eco 1986: 82). Both these understanding, for Eco, are exaggerations.

More important here than the question of agency by semiotics, however, is Eco's demonstration that architecture is an impoverished language, that the possibilities of architecture to articulate and communicate a position are finite and extremely limited. 'Communication' here goes beyond the narrow use of the term by Charles Jencks, and involves denotation of function and utility as well as symbolic connotations.

Empty Signifiers

The architectural firm Dogma argues through its production of hypothetical projects, that is, paper architecture, that architectural form is inherently political. Architectural theorist Ana Jeinic pointed out that this assertion is expressed by a very simple gesture: a focus in the work of Dogma on the binary of inclusion–exclusion, expressed by wall elements, restricted openings, and other formal devices (Jeinic 2014). Whether following Carl Schmitt's friend–enemy conception of the political, as Dogma's Aureli does, or simply acknowledging that a formation of a political community requires a process of inclusion and exclusion, the logic appears clear enough. Consequently, the idea of border is transposed in the firm's work into a formal, architectural limit.

In the 2007 paper–architecture project Stop City, eight colossal housing slabs of 500 × 500 × 25 metres are organized around a square-shaped piece of land containing a forest. Their purpose is to create a city edge, an abrupt limitation to city expansion and sprawl, preserving the town–country divide. It is imagined as a reaction to the conditions of Fordist consumer society described by Archizoom in their No-Stop City project. Instead of an analytical project unveiling the contemporary city as a spatial continuum and supermarket-like sprawl, a totalizing reduction of anything and everything to exchangeable goods, Stop City is a contrarian statement, positing division and boundary as a means of ending (capitalist) spatial expansion – Aureli's 'urbanization'.

Another project, A Simple Heart (2002–10), imagines a series of inhabitable 'walls' enclosing urban square-shaped spaces of 800 × 800 metres. The existing area, violently cut-off from the rest of the city fabric, is turned to an interior space by the walls and a transparent roof, a vast 'living room' (Figure 3.12). While the violence of the insertion of such enclosures into existing urban areas is reminiscent of OMA's Exodus, the visualizations of the wall are surprisingly less urban than the plans, and recall Superstudio's Continuous Monument, with infinite walls cutting through diverse natural environments. Or, alternatively, reminiscent of Rossi's Locomotiva 2 entry for the competition for the Centro Direzionale in Turin (1962):[17] a square-shaped, large-scale urban area defined by four colossal perimeter 'walls', a form which appears also in Dogma's homage to this project, Locomotiva 3 (2010). The project is more focused on the act of enclosure than on the promise of social exchanges in a more intimate urban space. A Simple Heart acts against urban fragmentation not so much by creating a continuum or unity, because unity here is limited to the interiority of the 800 × 800 metre square, but by the sheer scale of the architectural object. The effect on the city is similar to, yet distinct from, the megastructure – both of which are urban-scale architecture, though in the case of A Simple Heart the distinctions between architecture and infrastructure are never dissolved. Rather, it reorganizes the city in the manner an architect organizes the distribution of internal spaces in a building, albeit in a changed scale, hence the contained city fragments become an interior space of sorts. The 2005 City Walls project imagines a new town formed by a grid contained within a square. The grid is created by inhabited walls, and these walls act as limits, defining specific (square) urban territories and in effect subdividing the area of the city into particular units, each of which can be given a different character. Each of these, for Dogma, is 'a room', 'in which content is staged as furniture' (Dogma 2013: 52). In other words, here too scaling takes place, and the urban is conceived in terms of the architectural.

Architecture is finally reduced to walls in the Fields of Walls project (2012), an attempt to exacerbate Piranesi's Campo Marzio by inserting into the plan of Rome fifteen walls. The walls intensify the urban condition by being juxtaposed on an existing urban fabric, and while mostly permeable to pedestrians they nevertheless divide and define areas within the city. Juxtaposed on a somewhat informal urban area, they reorganize it, infuse order into urban chaos, and direct a reading of the city. Dogma here propose a second curatorial act, a sequel of sorts to the original curation of the city by Piranesi, an act that implies a critique of Campo Marzio's 'disorder'. Hence, Fields of Walls can be read first and foremost as an act of ordering the city.

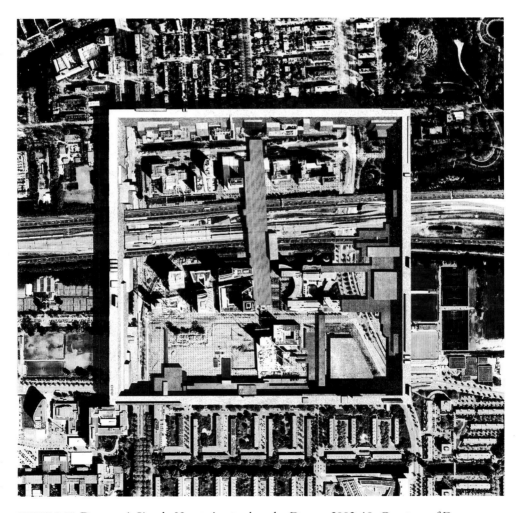

FIGURE 3.12 Dogma, A Simple Heart, Amsterdam, by Dogma 2002-10. Courtesy of Dogma.

Limits and boundaries are for Aureli and Tattara a means of confronting the 'flow' of urbanization, understood as economic-led urban development, the suburbanization and eventual sprawl which undermine the city and the conception of a city as a *cité*, a political community.[18] The limit constitutes (architectural) form and (political) subjectivity by preventing the singular unit (architecture, the individual subject, or social group) from merging with or being absorbed into the whole (urbanization). The limit, however, also establishes a relationship between the singular and the whole, and defines the type of relationship. 'The formal can be defined as the experience of limit,' writes Aureli, 'as the relationship between the "inside" and the "outside"' (Aureli 2011: 30).

For Aureli, the reformist idea of a building–city continuum is anathema, as his larger project is dedicated to 'freeing' architecture from 'urbanization'. Yet his reverence for the work of architects whose projects were to dissolve the architecture–urbanism dichotomy, such as Hilberseimer, complicates his position. This contradiction is overcome by accentuating the architecture, by positioning the architecture first and the urban second, in order to prevent subjugation by the urbanization. In this sense, Dogma's proposition is neither the kind of architectural autonomy created, according to Tafuri, by the iron grid, nor the continuum imagined by the architectural avant-garde. Architecture must remain unabsorbed by the urban, yet nevertheless has to engage with it on some level in order to achieve efficacy. Consequently, the balance Dogma attempt to achieve between a rigorous defence of autonomy, on the one hand, and efficacy via engagement with the city on the other, is rarely achieved: the projects oscillate between over-emphasizing autonomy, and therefore lack of efficacy, to, occasionally, over-engaging, and therefore loss of autonomy. Nevertheless, the attempt to reorder the urban as an architect arranges the internal organization of a building is a method which comes close to achieving this balance. 'A fundamental aspect of No-Stop City,' Aureli commented on the Archizoom project, 'is the disappearance of architecture and its replacement by furniture design, which was seen as a more effective form of urbanization because it is more flexible, and therefore more consumable and reproducible' (Aureli 2011: 20). He argued that in Hilberseimer, 'urbanity itself is conceived as one domestic space' (Aureli 2011: 16).

Despite the sophisticated, even if tenuous arguments articulated by Aureli and Dogma, the actual formal gesture that matters politically is a simple one: the creation of a boundary separating the architecture from its urban context, a boundary which is physical, though also psychological, symbolic, and ideological. Boundaries are undoubtedly powerful urban elements: walls, fences, rivers, canals, busy traffic arteries define neighbourhoods, urban enclaves and much more. Boundaries such as the Berlin Wall, the separation wall in the Occupied Territories or the UN Buffer Zone in Cyprus, give clear physical form to political separation and antagonism. But such boundaries, while unveiling an inside and outside of a political community, whether the excluded are homeless and poor or an antagonistic political community, are also very simple gestures that do not fully account for 'architecture'. Their expressive vocabulary is restrictive, and nuance is impossible. They identify inside and outside, inclusion and exclusion, but their actual content is dependent on what is included or excluded, on a relational condition. Hence, it is a powerful but limited language, producing strong statements but unable to create much nuance or more complex, multifaceted conditions. Dogma did not, of course, discover the use of formal limits and boundaries as devices of inclusion and exclusion. Aureli and Tattara were inspired by OMA's first project, Exodus, and its imaginary wall cutting through London, itself a transposed Berlin Wall. But gated communities or 'walk-through' neighbourhoods, permeable or 'sealed' buildings, accessible or inaccessible public spaces are all familiar from the contemporary city, whether the result of clients' briefs, of regulations, or architectural decision.

The Whale, a large residential building in Amsterdam by the Architekten Cie completed in 2000, was designed as a perimeter block with raised corners to facilitate public circulation, a pedestrian thoroughfare under and through the building, yet concerns raised by the city council regarding security resulted in fencing the courtyard and preventing such passage. A public housing project in Newark, New Jersey, was built with walls and defences against the threat of local gangs. New housing projects in London's Tower Hamlets are ostensibly 'street oriented', with main door entrances and supposedly direct street access, yet design is employed to veil their actual exclusive character, functioning, in effect, as gated communities. Oscar Newman's 'defensible space' theory and brand, still popular in the United States and Britain, or Crime Prevention Through Environmental Design (CPTED), utilize barriers, walls, vision and other means of defining space as inclusive or exclusive. Moreover, the idea of transitional spaces as spaces between private and public spaces has been incorporated into diverse governmental guidelines for place making, urban and architectural design. What really matters is who is included and who is excluded, or, in other words, the shape and form (and boundaries) of the political community.

All this demonstrates the incapacity of architecture to go beyond very general statements. While the deployment of walls as devices to delineate an inside–outside, inclusion–exclusion, is arguably political, it cannot be associated with a specific politics. The act, in its generality, remains ambiguous. The ambiguity can be overcome only by the specificity of its deployment. It speaks volumes of the limitations of architecture as language. At the end of the day, while the number of meanings language can create is almost infinite, in architecture, as Eco argued, they are very limited. Pawley commented:

> The idea that 'physical, social, personal, political, psychological, economic, civilizational and cultural factors' can all be expressed through 'the physical manifestation' is rather like expecting Beethoven's ninth symphony to be adequately recorded on a Dictaphone. The channel capacity is insufficient [...].
>
> *(Pawley 1971a: 88)*

It is therefore of little surprise that the relation of a specific form of architecture to a specific political movement and ideology is loose and associative at best. The architectural formulation is general and abstract. Its language is impoverished, and meanings are finite. Modernist architecture, or the use of concrete, were easily associated with 'the new', and thus deployed by political movements interested in forming a new society, in identifying themselves with renewal, progress, and change. Such architecture could be assimilated to a specific equivalential chain, yet its link to such a chain was necessarily weak, contingent and easily contested. This limitation also underlines the arguments posited by Jencks, Krier and others – namely, that architecture is not inherently political, that the correlation of a specific architecture to a specific political agenda is tenuous.

The first chapter in this section, studying the symbolic, is, to a degree, a response to these arguments. But while it claimed that architecture is political via its symbolic dimensions, it also becomes clear that architecture is political only in a marginal sense – its ability to articulate a precise ideology restricted. Instead, architecture is more easily identified with society, with worldview, with the political than with a political movement or narrow, specific ideology. It expresses and affirms society's self-image rather than that of a narrow movement; it is shaped by and therefore also expresses current political economy. The limitation of the meanings architecture can produce suggests that architecture is cumbersome and unrefined, from such a 'linguistic' perspective. It can speak generally or abstractly, but cannot articulate the specific.

This condition, however, is not necessarily as detrimental as may seem to political praxis. The systems theorist Niklas Luhmann argued that choice can be offered to voters in democratic elections only in the form of binaries: progressive/conservative, restrictive/expansive welfare state and so on (Mouffe 2005: 4–5). Crude binaries, the target of post-structuralist critiques, are required for democracy. Nuance, specificity, precision: all these are superfluous. Architecture's own vulgar language parallels that of the political. The symbolic at the heart of the political of which Laclau wrote, the 'empty signifier', is similar in its characteristics to architecture's linguistic limitations. The political–symbolic is unrefined, imprecise, abstract and contingent in meaning, similarly to Durkheim's understanding of collective consciousness in modern societies. Hence, the 'vulgarity' of architecture as a language, the coarse statements it can produce and the lack of nuance of 'refined' language, echo the condition of the political. All this gravitates towards an unexpected conclusion: despite the expectation and demands for cohesion, clarity, precision, and consistency voiced by political movements or by academics, the coarse language of architecture enables rather than prevents exchanges with a similarly coarse political.

In this section, architectural efficacy has been encountered in diverse contexts, in symbolic and in urban form. Throughout the book, efficacy appeared in countless forms: as a design of a university campus, as an experiment in urban planning, as a community garden, as a housing project, as a hypothetical design and much more. The ubiquity of architectural efficacy is challenged by the concern for the architect's agency, which, in contrast, is significantly restricted, limited, and dependent on external conditions. Yet here too, the book has brought to the fore instances in which architects have agency and demonstrate some level of control of the societal and political impact of their decisions and designs.

Everything is political – perhaps, though certainly not political to the same extent or in the same manner. The tighter the architect's control of a project, that is, the ability to steer it by decision without compromise, the lesser its socio-political impact, and vice versa. Many of the instances surveyed in this book in which efficacy is detected are of relatively minor consequence, no more than small pieces within an immense jigsaw puzzle. Rather than a demiurge, the architect is dependent on external conditions and powerful forces over which he or she has no control – only a limited ability to engage with them, to steer them somewhat in one direction or another. The cases in which the architect appears to have the power to significantly impact society through the design of buildings and cities stress the need for allegiances and alliances that cut across disciplinary and professional barriers, as well as the necessity of the dissemination of ideas, concepts and values which contrast dominant societal forms. Instead of architectural or individual freedom, the architect requires accomplices and collaborators in order to affect society. A collective and demanding task, then, but another *cité* is possible.

NOTES

Introduction

1. *AD* 1970/10: 507–22; 1970/11: 566–73; 1971/10: 619–30.
2. *AD* 1970/9: 431–46; 1970/10: 499–505; 1971/6: 332–33; 1971/10: 633–36, 659–64, 666–67; 1971/12: 727–36, 762–65.
3. *AD* 1970/7: 334–35; 1971/7: 441; 1971/8: 520. Reacting to an 'experts' seminar on housing, Pawley wrote that '[i]nevitably this statistical discourse has the effect of bringing all those who take part in it onto one side of the problem – the administrative, managerial side, the bureaucratic side, the side of "them" against a largely unrepresented "us"' (Pawley 1970a: 40).
4. *AD* 1970/4: 188–89; 1971/5: 264–65.
5. *AD* 1970/5: 220–21.
6. *AD* 1970/4: 169–70; 1970/10: 524–25.
7. *AD* 1970/6: 278.
8. *AD* 1970/11: 558–65; 1971/8: 472.
9. Reformism is discussed in Part One of this book, and follows Eduard Bernstein's conception of the term.
10. Including Pier Vittorio Aureli's questionable attempt to depict Aldo Rossi's project as political as well as his focus on Archizoom's critique of architecture, Felicity Scott's return to Ant Farm and the radical architecture of the late 1960s, BAVO, Cohabitation Strategies, the work of the Agency Group in Sheffield, Urban Asymmetries in Delft, Transgressive Architecture in London, Urban-Think Tank, City Min(e)d in Brussels, Raumlabor and many others.
11. The geographer Jamie Peck highlighted the case of dozens of city councils in the state of Michigan which have been placed under administrative control (Jamie Peck 2015). City councils in the United States with a high percentage of impoverished citizens end up with lower tax revenues and more expenses, and are therefore set up to fail. Once they falter, the right of their citizens to a democratically elected administration is withdrawn, and they are placed under a technocratic administration. Similar processes became visible in the negotiations with Greece on a bailout in June–July 2015, in which a democratically elected government, backed by a popular referendum, was humiliated by the European Union (EU). Even the International Monetary Fund, a bastion of neoliberalism, had by this time admitted that debt reduction for Greece is necessary, yet the EU pushed ahead with radical austerity remedies against economic rationale.
12. Proponents of participatory democracy, such as Jürgen Habermas, have focused on procedures rather than content, presuming the content should be left to the democratic process. Now, it seems, the democratic deficit is itself responsible for widening inequalities. See more in Part Two of this book.
13. There are, of course, more complex understandings of the political. See, among others, the work of Carl Schmitt, Ernesto Laclau, or Chantal Mouffe. These understandings will be outlined in later chapters.

14 The work of Foucault and 1970s feminism, for example, though also Barthes and Levi-Strauss's work on the myth, or Althusser's 'Ideology and State Apparatuses' essay. See also the work of Science and Technology Studies (STS) academics, such as Bruno Latour.
15 Actor-Network-Theory scholars differentiate between 'Politics' with a capital P, which refers to the type of official politics which take place within the specific territory delineated for power contestation, and 'politics' with a lower case p, the type of politics found outside that territory.
16 Deconstruction has been criticized for wilfully ignoring, even rejecting the locus of politics, preferring, instead, to focus solely on the political which takes place in the margins (Lilla 1998). Consequently, processes of de-naturalization were not followed by politicization in the full sense of the term. In the process, the official arena of politics is de-legitimized or rendered superfluous. Instead, a narrow and limited idea of the political emerged, restricted to the outer territories of politics.
17 To mention but a few: Jean-Louis Cohen (1992) *Le Corbusier and the Mystique of the USSR: Theories and Projects for Moscow, 1928–1936*, Princeton, N.J.; Oxford: Princeton University Press; Richard Pare, Jean-Louis Cohen (2007) *The Lost Vanguard: Russian Modernist Architecture 1922–1932*, New York: Monacelli Press; S. O. Khan-Magomedov (Selim Omarovich) (1986) *Alexandr Vesnin and Russian Constructivism*, London: Lund Humphries.
18 See, in particular, Mark Swenarton 1981.

Part One

1 Some of the material included in this section has been previously published as a chapter in the anthology *Critical Tools*. See Kaminer 2012.
2 Boltanski's focus is on 'sociological critical theory', yet his concerns and insights are relevant here beyond this limited area of sociological research.
3 Italics in citations are in the original unless stated otherwise.
4 A newer translation and complete version, translated by Henry Tudor, is available as Eduard Bernstein (1993) *The Preconditions of Socialism*.
5 Famously quoted by E.P. Thompson (1966: 56).
6 The coffee shops, as Richard Sennett has pointed out (1978), were the locus of intense discussions regarding culture and society, in which social rank was circumvented.
7 See also Hobsbawm 1984d: 206.
8 Secularism was an important ingredient of the labour movement's ideology, as Hobsbawm noted (1959: 128). But many of the movement's ideas were originally born in religious circles, and many of the nineteenth century middle-class reformers were animated by religious fervour.
9 Chadwick became aware of epidemics devastating the workhouses. The 1834 Poor Law Amendment Act, agitated by Chadwick, was a flawed law, which established a system of workhouses in order to address unemployment and homelessness. Nevertheless, the direct correlation of health, unemployment, and pauperism became painfully visible.
10 'Freedom' had an important place in collective consciousness in England. 'Free-born Englishmen' was a common phrase, and, as in today's America, the term 'freedom' was used to forward very different agendas, including patriotism, anti-Catholicism, and, in the nineteenth century, free trade. In 1849 Chadwick's enemies had the upper hand. Following London's poor performance during the Cholera epidemic he was dismissed from the Metropolitan Commission of Sewers. Chadwick and Shaftesbury were both dismissed in 1854 from the Board of Health (Hall 1998: 687).
11 In 1847, for example, it carried out the road improvements of New Oxford Street, and, in the process, cleared much of the St Giles slum. The empty lots acquired in projects such as these were resold to developers intent on for-profit construction.
12 It is necessary to mention, in this context, the important part *The Builder* had in spreading reformist ideas within the building industry.
13 Originally published in *The Builder* 1857, xiv/7: 77–78.
14 Typically, lodgers were not permitted in the new dwellings.
15 These arguments would be carried into the twentieth century – for example, in the dispute in the Royal Commission into the Operation of the Poor Laws (1905–9), which issued a majority report arguing for a weak state, individual responsibility, and charity, while a minority report, composed by Beatrice Webb, emphasized the role and responsibility of the state in solving poverty.
16 See the chapter 'Urban Form' in Part Three of this book.

17 'Town planning' became the term used in Britain, whereas 'urban planning' is the more common international term. Here both will be used interchangeably.
18 Peter Hall argued that planning's roots lie in anarchist theory: the ideal of a self-sustaining, non-capitalist, co-operative community (Hall 2014). But the step from perceiving a multiplicity of such communities as a social destination to scaling the ideal community to cover entire society is, on the level of thought and theory, easily made.
19 See also Martin Jay 1973: 64.
20 Yet it is important to note that Rudi Dutschke and some of the other leaders of the student movement in Germany were influenced and radicalized by the Frankfurt School before turning to other schools of thought or developing their own theories.
21 Lyotard identified critique's strong relation to bourgeois reformism, but ignored its deployment by Critical Theory or radical movements. The Frenchman's polemics became entangled in a general retreat into experimental but abstract theory which perfectly undermined many of the tenets of the Left.
22 Richard Rorty detected the influence of the Frankfurt School and post-structuralism in the transformation of an American reformist Left into a 'cultural left' (Rorty 1998: 77).
23 See Luc Ferry and Alain Renaut (1990), and to some extent Bruno Latour's realist–pragmatist argument in the widely read 'Why Has Critique Ran Out of Steam? From Matters of Fact to Matters of Concern' (2004).
24 In post-war Britain about a third of trained architects were directly employed by central or local government, and about 30 per cent of commissions received by private sector architects in the 1960s were from public sources (Lipman 1969: 203).
25 The English word 'recuperation' is very similar to its French counterpart, but not exactly the same. *Récupération* means, in addition to all other meanings of the English 'recuperation', also the hijacking of ideas. See the *Grand Larousse*, 1977, 4957 (5).
26 It is necessary to underline the fact that capitalism and states do not altogether avoid a less benign and more brutal treatment of opposition both within and without; 'inclusion' remains a process reserved for those elements of society which are considered 'respectable', or when the critique is too widespread to repress or ignore.
27 See also Butler 1997: 83–84.
28 It must be noted that Laclau's description of populism is based on his conception of the political, as outlined in earlier work. See, for example, Laclau and Mouffe (2001), especially pp. 63–64. Laclau's work on populism exacerbates and underlines certain aspects of the political, and for this reason is more useful for the purposes of this chapter.
29 Famously, it was Karl Marx who derogatorily described Fourier, Owen, and Saint-Simon as 'utopians' in order to highlight the futility and distance from reality of their thought.
30 As Kristin Ross has emphasized, there has been a struggle surrounding the shaping of the meanings associated with May '68. But while 'equality' may have indeed functioned as the uniting battle cry of workers and students, 'liberty' was nevertheless central to many of the participating students (Ross 2002: 169). In fact, Ross's book unfolds the *récupération* of the meaning of May '68.

Part Two

1 This chapter is expanded from Tahl Kaminer (2011c) 'The Ruins of the British Welfare State', *Footprint* 9.
2 Urban Splash commissioned Hawkins Brown Architects and Studio Egret West, with landscape architects Grant Associates.
3 Such as the exhibition 'Overlooked' (19 April–10 May 2015).
4 Architectural historian Helena Mattsson discussed in a lecture in Umea in 2013 the case of the Globen development in 1980s Stockholm, nowadays the Ericsson Globe. An example of 'popular' programming and crude corporate architecture, typical of the era's urban redevelopments. Even today, some cities are supporting such developments, such as the New Jersey Performing Arts Center (1997) or the Prudential Center indoor arena (2007) in Newark, or the Providence Place (1999) city centre shopping mall in Providence.
5 In 1981, two urban development corporations were created in Britain – the LDDC and another in Merseyside. The latter, up until its expansion in 1988, was dwarfed by the LDDC, both in scale of

Notes   **185**

employment and size of area. It was not until 1987 that an amalgam of urban development PPPs would be created, including large ones such as Black Country (Edwards 1992: 19).

6 Marcuse's argument merges the 'demand/supply' explanation of gentrification offered by David Ley with the 'production' explanation by Neil Smith. Here, structural changes are responsible for the return to the city – namely, the provision of an increasing number of white collar jobs – and gentrification is a means of motivating the employees via lifestyle and culture.

7 As in the cases of Jeanne van Heeswijk's Blue House, a temporary cultural initiative in Ijburg, the student accommodation offered in the Berlage Blocks of Amsterdam's Indische Buurt, or temporary student housing in the redevelopment area of NDSM in Amsterdam's north.

8 Though the issue titled 'Post-Traumatic Urbanism' from 2010 foregrounded concerns regarding the political and sustainability. Adrian Lahoud, Charles Rice and Anthony Burke (eds) (2010) Post-Traumatic Urbanism, *Architectural Design*, profile No 207, Sep/Oct.

9 More recently, in the November/December 2013 issue, titled 'The Architecture of Transgression' and guest-edited by Jonathan Mosley and Rachel Sara, Doina Petrescu and Constantin Petcou outline the emergence of their office Atelier d'Architecture autogérée (aaa) (pp. 58–65), Alastair Parvin calls for 'Open-Source Architecture and the Design Commons' (pp. 89–95), and Ulrich Beckefeld and Karsten Huneck describe the work of their Office for Subversive Architecture (OSA), invested in creating temporary green spaces and 'domesticating' the public space.

10 The sixth issue, 'Part 2: Power Building', addresses urban development in the Gulf States, Guantanamo, and the Occupied Territories. 'Architecture of Power Part 3', the seventh issue, includes, alongside articles on city branding, internet and media, an article on the commons and another by BAVO. Other topics addressed here include 'informed economy', surveillance, control, and Latin American politics.

11 'Craft the Agenda for a World to Come', the eighth issue, discusses China within an OMA-type of framework, and includes contributions by the Netherlands Architecture Institute (NAi), while the ninth issue, 'Suburbia After the Crisis', anticipating the collapse of the mortgage sector in the United States, includes an MIT study of New Jersey's urban sprawl. Whereas the tenth issue (*Volume* 2006/10) 'Agitation', focuses on digital modelling and technology, it also includes contributions by Lebanese architect Tony Chakar (pp. 37–39), discussion of Rio's informality and of Prishtina as post-conflict city, and a review of the Camp for Oppositional Architecture (pp. 152–53). The eleventh issue, titled 'Cities Unbuilt', highlights migration, informality and conflict with articles about the Caucasus, Kigali, Beirut and Palestine (*Volume* 2007/11).

12 Issue 14, after Arjen Oosterman replaced Bouman as chief editor, is dedicated to Bouman's manifesto for 'unsolicited architecture'. Bouman's list of necessary ingredients includes freedom from planning, giving voice to the under-represented, shelter for homeless, and colonizing unused spaces. Among the exemplary architects mentioned is Santiago Cirugeda (*Volume* 2007/14). The issue argues for an architecture which is subjugated indirectly to society – architecture which is directed at improvement and betterment and is not determined by the state or by corporate interests.

13 The only architectural publication so far in this territory to rigorously interrogate political theory is Teresa Hoskyns' (2014) *The Empty Place: Democracy and Public Space*, Oxon; New York: Routledge.

14 Contemporary urban participation is an urban alternative deployed by architects against planning. Among the influences on the contemporary movement were the Situationists and the work of de Certeau, with which architects were fascinated in the late 1990s: ideas and practices which avoid the question of 'making' the city in the physical sense, and instead focus on experiencing and interpreting the city. From this perspective, planning is the cause of rather than solution to the malaise of cities.

15 'I was obliged to persuade artists, learned men, and chiefs of industry,' wrote Saint-Simon, 'that their interests were essentially the same as those of the mass of the people; that they belonged to the class of laborers, at the same time that they were their natural chiefs; that the approbation of the mass of the people, for the services which they rendered them, was the only recompense worthy of their glorious exertions. I was obliged to insist much upon this point, […] since it is the only means of giving to the nations, guides who truly merit their confidence, guides who are capable of directing their opinions, and putting them into a state of judging fairly the political measures which are favorable or contrary to the interests of the greatest number' (Saint-Simon 2010: 87).

16 'Reason' is itself a weapon in such contestations, deployed as the privilege of the expert. Bourdieu has written that 'ideologies are always *doubly determined*, that they owe their most specific characteristics not only to the interest of the classes or class fractions they express (the function of

sociodicy), but also to the specific interests of those who produce them and to the specific logic of the field of production' (Bourdieu 1991: 169).
17 There are many others examples. Foucault's work, and particularly the concept of biopolitics, suggests an impossibility to be 'outside' society and its indoctrination.
18 For the PCI, the implementation of radical democracy in its own organization was exemplified by condoning an array of trade unions to compete for workers' memberships (Hobsbawm 1977) – which is disappointingly similar to liberal democracy. In any case, the absorption of Gramsci's theory into the PCI required a significant distortion of his writings (Müller 2013: 90).
19 Community councils in Scotland were set up as non-governmental representational bodies to enhance communication and exchanges between local government and residents. They provide an example of associative democracy.
20 Hannah Arendt's republicanism included ideas of 'deliberative democracy'. See Arendt 1963, 1972.
21 *Multitude*, in particular, offers a critique of the legitimacy of 'the people' as sovereign (Hardt and Negri: 2006).
22 For a more detailed discussion of the work of Negri, on which the following chapter is based, see Tahl Kaminer (2014) 'The Contradictions of Participatory Architecture and *Empire*', *Architecture Research Quarterly*, Vol 18, 1, pp. 31–37. By permission of Cambridge University Press.
23 Panzieri had preceded Tronti in positing the autonomy of the working class, a position developed from the official stance of the PSI that exalted 'autonomy', though without elaborating the meaning and context of autonomy (Wright 2002).
24 See Part One.
25 Marcuse studied the work of Schmitt as evidence of 'the authoritarian mind', yet nevertheless commented that 'Carl Schmitt gives a brilliant portrayal of liberalist rationalism' (Marcuse 2009: 206 note 27).
26 Mouffe is not the only scholar to use the term 'agonistic pluralism' or to focus on conflict and contestation as core aspects of the political. Jenny Mansbridge, Bonnie Honig, and Benjamin Barber articulate similar ideas to those of Mouffe.
27 Intellectual and social equality are not the same, according to Rancière – one is a basic condition, the other is demanded.
28 Rancière uses the term *le politique* (the political) to describe the territory of contestation between the police and the demands for emancipation, whereas the contestation for emancipation is referred to as *la politique* – 'politics'. 'So we have three terms,' Rancière wrote: 'policy, emancipation, and the political. If we want to emphasize their interplay, we can give to the process of emancipation the name of politics. I shall thus distinguish policy, politics, and the political – the political being the field for the encounter between emancipation and policy in the handling of a wrong' (Rancière 1992: 59). As Rancière's 'politics' is close in its meaning to what this book calls, following Mouffe, 'the political', to prevent confusion Rancière's 'politics' will be referred to, throughout the chapter, as 'the political'.
29 Architecture critic John Macarthur, at a seminar held in Edinburgh in 2014, similarly identified the Foucauldian and Adornian aspects in Rancière's aesthetic theory.
30 It is interesting to compare Rancière's argument to that of Constructivist literature critic Osip Brik, who wrote in 1928 that 'Democracy can have no division of art into "true" and "folk." All art workers are equal, no matter whose aesthetic taste they satisfy. [...] But, we may ask, who gave those eminent academics the monopoly of judgment on what's good or bad for art?' (Brik 2010: 78).
31 See the 2013 study by Ipsos-Mori, 'Generations', available at: http://www.ipsos-mori-generations.com/PartyPolitics (accessed 6 August 2013).
32 Tahl Kaminer, 'Interview with Amica Dall of Assemble' (London: 11 June 2015).
33 The idea of the commons as an alternative to the Enlightenment idea of public and private ownership has taken hold in participatory circles. See *Footprint* 16, Spring 2015; An Architecktur (2010); Dougald Hine (2013); David Bollier (2013).
34 The author has observed a community garden in Amsterdam's Belamiplein 2010–12. The non-exclusive and accessible character of the garden and the variety of uses – growing vegetables, using the lawn for recreation, or enjoying the bonfire/barbecue area – allowed diverse social groups to coincide with minimum friction, including homeless, middle class, migrants, and working class. See also Sarah Bell and Cristina Cerulli, 2012.
35 The online description of the ambience of the Elephant Park development in London by Lendlease emphasizes the communal spirit of the planned area: 'You'll find the concierge in a warm,

welcoming space that is framed by a living wall of vertical plants and crafted from natural materials, including timber panels and stone paving. Meanwhile, each of the rooftop gardens will play host to 40 plots, allowing residents to grow a wide range of fresh herbs and vegetables with a little help from their neighbours. Within each area of Elephant Park there will be a rooftop communal room, where residents will have the chance to stage film nights and parties with friends and family. The area's wooden deck will overlook the striking towers that make up London's distinctive skyline, providing a glimpse into the great possibilities that lie just beyond the development.' See http://www.elephantpark.co.uk/elephant-park/resident-facilities (accessed 3 December 2015).

36 The awarding of the 2015 Artes Mundi prize to American artist Theaster Gates for regeneration work in Chicago is a relevant precedent.
37 The 'nail house' is a term used for the Chinese who defy large-scale development and mass demolition and refuse to evict their homes (this term was not used by Assemble).
38 As stated by Fran Edgerley of Assemble in response to questions following a talk in Edinburgh, 26 September 2014.
39 See more about personalization later in this section.
40 U-TT wrote: 'One approach is what Ignasi de Sola-Morales has defined as "city acupuncture", which for our purposes means small-scale, highly localized interventions' (Brillembourg, Feireiss, Klumpner 2005: 107).
41 In the United States, for example, towns' budgets depend on taxation of residents' earnings, resulting in less redistribution – towns with less affluent residents have smaller budget per capita despite having more pressing expenses.
42 Among the propagators of politically committed architecture are figures such as Mike Lydon, co-editor of *Tactical Urbanism*, who is a member of the Congress for New Urbanism, a neoliberal urban ideology *par excellence*.
43 This thesis is advanced by, among others, Jean Baudrillard, particularly in his *The Mirror of Production*.
44 Avigail Sachs traces the emergence and modifications of the term 'users' in 1960s and 1970s United States as a result of a convergence between architecture, sociology, and psychology (Sachs 2013).
45 Byker was a pioneering project. The results were mixed: the percentage of original residents who returned was smaller than desired and anticipated, and the level of actual citizen empowerment was lower than some of those involved wished for.
46 The focus here is on participatory processes in the design of housing. There are other forms of participatory architecture, most commonly in the design of community buildings. In contrast to mass housing, such buildings are relatively marginal.
47 Pessac predated the implementation of mass-production techniques in the building industry, and while standardization certainly offered savings in the construction process, whether it actually did so in the case of Pessac has to be questioned.
48 Such housing was characterized in the late 1960s as 'petty commodity' in order to differentiate it from the formal housing sold on the market, which assumes the form of a fully fledged commodity. For this discussion, in which the work of John Turner was criticized, see, among others, Rod Burgess 1978.

Part Three

1 The concept of articulation, to a limited extent, relates to Althusser's 'over-determination', in which an event, occurrence or outcome is shaped not by a singular cause, but by a multiplicity, more than what would have been required to ensure its realization.
2 'The muffled boom in World Trade Centres,' wrote Martin Pawley in 1970, 'which has been going on since 1967 seems to be producing a monotonously anonymous kind of architecture' (Pawley 1970b: 55).
3 THINK team for the first round of the competition included Rafael Viñoly Architects, Frederic Schwartz Architects, Shigeru Ban Architects + Dean Maltz, Ken Smith, William Morrish, Jane Marie Smith, Rockwell Group, with Büro Happold, Arup and Jörg Schlaich.
4 The story of reconstruction is more intricate and complex than the concise account here. Of the numerous accounts available, Michael Sorkin's (2003) poignant and entertaining critique of the process is particularly recommended.
5 See also Pearce 2003: 2.

6 See also Richman 2003: 35.
7 Despite obvious influences, Breckman highlights the divergence of Lefort's categories of the symbolic and the real from Lacan's.
8 The 'misfit' between society and the symbolic parallels Mouffe's assertion that consensus is always exclusionary, achieved via hegemony.
9 In the nineteenth century, art for art's sake radicalized the idea of disinterestedness to the level of ridding aesthetics from any subjugation to morals.
10 Parts of the following chapter have been previously published in T. Kaminer (2013) 'In Search of Architectural Efficacy: Debate and Experimentation after May '68', in *Is There an (Anti-)Neoliberal Architecture?*, eds Jeinic, A., Wagner, A, Berlin: Jovis, pp. 46–61.
11 Lefebvre himself would give lectures at UP7, see Stanek 2008: 61.
12 This reading of *The Explosion* is greatly indebted to Lukasz Stanek's *Henri Lefebvre on Space* (see also Stanek 2008). While Lefebvre refers to the campus and its architecture, he does not offer a rigorous critique of the architecture, but rather suggests causality in a series of remarks and comments.
13 See also Miljacki 2012.
14 This comment is interpretative (Tafuri 1976).
15 The Soviet Union had, of course, abandoned capitalism and throughout the 1920s was busy installing a systematically planned state. But these were initial endeavours, with the 1920s NEP policies reversing some nationalizations and putting on hold other measures. The 'command economy' of the Soviet Union did not produce technocratic, managerial, or other significant innovations in the field of planned economy and society in those years. In any case, the first Five Year Plan, created by a centralized committee, was not born until the late 1920s. The Soviet Union, therefore, was far from being a model of economic and state planning in its immediate post-revolutionary era.
16 Planism was not immediately or uniformly adopted by social democratic parties in Europe. The Swiss and Czech parties turned to planism, as did the BWP and to a much lesser extent the Dutch SDAP. The German SPD (which approved in 1932 the *Umbau der Wirtschaft* with strong focus on planism) and its Austrian counterpart showed interest in such theories but were outlawed in the 1930s, and the interest in planism by the British Labour Party and the French SFIO and its rival communist party remained marginal throughout the 1930s. The Labour Plan of de Man is significant not just as a contributor to *planisme*, but because of its contribution to political thought. De Man understood the need of the BWP to lure the lower middle-class clerks and white-collar employees, not just the steel workers and miners – and believed the plan could thus be mobilized for a hegemonic operation (Hansen 1981).
17 The project's credits include Also Rossi, Gionugo Polesello, and Luca Meda.
18 In the workerist literature of the 1960s that inspires Aureli, the process of development is understood as capitalist-driven rather than as a technical progress associated with modernization, as ubiquitous at the time among Right and Left. Tafuri and his colleagues transposed this position to urban development, identifying the Fordist Plan as an expression of state capitalism (Tafuri 1976).

BIBLIOGRAPHY

AAA and PEPRAV (eds) (2007) *Urban Act: A Handbook for Alternative Practice*, Montrouge: Moutot Imprimeurs.
Ackerman, J. (1986) 'The Villa as Paradigm', *Perspecta,* Vol. 22, Paradigms of Architecture, pp. 10–31.
—— (1995) *The Villa: Form and Ideology of Country Houses*, London: Thames & Hudson.
Addison, P. (1975) *The Road to 1975: British Politics and the Second World War*, London: Pimlico.
Adorno, T. (1997) *Aesthetic Theory*, trans. Hullot-Kentor, R., London: The Athlone Press.
Adshead, S. (1916) 'The Standard Cottage', *The Town Planning Review*, Vol. 6, No. 4, April, pp. 244–49.
Althusser, L. (1969) *For Marx* [1965], trans. Brewster, B., London: Allen Lane.
—— (2001) 'Ideology and ideological state apparatuses' [1970], in *Lenin and Philosophy and Other Essays*, trans. Brewster, B., New York: Monthly Review Press, pp. 85–126.
Ambrosino, G., Bataille, G., Caillois, R. et al. (1988) 'Notes on the Foundation of a College of Sociology', in *The College of Sociology 1937–39* [1979], ed. Denis Hollier, Minneapolis: University of Minnesota Press, pp. 3–5.
An Architecktur (2008a) *An Architektur,* issue 19, Community Design. Involvement and Architecture in the US since 1963: Projects.
—— (2008b) *An Architektur*, issue 20, Community Design. Involvement and Architecture in the US since 1963: Texts.
—— (2010) 'On the Commons: A Public Interview with Massimo De Angelis and Stavros Stavrides', *e-flux*, available at: <http://www.e-flux.com/journal/on-the-commons-a-public-interview-with-massimo-de-angelis-and-stavros-stavrides/> (accessed 3 December 2015).
Arendt, H. (1960) 'Society and Culture', *Daedalus*, Vol. 89, No. 2, Mass Culture and Mass Media, spring, pp. 278–87.
—— (1963) *On Revolution*, New York: Viking Press.
—— (1972) *Crises of the Republic*, New York: Harcourt Brace Jovanovich.
Arnstein, S.R. (1969) 'A Ladder of Citizen Participation', *Journal of the American Institute of Planners*, 35, 4, pp. 216–24.
Attali, J. (1985) *Noise: The Political Economy of Music*, Manchester: Manchester University Press.
Aureli, P.V. (2007) 'The Difficult Whole', *Log,* Winter/Spring, pp. 39–61.
—— (2008) *The Project of Autonomy: Politics and Architecture Within and Against Architecture*, New York: Princeton Architectural Press.
—— (2011) *The Possibility of an Absolute Architecture*, Cambridge, Mass.: MIT Press.
Avilés, P. (2009) 'Autarky and Material Contingencies in Italian Architectural Debate (1936–1954)', *Footprint* 4, Agency in Architecture: Reframing Criticality in Theory and Practice, Spring, pp. 21–34.

Bibliography

Awan, N., Schneider, T., Till, J. (eds) (2011) *Spatial Agency: Other Ways of Doing Architecture*, London; New York: Routledge.
Ayers, A. (2012) 'Fun Palais', *The Architectural Review*, June; 231, 1384, pp. 45–51.
Baird, G. (2005) '"Criticality" and its Discontents', *The Harvard Design Magazine*, Fall 2004/Winter 2005, number 21, pp. 16–21.
Ballymore, 'London City Island', undated PR brochure, available at: <http://www.londoncityisland.com/brochures/city-island-brochure> (accessed 18 June 2015).
Banham, R. (2001) *Theory and Design in the First Machine Age* [1960], Oxford: Architectural Press.
——, Barker, P., Hall, P. and Price, C. (1969) 'Non-Plan: An Experiment in Freedom', *New Society*, 13, no. 338, 20 March, pp. 435–43.
Barber, B. (1996) 'Foundationalism and Democracy', in *Democracy and Difference: Contesting the Boundaries of the Political*, ed. Benhabib, S., Princeton: Princeton University Press, pp. 348–59.
Bataille, G. (1988) 'The Sorcerer's Apprentice', in *The College of Sociology 1937–39* [1979], ed. Hollier, D., Minneapolis: University of Minnesota Press, pp. 12–23.
Baudrillard, J. (1975) *The Mirror of Production*, St. Louis: Telos.
—— (2005) *The System of Objects* [1968], trans. Benedict, J., New York: Verso.
Bell, D. (1976) *The Coming of Post-Industrial Society* [1973], New York: Basic Books.
—— (1996) *The Cultural Contradictions of Capitalism* [1976], New York: Basic Books.
Bell, S. and Cerulli, C. (2012) 'Emerging Community Food Production and Pathways for Urban Landscape Transitions', in *E:CO*, Issue Vol. 14 No. 1, 2012, pp. 31–44.
Benhabib, S. (ed.) (1996a) *Democracy and Difference: Contesting the Boundaries of the Political*, Princeton, Princeton University Press.
—— (1996b) 'Towards a Deliberative Model of Democratic Legitimacy', in *Democracy and Difference: Contesting the Boundaries of the Political*, ed. Benhabib, S., Princeton, Princeton University Press, pp. 67–94.
—— (1996c) 'Introduction', in *Democracy and Difference: Contesting the Boundaries of the Political*, ed. Benhabib, S., Princeton, Princeton University Press, pp. 3–18.
Benjamin, W. (1968) 'The Work of Art in the Age of Mechanical Reproduction' [1936], *Illuminations*, New York: Schocken Books, pp. 217–51.
Berlage Institute (2009) 'Radicalizing the Local: Post Bubble Urban Strategies', Rotterdam: Berlage Institute, unpublished booklet.
Bernstein, E. (1978) *Evolutionary Socialism: A Criticism and Affirmation*, trans. Harvey, E.C., New York: Schocken Books.
—— (1993) *The Preconditions of Socialism*, trans. Tudor, H., Cambridge; New York: Cambridge University Press.
Betsky, A., Gandolfi, E. (eds) (2008) *Out There: Architecture beyond Building*, New York; Venice: Rizzoli.
Bialski, P., Derwanz, H., Otto, B., and Vollmer, H. (eds) (2015) *Ephemera*, 'Saving' the City: Collective Low-Budget Organizing and Urban Practice, Vol. 51(1), February.
Bishop, C. (2012) *Artificial Hells: Participatory Art and the Politics of Spectatorship*, London; New York: Verso.
Blau, E. (1999) *The Architecture of Red Vienna*, Cambridge, Mass.; London: MIT Press.
—— (2015) 'From Red Superblock to Green Megastructure: Municipal Socialism as Model and Challenge', in *Architecture and the Welfare State*, eds Swenarton, M., Avermaete, T. and van den Heuvel, D., Oxon; New York: Routledge, pp. 27–49.
Blundell Jones, P. (2011) 'Reframing Park Hill', *Architectural Review*, October, pp. 83–93.
——, Petrescu, D., and Till, J. (eds) (2005a) *Architecture and Participation*, London; New York: Taylor & Francis.
——, Petrescu, D., Till, J. (2005b) 'Introduction', in *Architecture and Participation*, eds Blundell Jones, P., Petrescu, D., Till, J., London; New York: Taylor & Francis, pp. xiii–xvii.
Boano, C., Keiling, E. (2013) 'Towards an Architecture of Dissensus: Participatory Urbanism in South-East Asia', The Participatory Turn in Urbanism, *Footprint 13*, Vol. 7/2, Autumn, pp. 41–62.
Bollier, D. (2013) 'The Quiet Realization of Ivan Illich's Ideas in the Contemporary Commons Movement', available at: <http://bollier.org/blog/quiet-realization-ivan-illichs-ideas-contemporary-commons-movement> (accessed 2 December 2015).

Boltanski, L. (2011) *On Critique: A Sociology of Emancipation*, Cambridge; Malden, MA: Polity.
——, Chiapello, E. (2005) *The New Spirit of Capitalism* [1999], trans. G. Elliott, London; New York: Verso.
Boudon, P. (1972) *Lived-in Architecture: Le Corbusier's Pessac Revisited* [1969], trans. Onn, G., London: Lund Humphries.
Bouman, O. (2005) 'Designing to Socialize', *Volume*, issue 4 (*Archis* Vol. 20 No. 4), pp. 5–13.
Bourdieu, P. (2002) *Language and Symbolic Power*, trans. Raymond, G. and Adamson, M., Cambridge: Polity Press.
—— (2003) *Distinction: A Social Critique of the Judgement of Taste* [1979], trans. Nice, R., London: Routledge.
Bradley, K. (2015) 'Open-Source Urbanism: Creating, Multiplying and Managing Urban Commons', in Commoning as Differentiated Publicness, *Footprint* 16, Spring, pp. 91–108.
Brand, S. (2010) 'How Slums Can Save the Planet', *Prospect*, 167, February, pp. 39–41.
Brik, O. (2010) 'The Democratization of Art', *October* 134, October, pp. 74–110.
Brillembourg, A., Feireiss, K., Klumpner, H. (eds) (2005) *The Informal City: Caracas Case*, Munich; London: Prestel.
Brillembourg, A., Klumpner, H. (eds) (2013) *Torre David: Informal Vertical Communities*, Zurich: Lars Müller.
Broady, M. (1966) 'Social Theory in Architectural Design', *Arena, the Architectural Association Journal*, Vol. 81 No. 898, January, pp. 149–54.
—— (1968) *Planning for People: Essays on the Social Context of Planning*, London: National Council of Social Service.
Breckman, W. (2013) 'Lefort and the Symbolic Dimension', in *Claude Lefort: Thinker of the Political*, ed. Plot, M., New York: Palgrave Macmillan, pp. 30–36.
British Government (2004) *Community Involvement in Planning: The Government's Objectives*, London: British Government, available at: <http://webarchive.nationalarchives.gov.uk/20120919132719/http://www.communities.gov.uk/documents/planningandbuilding/pdf/147588.pdf> (accessed 12 June 2015).
—— (undated) 'Setting up a Social Enterprise', available at: <https://www.gov.uk/set-up-a-social-enterprise> (accessed 23 July 2015).
Brown, B. (2015) 'Turner Prize 2015 Shortlist: Three Women – and a Housing Estate', *The Guardian*, 12 May, available at: <http://www.theguardian.com/artanddesign/2015/may/12/turner-prize-2015-shortlist-nominations-assemble-bonnie-camplin-janice-kerbel-nicole-wermers> (accessed 22 July 2015).
Brownill, S. & O'Hara, G. (2015) 'From Planning to Opportunism? Re-Examining the Creation of the London Docklands Development Corporation', *Planning Perspectives*, 30:4, pp. 537–70.
Brunkhorst, H. (2004) 'Critical Theory and the Analysis of Contemporary Mass Society', in *The Cambridge Companion to Critical Theory*, ed. by Rush, F. Cambridge; New York: Cambridge University Press, pp. 248–79.
Buckley, C. (2010) 'Modernity, Tradition and the Design of the "Industrial Village" of Dormanstown 1917–1923', *Journal of Design History*, Vol. 23 No. 1, pp. 21–41.
Budge, I. (2000) 'Deliberative Democracy versus Direct Democracy – Plus Political Parties!', in *Democratic Innovation*, ed. Saward, M., London; New York: Routledge, pp. 195–212.
The Builder, Vol. xiv, 7, February 1857, pp. 77–78.
Bull, M. (2001) 'You Can't Build a New Society with a Stanley Knife', *London Review of Books*, Vol. 23 No. 19, 4 October 2001, pp. 3–7; available at: <http://www.lrb.co.uk/v23/n19/print/bull01_.html> (accessed 24 August 2012).
Bürger, C. (1992) **'Modernity as Postmodernity: Jean Francois Lyotard'**, in *Modernity and Identity*, eds Lash, S. and Friedman, J., Oxford; Cambridge, Mass.: Blackwell, pp. 73–93.
Bürger, P. (1996) *Theory of the Avant-Garde* [1974], trans. Shaw, M., Minneapolis: University of Minnesota Press.
Burgess, R. (1978) 'Petty Commodity Housing or Dweller Control? A Critique of John Turner's Views on Housing Policy', *World Development*, No. 9/10, pp. 1105–33.
Butler, J. (1997) *The Psychic Life of Power*, Stanford: Stanford University Press.
Caillois, R. (1988) 'Introduction', in *The College of Sociology 1937–39* [1979], ed. Hollier, D., Minneapolis: University of Minnesota Press, pp. 9–11.

de Carlo, G. (2007) 'Architecture's Public' [1970], in *Architecture and Participation*, eds Blundell Jones, P., Petrescu, D. and Till, J., London; New York: Taylor & Francis, pp. 3–41.
Carter, A. (2002) 'Associative Democracy', in *Democratic Theory Today: Challenges for the 21st Century*, eds Carter, A. and Stokes, G., Cambridge: Polity, pp. 228–48.
—— and Stokes, G. (eds) (2002) *Democratic Theory Today: Challenges for the 21st Century*, Cambridge: Polity.
Casco & An Architektur (2006) 'Camp for Oppositional Architecture 2006: Theorizing Architectural Resistance', Utrecht/Berlin: unpublished booklet.
Chadwick, E. (1842) 'Report on the Sanitary Condition of the Labouring Population of Great Britain', in: *Poor Law Commissioners. Report on an Inquiry into the Sanitary Condition of the Labouring Population of Great Britain*, London: HMSO. Available at: <http://www.deltaomega.org/ChadwickClassic.pdf> (accessed 26 July 2011).
Chambers, S. (2004) 'The Politics of Critical Theory', in *The Cambridge Companion to Critical Theory*, ed. Rush, F., Cambridge; New York: Cambridge University Press, pp. 219–47.
Chase, J., Crawford, M., Kaliski, J. (eds) (1999) *Everyday Urbanism*, New York, N.Y.: Monacelli Press.
Choi, S. (2011) 'Newark and Community Development. An interview with Monsignor William J. Linder, founder of Newark's New Community Corporation', in *Urban Asymmetries: Studies and Projects on Neoliberal Urbanization*, eds Kaminer, T., Sohn, H., & Robles-Duran, M., Rotterdam: 010 Publishers, pp. 226–36.
Cohen, J. and Rogers, J. (1992) 'Secondary Associations and Democratic Governance', *Politics & Society* 20 (4), December, pp. 393–472.
Collymore, P. (1982) *The Architecture of Ralph Erskine*, London; New York: Granada.
Condorelli, C., Weizman, E. (2007) 'Support, Participation, & Relationships to Equity', in *The Violence of Participation*, ed. Miessen, M., Berlin; New York: Sternberg Press, pp. B28–36.
The Conservatives (c2009) 'Open Source Planning: Green Paper', Policy Green Paper No. 14; available: https://www.conservatives.com/~/media/Files/Green%20Papers/planning-green-paper.ashx (accessed 11 February 2015).
Coulson, A. (2003) 'Land-Use Planning and Community Influence: A Study of Selly-Oak, Birmingham', *Planning Practice and Research* 18 (2), pp. 179–95.
Cruz, T. (2005) 'Tijuana Case Study: Tactics of Invasion – Manufactured Sites', The New Mix: Culturally Dynamic Architecture, *Architectural Design*, Vol. 75, No. 4, Sep/Oct, pp. 32–37.
Cuff, D., Sherman, R. (eds) (2011) *Fast-Forward Urbanism: Rethinking Architecture's Engagement with the City*, New York: Princeton University Press.
Cullingworth, B. and Nadin, V., *Town and Country Planning in the UK*, 14th Edition (London; New York: Routledge, 2011).
Curry Stone Design Prize, available at: <www.currystonedesignprize.com/abour> (accessed 14 August 2015).
Cuyvers, L. (2015) 'Was Henri de Man an Early Post-Keynesian Neo-Marxist?', *Review of Radical Political Economics*, Vol. 47(1), pp. 90–105.
Davidoff, P. (1993) 'Democratic Planning', in *Architecture Culture 1943–1968*, ed. Ockman, J., New York: Rizzoli, pp. 442–45.
—— (2009) 'Advocacy and Pluralism in Planning', in *The Urban and Regional Planning Reader*, ed. Birch, E.L., London: Routledge, pp.148–55.
Deamer, P. (ed.) (2015) *The Architect as Worker: Immaterial Labor, the Creative Class, and the Politics of Design*, London: Bloomsbury.
Derrida, J. (1992) 'Force of Law: "The Mystical Foundation of Authority"', in *Deconstruction and the Possibility of Justice*, eds Cornell, D., Rosenfeld, M., Carlson, D.G., New York; London: Routledge, pp. 3–67.
Dogma (2013) *11 Projects*, London: AA Publications.
Dorfles, G. (1962) *Simbolo Comunicazione Consumo*, Turin: Einaudi, 1962.
Doucet, M.G. (2013) 'Thinking Democracy beyond Regimes: Untangling Political Analysis from the Nation-State', in *Claude Lefort: Thinker of the Political*, ed. Plot, M., New York: Palgrave Macmillan, pp. 157–75.

Dovey, K. (2011) 'Uprooting Critical Urbanism', *City*, 16:3–4, pp. 347–54.
Druot, F., Lacaton, A., & Vassal, J.P. (2007) *Plus*, Barcelona: Editorial Gustavo Gili.
Dryzek, J.S. (1990) *Discursive Democracy: Politics, Policy, and Political Science*, Cambridge: Cambridge University Press.
—— (2000a) *Deliberative Democracy and Beyond: Liberals, Critics, Contestations*, Oxford: Oxford University Press.
—— (2000b) 'Discursive Democracy vs. Liberal Constitutionalism', in *Democratic Innovation: Deliberation, Representation, and Association*, ed. Saward, M., Oxon: Routledge, pp. 78–89.
Durkheim, É. (1915) *The Elementary Forms of Religious Life*, London: Allen & Unwin.
—— (1957) *Professional Ethics and Civic Morals*, London: Routledge & Paul.
—— (1984) *The Division of Labour in Society*, Basingstoke: Macmillan.
—— (1998a) *Selected Writings*, ed. by Anthony Giddens, Cambridge; New York: Cambridge University Press.
—— (1998b) 'The Division of Labour and Social Differentiation', in *Selected Writings*, ed. by Anthony Giddens, Cambridge; New York: Cambridge University Press, pp. 141–54.
Edinburgh City Council (ECC) (2008) 'North West Portobello Development Brief', Edinburgh: Edinburgh City Council; available at: <https://www.edinburgh.gov.uk/directory_record/416123/north_west_portobello> (accessed 15 June 2015).
Eagleton, T. (1991) *Ideology: An Introduction*, London, New York: Verso.
—— (1996) *The Function of Criticism: From The Spectator to Post-Structuralism,* London; New York: Verso.
—— (2008) 'Marxism without Marxism', in *Ghostly Demarcations: A Symposium on Jacques Derrida's Specters of Marx*, ed. Sprinker, M., London; New York: Verso, pp. 83–87.
Eco, U. (1986) 'Function and Sign: Semiotics of Architecture', in *The City and the Sign: An Introduction to Urban Semiotics*, eds Gottdiener, M. and Lagopoulos, A.P., New York: Columbia University Press, pp. 55–86.
Edmunsdon, T. (1993) 'Public Participation in Development Control', *Town and Country Planning Summer School 1993 Proceedings*, London: Royal Town Planning Institute.
Edwards, B. (1992) *London Docklands: Urban Design in an Age of Deregulation*, Oxford; London: Butterworth Architecture.
Eisenschmidt, A. (ed.) (2012) City Catalyst: Architecture in the Age of Extreme Urbanisation, *Architectural Design*, Profile No. 219, Sep/Oct.
Elephant Park, urban development; available at: <http://www.elephantpark.co.uk/elephant-park/resident-facilities> (accessed 3 December 2015).
Engels, F. (1872) 'The Housing Question', available at: <https://www.marxists.org/archive/marx/works/download/Marx_The_Housing_Question.pdf> (accessed 19 November 2015).
Evans, R. (1997) 'Rookeries and Model Dwellings: English Housing Reform and the Moralities of Private Space', *Translations from Drawing to Building and Other Essays*, Cambridge, Mass.; London: MIT Press, pp. 93–117.
Fabricius, D. (2012) 'Revolution of the Ordinary', City Catalyst: Architecture in the Age of Extreme Urbanisation, ed. Alexander Eisenschmidt, *Architectural Design*, Profile No. 219, Sep/Oct, pp. 42–49.
Falasca-Zamponi, S. (2011) *Rethinking the Political: The Sacred, Aesthetic Politics, and the Collège de Sociologie*, Montreal & Kingston: McGill-Queen's University Press.
Fausch, D. (2011) 'She Said, He Said: Denise Scott Brown and Kenneth Frampton on Popular Taste', *Footprint* 8, Defying the Avant-Garde Logic: Architecture, Populism, and Mass Culture, Spring, pp. 77–90.
Ferry, L. and Renaut, A. (1990) *French Philosophy of the Sixties: An Essay on Antihumanism* [1985], University of Massachusetts Press.
Filippini, M. and Macchia, E. (2012) *Leaping Forward: Mario Tronti and the History of Political Workerism*, Maastricht: Jan van Eyck Academy/CRS.
Fisk, T. (1970) 'Student Power', *Architectural Review*, Vol. CXLVII No. 878, April, pp. 292–94.
Flierl, B. (1984) *Architektur und Kunst: Texte 1964–1983*, Dresden: VEB Verlag der Kunst.
Flierl, T. (2011) '"Possibly the Greatest Task an Architect Has Ever Faced": Ernst May in the Soviet Union (1930–1933)', in *Ernst May: 1886–1970*, eds Quiring, C., Voigt, W., Schmal, P.C., Herrel, E., Munich; London; New York: Prestel, pp. 157–95.

Florida, R. (2004) *The Rise of the Creative Class: and How it's Transforming Work, Leisure, Community and Everyday Life*, New York: Basic Books.
Flynn, B. (2005) *The Philosophy of Claude Lefort: Interpreting the Political*, Evanston, Northwestern University Press.
Forty, A. (2000) *Words and Buildings: A Vocabulary of Modern Architecture*, London: Thames and Hudson.
—— (2012) *Concrete and Culture: A Material History*, London: Reaktion Books.
Foucault, M. (1980) *Power/Knowledge*, ed. Colin Gordon, Brighton: Harvester.
—— (1991) *Discipline and Punish: The Birth of the Prison* [1979], trans. Sheridan, A., London: Penguin Books.
—— (2008) *The Birth of Biopolitics: Lectures at the Collège de France 1978–1979*, trans. Burchell, G., London: Palgrave Macmillan.
Gandolfi, E. (2009) 'Spaces of Freedom', *Architectural Design*, Vol. 79. No. 1, Jan/Feb, pp. 78–81.
Gavin, H. (1851) *The Habitations of the Industrial Classes*, London, Society for Improving the Condition of the Labouring Classes, available at <https://ia801507.us.archive.org/26/items/b22334622/b22334622.pdf> (accessed 16 November 2015).
—— (2015) *Sanitary Ramblings: Being Sketches and Illustrations of Bethnal Green* [1848], Milton Keynes: Lightening Source.
Giddens, A. (1971) *Capitalism and Modern Social Theory: An Analysis of the Writings of Marx, Durkheim, and Max Weber*, Cambridge; New York: Cambridge University Press.
—— (1985) *Durkheim*, London: Fontana.
Giuliani, R. (2001) 'Text of Mayor Giuliani's Farewell Address', *New York Times*, 27 December, available at: <http://www.nytimes.com/2001/12/27/nyregion/27CND-GIUL-TEXT.html?pagewanted=all> (accessed 20 December 2015).
Gladwell, M. (2001) *The Tipping Point: How Little Things Can Make a Big Difference*, London: Abacus.
Goetze, R. (1968) 'Recreating Responsive Environments', *Architectural Design*, Vol. XXXVIII August, p. 365.
——, Goodman, R., Grenell, P., Linn, C., Peattie, L., Terner, D. and Turner, J. (1968) 'Architecture of Democracy', *Architectural Design*, Vol. XXXVIII August, p. 354.
Goodburn, J. with Till, J. and Iossifova, D. (eds) (2012) Scarcity: Architecture in an Age of Depleting Resources, *Architectural Design*, Profile No. 218, July/Aug.
Goulet, P. (2002) 'A Conversation with Patrice Goulet', in Lacaton & Vassal, *2G*, No. 21, pp. 122–43.
Great Britain Royal Commission on the Housing of the Working Classes (1885) *Summary of the First Report*, Bristol Selected Pamphlets.
Habermas, J. (1974) *Theory and Practice*, trans. Viertel, J., Boston: Beacon Press.
—— (1995) 'Reconciliation Through the Public Use of Reason: Remarks on John Rawls's "Political Liberalism"', *Journal of Philosophy* XCII, Vol. 92(3), March, pp. 109–31.
—— (1996a) *Between Facts and Norms: Contributions to a Discourse Theory of Law and Democracy*, trans. Rehg, W., Cambridge: Polity Press.
—— (1996b) 'Three Normative Models of Democracy', in *Democracy and Difference: Contesting the Boundaries of the Political*, ed. Benhabib, S., Princeton, Princeton University Press, pp. 21–30.
Hall, P. (1998) *Cities in Civilization*, London: Weidenfeld & Nicolson.
—— (2014) *Cities of Tomorrow: An Intellectual History of Urban Planning and Design Since 1880* [1988], 4th ed., Oxford: Blackwell.
Hansen, E. (1981) 'Depression Decade Crisis: Social Democracy and Planisme in Belgium and the Netherlands 1929–1939', *Journal of Contemporary History*, Vol. 16 No. 2, April, pp. 292–322.
Hardin, G. (1968) 'The Tragedy of the Commons', *Science* 162, 1243–48.
Hardt, M. and Negri, A. (2000) *Empire*, Cambridge, Mass.: Harvard University Press.
—— (2006) *Multitude: War and Democracy in the Age of Empire*, London: Penguin Books.
—— (2009) *Commonwealth*, Cambridge, Mass.: Harvard University Press.
Hays, K.M. (1984) 'Critical Architecture: Between Culture and Form', *Perspecta* 21: The Yale Architectural Journal, pp. 14–29.
Healey, P. (1971) 'Barrios Are Not Romantic', *Architectural Design,* October, p. 631.

Hetherington, P. (2002) 'Manchester Unveils Plans for a Radically New Islington', *The Guardian*, Tuesday 17 September, available at: <http://www.guardian.co.uk/uk/2002/sep/17/communities.arts?INTCMP=SRCH> (accessed 30 November 2011).

van den Heuvel, D. (2015) 'The Open Society and Its Experiments: The Case of the Netherlands and Piet Blom', in *Architecture and the Welfare State*, eds Swenarton, M., Avermaete, T. and van der Heuvel, D., Oxon; New York: Routledge, pp. 135–52.

Hidalgo, R. (2011) 'Socioterritorial Changes in Santiago de Chile and the New Outline for the Metropolitan Periphery', in *Urban Asymmetries: Studies and Projects on Neoliberal Urbanization*, eds Kaminer, T., Sohn, H. & Robles-Duran, M., Rotterdam: 010 Publishers, pp. 152–69.

Hide, R. (ed.) (2012) *Future Practice: Conversations from the Edge of Architecture*, London; New York: Routledge.

Hindess, B. (1996) *Discourses of Power: From Hobbes to Foucault*, Oxford: Blackwell.

Hine, D. (2013) 'Commoning the City', in *STIR*, 2, Summer, available at: <http://dougald.nu/commoning-in-the-city-stir-magazine/> (accessed 3 December 2015).

Hirst, P. (1994) *Associative Democracy: New Forms of Economic and Social Governance*, Cambridge: Polity.

Hobsbawm, E. (1959) *Primitive Rebels: Studies in Archaic Forms of Social Movements in the 19th and 20th Centuries*, Manchester: Manchester University Press.

—— (1964) 'The Labour Aristocracy in Nineteenth-Century Britain' [1954], *Labouring Men: Studies in the History of Labour*, London: Weidenfeld and Nicolson, pp. 272–315.

—— (1977) *The Italian Road to Socialism: An Interview by Eric Hobsbawm with Giorgio Napolitano*, London: MW Books/Journeyman P.

—— (1984a) 'Debating the Labour Aristocracy' [1979], *Workers: Worlds of Labor*, New York: Pantheon Books, pp. 214–26.

—— (1984b) 'The Aristocracy of Labour Reconsidered' [1979], *Workers: Worlds of Labor*, New York: Pantheon Books, pp. 227–51.

—— (1984c) 'The Formation of British Working Class Culture' [1979], *Workers: Worlds of Labor*, New York: Pantheon Books, pp. 176–93.

—— (1984d) 'The Making of the Working Class 1870-1914' [1981], *Workers: Worlds of Labor*, New York: Pantheon Books, pp. 194–213.

—— (2011) *How to Change the World: Tales of Marx and Marxism*, London: Abacus.

Hollein, H. 'Nuts and Bolts at Aspen', *Architectural Design*, Vol. XXXVIII September 1968/9, p. 397.

Hollier, D. (ed.) (1988) *The College of Sociology 1937–39* [1979] Minneapolis: University of Minnesota Press.

Honig, B. (1996) 'Difference, Dilemmas, and the Politics of Home', in *Democracy and Difference: Contesting the Boundaries of the Political*, ed. Benhabib, S., Princeton: Princeton University Press, pp. 257–77.

Honneth, A. (2004) 'Organized Self-Realization Some Paradoxes of Individualization', *European Journal of Social Theory*, 7(4), pp. 463–78.

Hook, M. (2015) 'The Affirmative Qualities of a Temporal Architecture', *Architectural Design*, Vol. 85 (3), pp. 118–23.

Horkheimer, M., Adorno, T. (2002) *Dialectic of Enlightenment*, trans. Jephcott, E., Stanford: Stanford University Press.

Hoskyns, T. (2014) *The Empty Place: Democracy and Public Space*, Oxon; New York: Routledge.

Hou, J. (2010) *Insurgent Public Space: Guerrilla Urbanism and the Remaking of Contemporary Cities*, London: Routledge.

—— and Rios, M. (2003) 'Community-Driven Place Making: The Social Practice of Participatory Design in the Making of Union Point Park', *Journal of Architectural Education*, Vol. 57, No. 1, September, pp. 19–27.

Humphries, P. (2013) 'Pride of Place', *Inside Housing*, January, pp. 25–26.

HM Government (2010) 'The Coalition: Our Programme for Government', London: HM Government; available at: <http://webarchive.nationalarchives.gov.uk/20100919110641/http://programmeforgovernment.hmg.gov.uk/communities-and-local-government/index.html> (accessed 11 February 2015).

Ipsos-Mori, 'Generations', available at: <http://www.ipsos-mori-generations.com/PartyPolitics> (accessed 6 August 2013).

Jameson, F. (1985) 'Architecture and the Critique of Ideology', in *Architecture, Criticism, Ideology*, Ockman, J., New Jersey: Princeton Architectural Press, pp. 51–87.
—— (1999) 'Marx's Purloined Letter', in *Ghostly Demarcations: A Symposium on Jacques Derrida's Specters of Marx*, ed. Sprinker, M., London: Verso, pp. 26–67.
Jay, M. (1973) *The Dialectical Imagination: A History of the Frankfurt School and the Institute of Social Research, 1923–1950,* Berkeley, Los Angeles: University of California Press.
—— (1984) *Marxism & Totality: The Adventures of a Concept from Lukács to Habermas,* Berkley; Los Angeles: University of California Press.
Jeffrey, N. (1969a) 'Determinism', *Architectural Design*, Vol. XXXIX May 1969/5, p. 237.
—— (1969b) 'Techniques for Democratic Planning', *Architectural Design*, Vol. XXXIX November 1969/11, pp. 584–85.
Jeinic, A. (2014) 'The Dead End of the Political … In Architecture and in Politics', lecture at ESALA, University of Edinburgh, April.
Jencks, C. (1973) *Modern Movements in Architecture*, Harmondsworth, Middlesex: Penguin Books.
—— (1977) *The Language of Post-Modern Architecture,* London: Academy Editions.
—— and Baird, G. (eds) (1969) *Meaning in Architecture*, London: Barrie and Rockliff.
Jenkins, P., Forsyth, L. (eds) (2010) *Architecture, Participation and Society*, Oxon: Routledge.
Jones, P. & Card, K. (2011) 'Constructing "Social Architecture": The Politics of Representing Practice', *Architectural Theory Review*, 16:3, pp. 228–44, DOI: 10.1080/13264826.2011.621543
Kafka, B. (2012) 'The Administration of Things: A Genealogy', *W86th*, May 21, available at: <http://www.west86th.bgc.bard.edu/articles/the-administration-of-things.html#> (accessed 23 May 2014).
Kaminer, T. (2010) 'City and Society: The Keynesian New Town and the Resurrection of Capitalism', in *The Planned and Unplanned City*, ed. Provost, M., Amsterdam: SUN, pp. 38–43.
—— (2011a) *Architecture, Crisis and Resuscitation: The Reproduction of Post-Fordism in Late-Twentieth-Century Architecture,* London; New York: Routledge.
—— (2011b) 'An Introduction to Newark: The Continuous Crisis of the Obsolete City', in *Urban Asymmetries: Studies and Projects on Neoliberal Urbanization*, eds Kaminer, T., Sohn, H. & Robles-Duran, M., Rotterdam: 010 Publishers, pp. 192–207.
—— (2011c) 'The Ruins of the British Welfare State', *Footprint*, issue 9, Autumn, pp. 95–102.
—— (2012) 'Reformism, Critique, Radicalism', in *Critical Tools*, eds Heynen, H., Genard, J.L. & Kaminer, T., Brussels: La Lettre vole, pp. 189–97.
—— (2013) 'In Search of Architectural Efficacy: Debate and Experimentation after May '68', in *Is There an (Anti-)Neoliberal Architecture?*, eds Jeinic, A., Wagner, A., Berlin: Jovis, pp. 46–61.
—— (2014) 'The Contradictions of Participatory Architecture and Empire', *Architecture Research Quarterly*, Vol. 18, 1, pp. 31–37.
—— (2015) 'Interview with Amica Dall of Assemble', London: unpublished, 11 June.
Kant, I. (1966) *Critique of Pure Reason*, New York: Anchor Books.
Kautsky, K. (1902) 'The Aims and Limitations of the Materialist Conception of History', *Social Democrat*, Vol. 6 No. 8, August, pp. 242–48; available at: <https://www.marxists.org/archive/kautsky/1902/08/aims-limitations.htm> (accessed 3 November 2015).
Koselleck, R. (1988) *Critique and Crisis: Enlightenment and the Pathogenesis of Modern Society* [1959], Cambridge, Mass.: MIT Press.
Krier, L. (1998) 'Vorwärts, Kameraden, Wir Mässen Zurück (Forward, Comrades, We Must Go Back)', in *Oppositions Reader*, ed. Hays, K.M., New York: Princeton Architectural Press, pp. 400–21.
Krüger, M. (2009) 'Notes on Critical Theory in Germany', in *The German Issue* [1982], ed. Lotringer, S., New York; Los Angeles: Semiotext(e), pp. 122–33.
Kuhn, T. (1962) *The Structure of Scientific Revolutions*, Chicago: University of Chicago Press.
Lacaton & Vassal (2002) *2G*, No. 21, Barcelona: Gustavo Gili.
—— (2007) *G2: Lacaton & Vassal*, Barcelona: Gustavo Gili.
—— (2012) *2G: Recent Works*, No. 60 Barcelona: Gustavo Gili.
Laclau, E. (2004) 'Can Immanence Explain Social Struggles', in *Empire's New Clothes: Reading Hardt and Negri*, eds Passavant, P. & Dean, J., London; New York: Routledge, pp. 21–30.

—— (2005) *On Populist Reason*, London: Verso.
—— (2007) 'Why Do Empty Signifiers Matter to Politics?', *Emancipations(s)* [1996], London; New York: Verso, pp. 36–46.
——, Mouffe, C. (2001) *Hegemony and Socialist Strategy: Towards a Radical Democratic Politics* [1985], London; New York: Verso.
Landry, C. (2008) *The Creative City: A Toolkit for Urban Innovators*, Near Stroud: Comedia.
Latour, B. (2004) 'Why Has Critique Ran Out of Steam? From Matters of Fact to Matters of Concern', *Critical Inquiry*, Volume 30 number 2, Winter, pp. 225–48.
Leach, E. (1969) 'What Kind of Community?', *Architectural Design*, Vol. XXXIX July, pp. 353–54
Le Corbusier (2008) *Towards a New Architecture* [1923], BN Publishing.
Lefebvre, H. (1969) *The Explosion: Marxism and the French Upheaval*, trans. Ehrenfeld, A., New York; London: Monthly Review Press.
—— (1991) *The Production of Space*, trans. Nicholson-Smith, D., Oxford: Blackwell.
—— (2000) *Everyday Life in the Modern World* [1971], tran. Rabinovitch, S., London: Athlone.
—— (2005) *The Critique of Everyday Life, Vol. III: From Modernity to Modernism (Towards a Metaphilosophy of Daily Life)* [1981], trans. Elliott, E., London; New York: Verso.
Lefort, C. (1986) *The Political Forms of Modern Society: Bureaucracy, Democracy, Totalitarianism* [1971, 1978], Cambridge: Polity Press.
—— (1988) *Democracy and Political Theory*, trans. Macey, D., Cambridge: Polity Press.
Leguia, M. (ed.) (2011) Latin America at the Crossroads, *Architectural Design*, Profile No. 211, May/June.
Lenin, V. (1964) 'Imperialism and the Split of Socialism', *Collected Works* Vol. 23, Progress Publishers; available at: <http://www.marxists.org/archive/lenin/works/1916/oct/x01.htm> (accessed 1 August 2011).
Lévi-Strauss, C. (1963) 'Do Dual Organizations Exist?', in *Structural Anthropology*, New York: Basic Books, pp. 132–63.
—— (2011) *Tristes Tropiques* [1955], trans. Weightman, J. and Weightman, D., London; New York: Penguin Books.
Lilla, M. (1998) 'The politics of Jacques Derrida'. *The New York Review of Books*, 25 June. Available at: <http://www.nybooks.com.ezproxy.is.ed.ac.uk/articles/archives/1998/jun/25/the-politics-of-jacques-derrida/> (accessed 1 October 2015).
Lipman, A. (1969) 'The Architectural Belief System and Social Behaviour', *The British Journal of Sociology*, Vol. 20, No. 2, Jun., pp. 190–204.
Locke, J. (1988) *Two Treatises of Government* [1689], Cambridge: Cambridge University Press.
Lotringer, S. (ed.) (2009) *The German Issue* [1982], New York; Los Angeles: Semiotext(e).
—— and Marazzi, C. (eds) (2007) *Autonomia: Post-Political Politics* [c. 1979], New York; Los Angeles: Semiotext(e).
Lydon, M. et al. (eds) (2012) *Tactical Urbanism 2: Short-Term Action, Long-Term Change*, Miami; New York: Street Plans Collective, available at <http://issuu.com/streetplanscollaborative/docs/tactical_urbanism_vol_2_final> (accessed 15 February 2013).
Marcuse, H. (1969) *One Dimensional Man* [1964], London: Sphere Books.
—— (1999) *Reason and Revolution* [1941], New York: Humanity Books.
—— (2007) 'The Affirmative Character of Culture' [1937] in *The Essential Marcuse: Selected Writings*, eds Feenberg, A. and Leiss, W. Boston: Beacon, pp. 201–32.
—— (2009) *Negations: Essays in Critical Theory*, [1968] trans. Shapiro, J.J., London: Mayfly.
Marcuse, P. (1988) 'Do Cities Have a Future?', in *The Imperiled Economy: Through the Safety Net*, ed. Chery, R., New York: Union of Radical Political Economists, pp. 189–200.
—— (2013) 'Housing Policy and the Myth of the Benevolent State', in *The Affordable Housing Reader*, eds Tighe, R., Mueller, E., Oxon: Routledge, pp. 36–43.
Marmot, A. (2002) 'Architectural Determinism: Does Design Change Behaviour?', *The British Journal of General Practice,* Vol. 52 (476), pp. 252–53.
Martin, L. (1990) 'Transpositions: On the Intellectual Origins of Tschumi's Architectural Theory', *Assemblage*, no. 11, April, pp. 23–37.

Marx, K. (2003a) 'Preface to A Critique of Political Economy', in *Karl Marx: Selected Writings*, 2nd ed., ed. McLellan, D., Oxford; New York: Oxford University Press, pp. 424–28.
—— (2003b) 'The Eighteenth Brumaire of Louis Bonaparte', *Karl Marx: Selected Writings*, 2nd ed., ed. McLellan, D., Oxford: Oxford University Press, pp. 329–55.
Mauss, M. (1970) *The Gift: Forms and Functions of Exchange in Archaic Societies*, London: Routledge & Kegan Paul.
Mayer, M. (2011) 'Neoliberal Urbanization and the Politics of Contestation', in *Urban Asymmetries: Studies and Projects on Neoliberal Urbanization*, eds Kaminer, T., Sohn, H. & Robles-Duran, M., Rotterdam: 010 Publishers, pp. 46–61.
Mearns, A. (1970) *The Bitter Cry of Outcast London* [1883], Leicester: Leicester University Press; available at: <http://www.attackingthedevil.co.uk/related/outcast.php> (accessed 18 November 2015).
Merle, J. (2012) 'Architectural Contestation', TU Delft, unpublished dissertation.
Merrill, M. (2010) 'Commonwealth and "Commonism"', *International Labor and Working-Class History*, Vol. 78, Iss. 01, September, pp. 149–63.
Miessen, M. (ed.) (2007) *The Violence of Participation*, Berlin; New York: Sternberg Press.
—— (2010a) *The Nightmare of Participation*, Berlin; New York: Sternberg Press.
——, Basar, S. (eds) (2006) *Did Someone Say Participate? An Atlas of Spatial Practice*, Cambridge, Mass.: MIT Press.
—— and Mouffe, C. (2007) 'Articulated Power-Relations', in *The Violence of Participation*, ed. Miessen, M., Berlin; New York: Sternberg Press, pp. B37–48.
Miljacki, A. (2012) 'The Logic of the Critical and the Dangers of "Recuperation", or, Whatever Happened to the Critical Promise of Tschumi's Advertisements for Architecture', in *Critical Tools*, eds Heynen, H., Genard, J.L. & Kaminer, T., Brussels: La Lettre vole, 141–53.
Mohr, C. (2011) 'The New Frankfurt', in *Ernst May: 1886–1970*, eds Quiring, C., Voigt, W., Schmal, P.C., Herrel, E., Munich; London; New York: Prestel, pp. 51–67.
Molinari, L. (2015) 'Matteotti Village and Gallaratese 2: Design Criticism of the Italian Welfare State', in *Architecture and the Welfare State*, eds Swenarton, M., Avermaete, T. and van den Heuvel, D., Oxon; New York: Routledge, pp. 259–75.
Moreno, C.D., Grinda, E.G. (2015) 'A Conversation with Anne Lacaton and Jean-Philippe Vassal', Lacaton & Vassal 1993–2015: Post-Media Horizon, *El Croquis* 177/178, pp. 5–31.
Morris, W. (1888) 'A Dream of John Bell', available at: <http://www.marxists.org/archive/morris/works/1886/johnball/chapters/chapter4.htm> (accessed 2 January 2012).
Morrow, R. (2007) 'ECObox. Mobile Devices and Urban Tactics', *Domus* 908, November, pp. 50–53.
Mosley, J. and Sara, R. (eds) (2013) The Architecture of Transgression, *Architectural Design*, November/December.
Mota, N. (2011) 'Between Populism and Dogma: Álvaro Siza's Third Way', Defying the Avant-Garde Logic, *Footprint* 8, spring, pp. 35–58.
Mouffe, C. (1996a) 'Democracy, Power, and the "Political"', in *Democracy and Difference: Contesting the Boundaries of the Political*, ed. Benhabib, S., Princeton, Princeton University Press, pp. 245–56.
—— (1996b) 'Radical Democracy or Liberal Democracy?', in *Radical Democracy: Identity, Citizenship, and the State*, ed. Trend, D., New York; London: Routledge, pp. 19–26.
—— (1999) 'Deliberative Democracy or Agonistic Pluralism', *Social Research*, 66, 3, pp. 745–58.
—— (2005) *The Return of the Political* [1993], London; New York: Verso.
—— (2013a) *Hegemony, Radical Democracy and the Political*, ed. by James Martin, Oxon: Routledge.
—— (2013b) 'For an Agonistic Model of Democracy' [2000], in *Hegemony, Radical Democracy and the Political*, ed. by James Martin, Oxon: Routledge, pp. 191–206.
Mount, H. (2014) 'London's Ultimate Village: Greenwich Peninsula', *The Evening Standard*, 9 October, available at: <http://www.standard.co.uk/lifestyle/esmagazine/londons-ultimate-village-greenwich-peninsula-9784838.html> (accessed 14 August 2015).
Müller, J.W. (2013) 'The Paradoxes of Post-War Italian Political Thought', *History of European Ideas*, Vol. 39, No. 1, pp. 72–102.
Mumford, L. (1989) *The City in History* [1961], San Diego; New York; London: Harvest Books.

Murphy, T.S. (2010) 'The Workerist Matrix: Introduction to Mario Tronti's Workers and Capital and Massimo Cacciari's "Confrontation with Heidegger"', *Genre*, September, Vol. 43 (3–4), pp. 327–36.

Negri, A. (2003) 'Keynes and the Capitalist Theory of the State' [1967], in Hardt, M. and Negri, A., *Labor of Dionysus: A Critique of State-Form*, Minneapolis: University of Minnesota Press, pp. 23–51.

—— (2005) *Books for Burning: Between Civil War and Democracy in 1970s Italy*, London; New York: Verso.

—— (2009) 'On Rem Koolhaas', *Radical Philosophy*, 154, March/April, pp. 48–50.

Norberg-Schulz, C. (1963) *Intentions in Architecture*, London: Allen and Unwin.

—— (1968) 'Less or More?', *Architectural Review*, Vol. 143 No. 354, April, pp. 257–58.

Ockman, J. (2008) 'Talking with Bernard Tschumi', *Log* 13/14, pp. 159–70.

Osten, M. van (2007) 'Sex & Space: Space / Gender / Economy', in Doina Petrescu (ed.), *Altering Practices: Feminist Politics and Poetics of Space*, London; New York: Routledge, pp. 213–40.

Oswalt, Ph., Overmeyer, K., Misselwitz, Ph. (eds) (2013) *Urban Catalyst: The Power of Temporary Use*, Berlin: DOM.

Park, K. (2012) 'Localising the Global', in City Catalyst: Architecture in the Age of Extreme Urbanisation, ed. Eisenschmidt, A., *Architectural Design*, Profile No. 219, pp. 36–41.

Parrinello, G. (2013) 'The City–Territory: Large-Scale Planning and Development Policies in the Aftermath of the Belice Valley Earthquake (Sicily, 1968)', *Planning Perspectives*, 28:4, pp. 571–93.

Parvin, A. (2013) 'Open-Source Architecture and the Design Commons', *Architectural Design*, The Architecture of Transgression, eds Mosley, J. and Sara, R., November/December, pp. 89–95.

Patton, P. (2008) 'After the Linguistic Turn: Post-Structuralist and Liberal Pragmatist Political Theory', in *The Oxford Handbook of Political Theory*, eds Dryzek, J.S., Honig, B. and Phillips, A., Oxford: Oxford University Press, pp. 125–41.

Pawley, M. (1969) 'Agora', *Architectural Design*, Vol. XXXIX July, pp. 358–62.

—— (1969) 'The Time House', in *Meaning in Architecture*, eds Jencks, C. and Baird, G., London: Barrie and Rockliff, pp. 120–48.

—— (1970a) 'In Housing everybody's a Conservative', *Architectural Design*, January, pp. 40–41.

—— (1970b) 'The Shape of Trade', *Architectural Design*, February, p. 55.

—— (1971a) *Architecture versus Housing*, New York; Washington: Praeger.

—— (1971b) 'Inside the AA', *Architectural Design*, March, pp. 190–91.

——, Bernard Tschumi (1971) 'The Beaux Arts since '68', *Architectural Design*, September, pp. 533–66.

Pearce, F. (2003) 'Introduction: the Collège de Sociologie and French Social Thought', *Economy and Society*, Vol. 32 No. 1 February, pp. 1–6.

Peck, J. (2015) 'Framing Detroit', lecture at the University of Edinburgh, 28 October.

Petcou, C. and Petrescu, D. (2007) 'Acting Space: Transversal Notes, On-the-Ground Observations and Concrete Questions for Us All', in AAA and PEPRAV (eds), *Urban Act: A Handbook for Alternative Practice*, Montrouge: Moutot Imprimeurs, pp. 319–28.

—— (2015) 'R-URBAN or How to Co-Produce a Resilient City', *Ephemera*, 'Saving' the City: Collective low-budget organizing and urban practice, Vol. 15 (1), February, pp. 248–62; available at <http://www.ephemerajournal.org/contribution/r-urban-or-how-co-produce-resilient-city> (accessed 13 July 2015).

——, Nishat Awan (eds) (2010) *Trans-Local-Act: Cultural Practices Within and Across*, Sheffield/Paris: aaa/peprav.

Petrescu, D. (2007a) 'How to Make a Community as well as the Space for It', *Re-public: Reimagining Democracy*, available at <http://seminaire.samizdat.net/IMG/pdf/Doina_Petrescu_-2.pdf> (accessed 13 July 2015).

—— (ed.) (2007b) *Altering Practices: Feminist Politics and Poetics of Space*, London: Routledge.

Plot, M. (ed.) (2013) *Claude Lefort: Thinker of the Political*, New York: Palgrave Macmillan.

Porter, R. (2000) *London: A Social History* [1994], London: Penguin.

Powers, A. (1981) '"Architects I Have Known": The Architectural Career of S. D. Adshead', *Architectural History*, Vol. 24, pp. 103–23, 160–64.

Price, C. (1968) 'Architecture in the UK, 1945–1965', *Architectural Design*, Vol. XXXVIII February, p. 5.

Provost, M. and Vanstiphout, W. (2012) 'Make No Big Plans', in City Catalyst: Architecture in the Age of Extreme Urbanisation, ed. Eisenschmidt, A., *Architectural Design*, Profile No. 219, Sep/Oct, pp. 104–7.
Puglisi, L.P. (ed.) (2009) Theoretical Meltdown, *Architectural Design*, Vol. 79. No. 1, Jan/Feb.
Querrien, A. (2007) 'The Exodus Lives on the street Corner', in *Urban Act: A Handbook for Alternative Practice*, eds AAA and PEPRAV, Montrouge: Moutot Imprimeurs, pp. 307–13.
——, Doina Petrescu, Constantin Petcou (2007) 'What Makes a Biopolitical Place? A Discussion with Antonio Negri', in *Urban Act: A Handbook for Alternative Practice*, eds AAA and PEPRAV, Montrouge: Moutot Imprimeurs, pp. 290–99.
Quiring, C., Voigt, W., Cachola Schmal, P. Herrel, E. (eds) (2011) *Ernst May: 1886–1970*, Munich; London; New York: Prestel.
Rancière, J. (1991) *The Ignorant Schoolmaster: Five Lessons in Intellectual Emancipation*, trans. Ross, K., Stanford: Stanford University Press.
—— (1992) 'Politics, Identification, and Subjectivization', *October*, Vol. 61, The Identity in Question, Summer, pp. 58–64.
—— (2004) *The Politics of Aesthetics*, trans. Rockhill, G., New York: Continuum.
—— (2007) *On the Shores of Politics*, trans. Heron, L., London: Verso.
—— (2009) *Aesthetics and its Discontents*, trans. Corcoran, S., Cambridge: Polity Press.
—— (2014) *Dissensus: On Politics and Aesthetics*, trans. Corcoran, S., London; New Delhi: Bloomsbury.
Rapoport, A. (1968) 'The Personal Element in Housing: An Argument for Open-Ended Design', *RIBA Journal*, July, Vol. 75 No. 7, pp. 300–7.
Ravetz, A. (2001) *Council Housing and Culture: The History of a Social Experiment*, London; New York: Routledge.
Redfield, J. (1968) 'Response', *Architectural Design*, Vol. XXXVIII August, p. 389.
Rice, Ch. and Burke, A. (eds) (2010) Post-Traumatic Urbanism, *Architectural Design*, profile No. 207, Sep/Oct.
Richman, M. (2003) 'Myth, Power and the Sacred: Antiutilitarianism in the Collège de Sociologie 1937–9', *Economy and Society*, 32:1, pp. 29–47.
Roberts, H. (1853) *The Dwellings of the Labouring Classes, Their Arrangements and Constructions* [1851], London: Society for Improving the Conditions of the Labouring Class.
—— (2007) *The Dwellings of the Labouring Classes, Their Arrangements and Constructions* [1851], Elibron Classics.
Roberts, R. (1971) *The Classic Slum: Salford Life in the First Quarter of the Century*, Manchester: Manchester University Press.
Rorty, R. (1998) *Achieving Our Century: Leftist Thought in Twentieth-Century America*, Cambridge, Mass.: Harvard University Press.
Kristin Ross (2002) *May 68 and Its Afterlives*, Chicago; London: University of Chicago Press.
Rossi, A. (1991) *The Architecture of the City*, Cambridge, Mass.: MIT Press.
Rowe, C. and Koetter, F. (1978) *Collage City*, Cambridge, Mass.: MIT Press.
—— (2000) 'Collage City', in *Architecture Theory since 1968*, ed. K. Michael Hays, London; Cambridge, Mass: MIT Press, pp. 92–111.
Ruby, I. and Ruby, A. (2002) 'Naïve Architecture: Notes on the Work of Lacaton & Vassal', Lacaton & Vassal, *2G*, No. 21, pp. 4–19.
—— (2005) 'Reprogramming Architecture', *Volume*, issue 2 (*Archis* Vol. 20 No. 2), pp. 5–20.
—— (2007) 'Extra Space, Extra Large: On the Recent Work of Lacaton & Vassal', in Lacaton & Vassal, *G2: Lacaton & Vassal*, Barcelona: Gustavo Gili, pp. 6–23.
Sachs, A. (2013) 'Architects, Users, and the Social Sciences in Postwar America', *Use Matters: An Alternative History of Architecture*, ed. Cupers, K., Oxon: Routledge, pp. 69–84.
Saint-Simon, H. (2010) 'New Christianity: Dialogues between a Conservative and an Innovator (Selected Excerpts) 1' [1825], *Sociological Origins*, 6.2, Fall, pp. 73–89.
Saward, M. (ed.) (2000) *Democratic Innovation: Deliberation, Representation, and Association*, Oxon: Routledge.
Scheuerman, W.E. (2006) 'Critical Theory Beyond Habermas', in *The Oxford Handbook of Political Theory*, eds Dryzek, J.S., Honig, B., Phillips, A., Oxford: Oxford University Press, pp. 85–104.

Schmelzkopf, K. (2002) 'Incommensurability, Land Use, and the Right to Space: Community Gardens in New York City', *Urban Geography*, 23:4, pp. 323–43.
Scott, F.D. (2007) *Architecture or Techno-Utopia: Politics After Modernism*, Cambridge, Mass.: MIT Press.
Scott Brown, D. (1992) 'Remedial Housing for Architecture Studio', in Venturi Scott Brown & Associates, *On Houses and Housing*, Architectural Monographs No. 21, London: Academy Editions, pp. 51–57.
Searle, A. (2015) 'Power to the People! Assemble Win the Turner Prize by Ignoring the Art Market', *The Guardian*, 7 December, available at: <http://www.theguardian.com/artanddesign/2015/dec/07/turner-prize-2015-assemble-win-by-ignoring-art-market> (accessed 8 December 2015).
Secchi, B. (2007) 'Rethinking and Redesigning the Urban Landscape', *Places*, 19 (1), pp. 6–11.
Sennett, R. (1978) *The Fall of Public Man*, London; New York: Penguin.
Frances, S. (2013) *The Diary of Frances Lady Shelley* [1913], ed. E. Edgecumbe, London: Forgotten Books, available at: <http://www.forgottenbooks.com/readbook_text/The_Diary_of_Frances_Lady_Shelley_1913_1000263113/1 > (accessed 3 March 2016).
Simmel, G. (2002) 'The Metropolis and Mental Life' [1903], in *Rethinking Architecture: A Reader in Cultural Theory*, ed. Leach, N., London; New York: Routledge, pp. 69–79.
—— (2003) *The Philosophy of Money* [1907], 3rd ed., trans. Bottomore, T., Frisby, D., Mengelberg, K., London; New York: Routledge.
Slater, T. (2011) 'Gentrification of the City', *The New Blackwell Companion to the City*, Oxford: Blackwell, pp. 571–85.
Slessor, C. (2009) '045: Nantes school of architecture', *The Architectural Review*, June, 225, 1348, pp. 68–73.
Smith, N. (1987) 'Gentrification and the Rent Gap', *Annals of the Association of American Geographers*, Vol. 77, No. 3, Sep., pp. 462–65.
—— (1996) *The New Urban Frontier: Gentrification and the Revanchist City*, London; NYC: Routledge.
—— (2008) 'The Evolution of Gentrification', in *Houses in Transformation: Interventions in European Gentrification*, eds Berg, J.J., Kaminer, T., Schoonderbeek, M., Zonneveld, J., Rotterdam: NAi Publishers, pp. 15–25.
Smithson, A. (1968) 'Local Character', *Architectural Design*, Vol. XXXVIII September, 9, pp. 416–17.
Somol, R. and Whiting, S. (2002) 'Notes Around the Doppler Effect and Other Moods of Modernism', *Perspecta* 33: The Yale Architectural Journal, pp. 72–77.
Sorkin, M. (2003) *Starting from Zero: Reconstructing Downtown New York*, London; New York: Routledge.
Speaks, M. (2003) 'Design Intelligence', *Hunch* 6/7, summer, pp. 416–21.
Spriggs, E.A. (1984) 'Hector Gavin, MD, FRCSE (1815–1855) – His Life, His Work for the Sanitary Movement, and His Accidental Death in the Crimea', *Medical History*, 28: 283–92. Also available: http://www.ncbi.nlm.nih.gov/pmc/articles/PMC1139447/pdf/medhist00078-0061.pdf> (accessed 27 July 2011).
Stanek, L. (2008) 'Lessons from Nanterre', *Log* 13/14, fall, pp. 59–67.
—— (2011) *Henri Lefebvre on Space: Architecture, Urban Research and the Production of Theory*, Minneapolis: University of Minnesota Press.
—— (2015) 'Who Needs "Needs"? French Post-War Architecture and Its Critics', in *Architecture and the Welfare State*, eds Swenarton, M., Avermaete, T. and van der Heuvel, D., Oxon; New York: Routledge, pp. 113–30.
Steffel, R.V. (1973) 'The Slum Question: The London County Council and Decent Dwellings for the Working Classes, 1880–1914', *Albion: A Quarterly Journal Concerned with British Studies*, Vol. 5, No. 4, Winter, pp. 314–25.
—— (1976) 'The Boundary Street Estate: An Example of Urban Redevelopment by the London County Council, 1889–1914', *The Town Planning Review*, Vol. 47, No. 2, Apr., pp. 161–73.
Stenberg, J. (2013) 'Citizens as Knowledge Producers in Urban Change: Can Participation Change Procedures and Systems?' in *Footprint* 13, Vol. 7 No. 2, Autumn, pp. 131–42.
Stengers, I. and Pingarre, Ph. (2011) *Capitalist Sorcery: Breaking the Spell*, New York: Palgrave MacMillan.
Stephens, S. (2004) *Imagining Ground Zero: Official and Unofficial Proposals for the World Trade Centre Competition*, London: Thames & Hudson.

Stern, R.A.M., Fishman, D., Tilove, J. (2013) *Paradise Planned: The Garden Suburb and the Modern City*, New York: Monacelli Press.
Stolnitz, J. (1961) 'On the Origins of Aesthetic Disinterestedness', *The Journal of Aesthetics and Art Criticism* 20, nr 2, Winter, pp. 131–43.
Stratford, H. with Petrescu, D. and Petcou, C. (2008) 'Form-Trans-Form: The "Poetic" Resistance in Architecture', *ARQ*, Vol. 12, No. 2, pp. 149–58.
Swenarton, M. (1981) *Homes Fit for Heroes: The Politics and Architecture of Early State Housing in Britain*, London: Heinemann Educational books.
—— (2008a) 'Introduction', in *Building the New Jerusalem*, Bracknell: HIS BRE Press, pp. 1–11.
—— (2008b) 'The Education of an Urbanist', in *Building the New Jerusalem: Architecture, Housing and Politics 1900–1930*, Bracknell: HIS BRE, pp. 95–124.
——, Avermaete, T. and van der Heuvel, D. (eds) (2015) *Architecture and the Welfare State*, Oxon; New York: Routledge.
Swyngedouw, E. (2016) 'On the Impossibility of an Emancipatory Architecture: The Deadlock of Critical Theory, Insurgent Architects, and the Beginning of Politics', in *Can Architecture be an Emancipatory Project? Dialogues on Architecture and the Left*, ed. Lahiji, N.Z., Hants: Zone Books, pp. 48–69.
Symonds, C. (2015) 'Paul Beswick: Why I Joined Planning Democracy', *Planning Democracy*, 20 Feb, available at: <http://www.planningdemocracy.org.uk/2015/why-i-joined-planning-democracy/> (accessed 12 June 2015).
Tafuri, M. (1976) *Architecture and Utopia: Design and Capitalist Development* [1973], trans. Luigia La Penta, B., Cambridge, Mass.; London: MIT Press.
—— (1980) *Theories and Histories of Architecture*, trans. Verrecchia, G., New York: Harper & Row.
—— (2000a) 'Towards a Critique of Architectural Ideology', in *Architecture Theory since 1968*, ed. Hays, K.M., Cambridge, Mass.; London: MIT Press, pp. 6–35.
—— (2000b) 'L'architecture dans le boudoir: The Language of Criticism and the Criticism of Language' [1974], in *Architecture Theory since 1968*, ed. Hays, K.M., Cambridge, Mass.; London: MIT Press, 2000, pp. 148–73.
Tanke, J.J. (2011) *Jacques Rancière: An Introduction*, London; New York: Continuum.
Taylor, M. (2014) '"Being Useful" After the Ivory Tower: Combining Research and Activism with Brixton Pound', *Area*, 46.3, pp. 305–12.
Teyssot, G. (1981) 'Neoclassic and "Autonomous" Architecture: the Formalism of Emil Kaufmann', *Architectural Design*, 51, 6/7, pp. 24–9.
Thompson, E.P. (1966) *The Making of the English Working Class* [1963], New York: Vintage Editions.
Till, J. (2006) 'The Architect and the Other', *open Democracy*, 25 June, available at: <https://www.opendemocracy.net/ecology-landscape/architecture_3680.jsp> (accessed 8 July 2013).
Tonka, H. (2011) 'Critique of Urban Ideology' [1968], in *Utopie: Texts and Projects 1967–1978*, eds Buckley, C., Violeau, J.L., New York: Semiotext[e], pp. 155–79.
——, Jungmann, J.P. and Aubert, J. (2011) 'Architecture as a Theoretical Problem', in *Utopie: Texts and Projects, 1967–1978*, eds Buckley, C., Violeau, J.L., Cambridge, Mass.: MIT Press, pp. 124–45.
Tonkiss, F. (2012) 'Informality and Its Discontents', in *Informalize! Essays on the Political Economy of Urban Form Vol. 1*, eds Angelil, M., Heul, R., Berlin: Ruby Press, pp. 55–70.
—— (2013) *Cities by Design: The Social Life of Urban Form*, Cambridge; Malden, MA: Polity.
Toorn, R. van (1997) 'Fresh Conservatism and Beyond. Second Modernity', in *Archis*, no. 11, pp. 15–22.
Touraine, A. (1971) *The Post Industrial Society: Tomorrow's Social History – Classes, Conflicts, and Culture in the Programmed Society* [1969], trans. Mayhew, L.F.X., New York: Random House.
—— (1995) *A Critique of Modernity*, Oxford: Blackwell.
Trend, D. (ed.) (1996) *Radical Democracy: Identity, Citizenship, and the State*, New York; London: Routledge.
Tronti, M. (2009) 'Towards a Critique of Political Democracy', *Cosmos and History: The Journal of Natural and Social Philosophy*, Vol. 5, no. 4, pp. 68–75.
—— (2010) 'Selections from Workers and Capital', *Genre*, September, Vol. 43 (3–4), pp. 337–52.
—— (2012a) 'La Fabbrica e la societa' [1962], in *Leaping Forward: Mario Tronti and the History of Political Workerism*, eds Filippini, M. and Macchia, E., Maastricht: Jan van Eyck Academy/CRS, pp. 7–13.

—— (2012b) 'Il Piano del Capitale' [1963], in *Leaping Forward: Mario Tronti and the History of Political Workerism*, eds Filippini, M. and Macchia, E., Maastricht: Jan van Eyck Academy/CRS, pp. 42–58.
Tschumi, B. (1975) 'The Environmental Trigger', in *A Continuing Experiment: Learning and Teaching at the Architectural Association*, ed. Gowan, J., London: Architectural Press, pp. 89–100.
—— (1994) *The Manhattan Transcripts*, London, Academy Editions, XX.
—— and Montés, F. (1970) 'Do-It-Yourself-City', *L'Architecture d'aujourdhui* 148, Feb–March, pp. 98–105.
Turner, J. (1968) 'Housing Priorities, Settlement Patterns, and Urban Development in Modernizing Countries', *Journal of the American Institute of Planners*, November, 34/6, pp. 354–63.
United Nations (1992) 'Agenda 21', Rio de Janeiro: UN; available online at: <http://www.unep.org/Documents.Multilingual/Default.asp?DocumentID=52&ArticleID=58&l=en> (accessed 12 June 2015).
Unwin, R. (1967) *The Legacy of Raymond Unwin: A Human Pattern for Planning*, ed. Creese, W.L., Cambridge, Mass.: MIT Press.
UoB (2015) 'University of Bristol; It's Sound – Bristol Pound Encourages Community Unity', *Computer Weekly News*, Mar 26, p. 710.
Ure, A. (1835) *The Philosophy of Manufactures*, London: Charles Knight; available at: <https://ia902707.us.archive.org/27/items/philosophyofmanu00urea/philosophyofmanu00urea.pdf> (accessed 12 November 2015).
Valentine, J. (2013) 'Lefort and the Fate of Radical Democracy', in *Claude Lefort: Thinker of the Political*, ed. Plot, M., New York: Palgrave Macmillan, pp. 203–17.
Vaneigem, R. (2006) *The Revolution of Everyday Life* [1967], trans. Nicholson-Smith, D., London: Rebel Press.
Venturi, R. (1977) *Complexity and Contradiction in Architecture* [1966], 2d ed., New York: Museum of Modern Art.
——, Scott Brown, D. and Izenour, S. (1977) *Learning from Las Vegas: The Forgotten Symbolism of Architectural Form* [1972], revised ed., Cambridge, Mass.; London: MIT Press.
——, Steven Izenour, and Denise Scott Brown, 'The Home', in Venturi Scott Brown & Associates, *On Houses and Housing*, Architectural Monographs No. 21 (London: Academy Editions, 1992), pp. 58–65.
Vidler, A. (2008) *Histories of the Immediate Present: Inventing Architectural Modernism*, London; Cambridge, Mass.: MIT Press.
Viganò, P. (2012) 'The Contemporary European Urban Project: Archipelago City, Diffuse City and Reverse City', in *The SAGE Handbook of Architectural Theory*, eds Crysler, C.G., Cairns, S. & Heynen, H., London: SAGE, pp. 657–71.
Viñoly, R. (2003) 'Master Planner or Master Builder?', *New York Times*, December 12.
Violeau, J.L. (2007) 'Why and How "to Do Science"? On the Often Ambiguous Relationship between Architecture and the Social Sciences in France in the Wake of May '68', *Footprint* issue 1, autumn, pp. 7–22.
Wainwright, O. (2015) 'The Street that Might Win the Turner Prize: How Assemble Are Transforming Toxteth', *The Guardian*, 15 May, available at: <http://www.theguardian.com/artanddesign/architecture-design-blog/2015/may/12/assemble-turner-prize-2015-wildcard-how-the-young-architecture-crew-assemble-rocked-the-art-world> (accessed 22 July 2015).
Weber, M. (2012) *The Protestant Ethic and the Spirit of Capitalism* [1905], US: Renaissance Classics.
Wellner, M. (2012) 'Surplus: In Conversation with Anne Lacaton and Jean-Philippe Vassal', in *Reduce Reuse Recycle*, eds. Petzet, M., Florian Heilmeyer, F., Germany: Hatje Cantz, pp. 13–26.
Williams, R. (2005) 'Base and Superstructure in Marxist Cultural Theory' [1973], in *Culture and Materialism*, London; New York: Verso, pp. 31–49.
Wilson, J., Swyngedouw, E. (eds) (2014a) *The Post-Political and Its Discontents: Spaces of Depoliticization, Spectres of Radical Politics*, Edinburgh: Edinburgh University Press.
—— (2014b) 'Seeds of Dystopia: Post-Politics and the Return of the Political', in *The Post-Political and Its Discontents: Spaces of Depoliticization, Spectres of Radical Politics*, eds Wilson, J., Swyngedouw, E., Edinburgh: Edinburgh University Press, pp. 1–22.
Wilson, R. (2003) 'Art in Process', *The Architectural Review*, Feb; 213, 1272, pp. 56–61.

—— (2013) 'Not Doing/Overdoing: "Omission" and "Excess"', The Architecture of Transgression, *Architectural Design*, Profile 226, November, pp. 45–51.

Wohl, A.S. (1977) *The Eternal Sum: Housing and Social Policy in Victorian London*, London: Edward Arnold.

Wolin, S.S. (1996) 'Fugitive Democracy', in *Democracy and Difference: Contesting the Boundaries of the Political*, ed. Benhabib, S., Princeton, Princeton University Press, pp. 31–45.

Woolf, V. (2015) *A Room of One's Own*, Adelaide: University of Adelaide, available at: <https://ebooks.adelaide.edu.au/w/woolf/virginia/w91r/chapter1.html? (accessed 2 November 2015).

Wortham-Galvin, B.D. (2013) 'An Anthropology of Urbanism: How People Make Places (and What Designers and Planners Might Learn from It)', The Participatory Turn in Urbanism, *Footprint* 13, Vol. 7, No. 2, autumn, pp. 21–40.

Wright, S. (2002) *Storming Heaven: Class Composition and Struggle in Italian Autonomist Marxism*, London; Sterling, VA.: Pluto Press.

Young, I. (1996) 'Communication and the Other: Beyond Deliberative Democracy', in *Democracy and Difference: Contesting the Boundaries of the Political*, ed. Benhabib, S., Princeton, Princeton University Press, pp. 120–35.

Žižek, S. (2006) *The Parallax View*, Cambridge, Mass.: MIT Press.

Zukin, S. (1989) *Loft Living: Culture and Capital in Urban Change* [1982], New Brunswick: Rutgers University Press.

—— (1995) *The Cultures of Cities*, Cambridge, Mass.; Oxford: Blackwell.

INDEX

Adorno, Theodor 47, 55, 102, 160
aesthetics 98, 100–3, 114, 144–5, 147, 188n9
agency 1, 2, 9–11, 13, 46, 48, 79, 93, 98, 148, 156, 177; architectural 3, 7–11, 13, 14, 16, 120, 136, 156, 181
Althusser, Louis 2, 10, 12, 93, 98, 137
anti-statism 3, 77, 89, 120–1
Aravena, Alejandro *see* Elemental
Architectural Design (*AD*) 4–7, 75, 76, 185n8–9
The Architectural Review (*AR*) 4, 75, 116, 155
aristocracy of labour *see* labour aristocracy
Arnstein, Sherry 77, 82, 88
articulation 96, 136, 137, 139, 146, 148, 187n1
Arts and Crafts 40–2, 45
Assemble 14, 77–8, 108, 113–16, 186n32, 187n37
Atelier d'architecture autogérée (aaa) 75–9, 103, 108–13, 116–17, 185n9
Aureli, Pier Vittorio 76, 159–62, 177, 179, 182n10, 188n18
austerity 10–11, 85, 182n11
autonomy 9, 21, 55, 62, 81, 82, 93, 95, 120, 146, 167; architectural 10, 51, 80, 150, 160–1, 167, 169, 171, 179; artistic 102, 149
avant-garde 19, 53, 80–1, 101, 140, 171, 179; historic 80, 105, 123, 147; neo- 10; political 80

Banham, Reyner 4, 82, 83, 135
Baudrillard, Jean 54, 131, 187n43
Benhabib, Seyla 82, 86, 88–90, 106
Bernstein, Eduard 23–6, 182n9, 183n4
biopolitics 56–7, 186n17; *see also* Foucault
Boltanski, Luc 12, 22, 49, 51, 57, 60, 104–5, 121, 183n2

Bordieu, Pierre 81–2, 98, 100, 135, 137, 185n16
Boudon, Philippe 127–31; *see also* Pessac; Le Corbusier
The Boundary Estate 38
Broady, Maurice 3, 9–10, 83
Bruchfeldsstrasse 166, 168, 171; *see also* May
The Builder 32, 36, 183n12–13
Bürger, Peter 100–1, 147, 171

Cacciari, Massimo 8–9
Caillois, Roger 144–5, 147; *see also* Collège de Sociologie
de Carlo, Giancarlo 3, 4, 16, 76–7, 79, 82, 123–4
Chadwick, Edwin 31–2, 35, 36, 183n9–10
civil society 20, 54, 82, 86–9, 107, 138, 148, 162
collage city 59, 150, 161
Collège de Sociologie 144–5, 157
community gardening 14–15, 75, 103, 108–13, 116, 181, 186n34
consultation *see* planning consultation
co-optation 15, 20, 53–63, 76, 89, 106–7, 111, 113, 120, 148, 151, 184n25, 184n30
crisis: economic 11, 110, 116, 120, 172–3; of socialism 92; urban 70
critical theory 22, 46–7, 49, 51, 88, 183n2, 184n21
critique 13, 15, 19–22, 25, 48–55, 57, 77, 84, 96–8, 106–7, 137, 149, 181, 184n21, 184n23, 184n26, 186n21; 1960s 10, 59–60, 62, 83, 87, 125, 131, 155; architectural 6–7, 9, 50, 60, 83, 87, 103, 120, 171, 182n10; 'ordinary' 22, 28; reformist 22, 26, 27, 32, 37, 46, 47, 49, 51, 57
Cruz, Teddy 74–5, 77, 114, 117

Davidoff, Paul 77, 83
deconstruction 47–8, 75, 183n16; *see also* Derrida; post-structuralism
democracy 3, 5, 11, 24, 79–83, 86, 87, 89, 100, 104, 109, 144, 146, 181, 186n30; agonistic 96–8, 103; associative 86, 113, 186n19; deliberative 82, 88–90, 92, 96, 98, 106, 182n12, 186n20; liberal 24, 84–5, 88–9, 90, 96–8, 107, 144–5, 151, 162, 166, 186n18; radical 15, 77, 78, 84–6, 88, 96–9, 105–6, 186n18
democratic deficit 11, 84, 98, 150, 182n12
Derrida, Jacques 47–8, 105; *see also* deconstruction; post-structuralism
determinism 9–10, 16, 48
dissensus 99–100; *see also* Rancière; distribution of the sensible
distribution of the sensible 99–101; *see also* Rancière; dissensus
Dogma 159, 177–9; *see also* Aureli
Dormanstown 40, 42
Dryzek, John 80, 84, 88–9, 106
Durkheim, Émile 137–40, 144–5, 157, 181

Eagleton, Terry 12, 20–2, 48
Eco, Umberto 16, 175–7, 180
Eisenman, Peter 10, 51, 60, 61, 74, 93, 105
Elemental 74–5, 77, 131
empty signifiers 58–9, 61, 63, 140, 146, 150–1, 177, 181
Engels, Friedrich 33, 36, 81, 120
equivalential chain 57–9, 63, 136, 148–51, 180
everyday urbanism 75, 77
evolutionary socialism 23–6, 159, 165

Fordism 40, 60, 70, 126, 139–40, 160; post- 49, 67, 120, 132, 139, 149, 159–60
Foucault, Michel 2, 10, 56–7, 82, 94
fragments: social 80, 131, 137, 144, 146, 148–9, 162, 167; urban 80, 131, 161–2, 167, 169, 171, 177

The Garden City 40, 42, 44–6, 166, 171
gentrification 14, 62, 68, 71, 73, 112–13, 115, 119, 185n6
Gramsci, Antonio 58, 85, 186n18
Ground Zero 140–1; *see also* World Trade Center

Habermas, Jürgen 77, 82, 86, 88–91, 103, 106, 182n12
hegemony 12, 15–16, 19, 25, 58, 92, 96–8, 100, 104–5, 136, 144–6, 148–50, 165, 172, 174, 188n8, 188n16
Hilberseimer, Ludwig, 20, 140, 171–3, 179
housing 41–4, 50, 67–73, 88, 112, 116, 122–8, 121, 158–9, 171, 177, 182n3, 185n7, 187n48; council 41, 42, 43, 67–9; mass 50, 60–1, 123–32, 150, 187n46; social 50, 60, 70, 72, 87, 117, 119, 124, 130, 159, 165, 171, 188
housing acts 41, 44–5
Howard, Ebenezer 44; *see also* The Garden City

ideology 2, 7, 12, 25, 29, 37, 40, 48, 54, 57, 70, 137, 154, 156, 171, 174, 176, 180–1, 183n8; bourgeois 25, 29; dominant 12, 48, 56, 156; free-market 37, 74, 94, 187n42

Jencks, Charles 7–9, 135, 136, 144, 150, 177, 180

Kant, Immanuel 21–2, 26–7, 46, 81–2, 100, 102, 131, 147, 167
Karl Marx Hof *see* Red Vienna
Kautsky, Karl 2, 24–5
Keynes, John Maynard 166, 173
Keynesian economics 8, 10, 11, 47, 50, 60–3, 70, 74, 92, 93, 149, 153, 165–6, 171–3
Koolhaas, Rem 10, 61, 76, 95, 119; *see also* OMA
Korsch, Karl 20, 26–7, 46–7, 49
Krier, Léon 1, 8, 180

labour aristocracy 29, 30, 39, 41–2
Labour (party) 43, 45, 172, 188n16
Lacaton and Vassal 75–8, 116–19, 130–1
Laclau, Ernesto 25, 57–8, 61, 80, 93, 95–7, 100, 106, 136, 139, 140, 146, 148–9, 165, 181, 182n13, 184n28
Le Corbusier 7, 50, 61, 117, 127–8, 135, 171, 176, 183n17
Lefebvre, Henri 2, 3, 61, 77, 82, 87, 112, 127–8, 120, 137, 152–6, 188n11–12
Lefort, Claude 145–6, 188n7
Lenin, Vladimir Ilyich 25, 29, 80
Letchworth 40, 43–4
Lévi-Strauss, Claude 157–8, 183n14
Levittown 126–7, 170
Lloyd George, David 25, 41, 172
localism 74–5, 84, 87–8, 92, 103, 109–13, 121–2, 124, 162, 186n19, 187n40; glocal 110, 162
London City Island 72, 121
London Docklands 70–2, 163–5
London Docklands Development Corporation (LDDC) 70, 163, 165, 184n5
Lukács, Georg 2, 106

de Man, Henri 166, 172–3, 188n16
Marcuse, Herbert 5, 47, 55–6, 94, 97, 186n25
Marcuse, Peter 71, 83, 185n6
Marx, Karl 2, 3, 23, 54–5, 59, 92–4, 184n29
Marxism 46–7; orthodox 2, 23, 24, 93
Mauss, Marcel 139, 145, 157–8

May '68 3, 4, 6, 19, 46, 48, 60–1, 85, 122, 152, 154, 184n30
May, Ernst 20, 166–9, 171–4
Miessen, Markus 74, 76, 80, 95, 103–7
model housing 32–7
Mouffe, Chantal 12, 13, 25, 77, 80, 82, 85, 88, 91, 93, 96–8, 103–5, 106–7, 136, 139, 146, 162, 165, 181, 182n13, 186n26, 186n28, 188n8

Nanterre 154–6; *see also* Lefebvre
needs 7–8, 61–2, 79–80, 83, 91, 121, 123, 130–1, 153, 169
Negri, Antonio 29, 99, 106, 120–3, 186n22; and Hardt 77, 82, 91–6, 123, 186n21
neoliberal 10, 11, 57, 63, 69, 74, 78, 85, 93, 105, 111, 119, 122, 132, 150–1, 159, 174, 182n11; ideology 15, 62, 94, 120–2, 187n42; policies 74, 92, 121, 162; theories 92, 94, 104, 107, 165
Norberg-Schulz, Christian 7, 135, 161

Occupy 84–5
OMA (Office for Metropolitan Architecture) 76, 114, 177, 179, 185n11

Park Hill 67–9, 72
participation: architectural 15, 74–82, 86, 91, 103, 109, 114, 120, 123–5, 131, 132, 187n46; citizens' 3, 5, 7, 11, 15, 77, 79, 82–5, 87, 103–5, 108–9, 113, 185n14
participatory movement 3, 10, 15, 74–82, 88, 92, 108–9, 116–17, 121–2, 131, 150; democracy 13, 78, 80–2, 85, 86, 88–92, 105, 182n12, 186n33
Partito Comunista Italiano (PCI) 85, 92, 186n18
pavillionsystem 167, 169–70
Pawley, Martin 6, 7, 125–6, 152, 154, 180
personalization 50, 78, 117, 119, 123, 125–31
Pessac 127–9, 131, 135, 187n47
Petrescu, Doina and Petcou, Constantin 87, 92, 108–9, 111–13, 116, 121, 185n9; *see also* Atelier d'architecture autogérée (aaa)
The Plan *see* planning
planism 92, 121, 159, 166, 171, 173, 188n16, 188n18
planisme see planism
planning: advocacy 83; consultation 40, 78, 83–4, 87–8, 90, 140; economic 8, 38, 45, 50, 92, 153, 173, 188n15; social 8, 46, 50, 92–3, 153, 172–3, 188n15; spatial 6, 7, 19, 20, 40, 43–6, 50, 61, 70, 74, 75, 78, 83, 84, 86–8, 90, 103, 109, 120–1, 153, 159, 160, 162–5, 173, 181, 184n17–18, 185n12, 185n14
politics 1, 4–5, 7–13, 21, 30, 41, 43, 46–9, 51, 54, 56–7, 74–5, 77, 86, 88–9, 93, 95–8, 101, 104, 107–8, 111, 120–1, 138–40, 142, 144–5, 148, 151–2, 162, 171, 180, 183n15–16, 185n10, 186n28; aesthetics of 100–2, 147; bourgeois 25; hegemonic 16
populism 57–8, 184n28
post-Fordism *see* Fordism
post-humanism 82, 90, 125
postmodernism 47, 95, 102, 105; architectural 10, 136
the post-political condition 13, 51, 74, 96, 120, 160
post-structuralism 47, 49, 51, 105, 153, 181, 184n22

Rancière, Jacques 13, 77, 82, 91, 98–103, 120, 123, 186n27–30; *see also* distribution of the sensible; dissensus
récupération see co-optation
Red Vienna 158–9
reform 6, 15, 19–22, 30, 43, 45–7, 49, 50, 69, 92, 150, 171, 173, 184n21; architectural 157, 159, 163, 171, 174, 179, 183n12; housing 29, 31, 32, 38, 39, 41, 42; political 9, 14, 21–9, 33, 37, 41, 46–7, 51, 159, 182n9, 183n8, 184n22; sanitary 28, 31–2; social 24–5, 27–32, 38, 44
Roberts, Henry 33–6, 40, 42
Royal Institute of British Architects (RIBA) 20, 163

Saint-Simon, Henri Comte de 80–1, 120, 184n29, 185n15
the sanitary movement 26, 31–3, 44
Schmitt, Carl 96–7, 159, 162, 177, 182n13, 186n25
secret societies 20–1, 29, 145, 147
Semiotext(e) 48–9
Shaftesbury, Anthony Ashley-Cooper, seventh Earl of 27, 33, 35, 37, 147, 183n10
Situationist 61, 103, 185n14
Skidmore, Owings Merrill (SOM) 140, 143, 163–4
social democracy 14, 24, 25, 150, 171
superstructure 2, 8, 10
Swyngedouw, Erik 1, 13

Tafuri, Manfredo 8–9, 14, 20, 50, 51, 77, 136, 156, 159, 160, 166–71, 174, 179
technocracy 80–1, 96, 154
Tonka, Hubert 3, 53, 152
Tronti, Mario 8–10, 92, 93, 95, 97, 120, 159
Tschumi, Bernard 7, 105, 117, 152–6
Tudor Walters Report 40–2, 45
Turner, John 5, 83, 131, 187n48

Ungers, Oswald Matthias 4, 161
Unwin, Raymond 40–2, 44–5, 171

Index

Urban Splash 67–9, 184n2
Urban-Think Tank (U-TT) 74–7, 117, 122, 182n10, 187n40

vanguard *see* avant-garde
Volume 76, 185n11–12

Weber, Max 2, 21, 145, 149

The Weimar Republic 14, 20, 128, 136, 159, 166, 172
Weissenhofsiedlung 14, 128, 166–71
Williams, Raymond 2, 10
Woolf, Virginia 1
World Trade Center 140–4; *see also* Ground Zero

Žižek, Slavoj 13, 157–8, 175